THE ASIAN BARBECUE BOOK

From Teriyaki to Tandoori
125 Tantalizing Recipes for Your Grill

Alex Skaria

Photography by **Alberto Cassio**

TUTTLE Publishing

Tokyo | Rutland, Vermont | Singapore

To my mother, Anita, my father, Arankathu, and my brother Andreas

Acknowledgments

It has taken quite a few years to write this book and I wish to thank all those who helped and inspired me throughout this period. This book would not have been possible without my good friend Alberto Cassio who did the food photography for the book. The photographs were made during an intensive three-week session. I owe a word of thanks to our kitchen assistant Nasima, who helped us prepare the food, and to the food stylist Khun Pat Chulaka, who was of great assistance and helped to give the photographs their subtle appearance.

I also wish to thank my publisher Eric Oey and his wife Christina who gave numerous very inspiring ideas and input. Special thanks go to my editor Holly Jennings who patiently reviewed the text, asked often very critical questions, clarified various inconsistencies, and helped to make the text lean and easily legible. Furthermore, I wish to express my thanks to my sister-in-law Mouna who gave me a lot of insight into the secrets of Lebanese cuisine. I also wish to thank the staff and friends of the Royal Varuna Yacht Club who helped me to organize numerous BBQ parties, which were the original source of inspiration of this book. Finally to my wife Yanping and daughter Surya who supported me throughout this period with calm advice and many suggestions.

contents

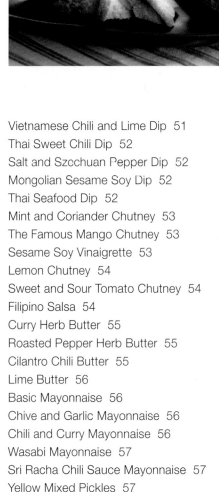

A Love of Good Food

Like many passionate cooks, my first fond memories of food go back to my childhood. I learned the basics of cooking from my German mother, who comes from a family of restaurateurs. I remember sitting next to the stove while she cooked my favorite dish—beef goulash with red cabbage. She always said that the most important factor was frying the meat at a sufficiently high temperature in a heavy cast-iron pot, which gave the sauce its excellent rich brown color and flavor. And she was not shy with spices like juniper, bay leaf, cloves and other spices like nutmeg and mace. I still get a good helping when I return home from overseas. My father took us to his homeland in south India every other year. There I had the rare opportunity to witness my grandmother cook original Kerala food on a stove fired with palm leaf stems. I started collecting her recipes when I was eighteen years old, beginning a lifelong pursuit of delicious Asian recipes. My favorite recipe was (and in fact still is) her beef Oolarthiathu, a spicy dish of stir-fried beef with slices of fried coconut and lots of onions that are cooked until the sauce becomes wonderfully thick. The crispy texture of the fried coconut slices combined with the thick consistency of the spicy curry sauce is unforgettable. It was during these family trips to India that I really began to delve into the secrets of spices and how to best use them. I remember that the women raised their eyebrows when seeing me in the kitchen—it simply was not a place for a young man! But it was worth it, and I collected recipes year after year during each visit.

Later, during my university studies, I became friends with some Chinese students. I joined a Chinese student association where the major pastime was to cook dinner on Sunday afternoons. We often held larger cooking events and sometimes cooking competitions where each student showed off some of the specialties from his province. Many years later I met my wife who taught me finer details of her regional Chinese cuisine—Shanghai cooking. Now we live in Thailand, which has been a boon to exploring an even wider array of Asian cooking styles. Thailand is a vast melting pot of the culinary arts. Thais have incorporated Indian, Thai, Chinese, Vietnamese, Malaysian and Laotian, and strangely enough Spanish and Portuguese, elements into their cuisine and thus most ingredients are readily available. Contemporary cooks in Thailand, and elsewhere in Asia, now often successfully combine Western ingredients with Asian spices to create a wonderful new specialty. Shopping in Thailand is always an adventure. I often find new ingredients, vegetables and spices that I'm unfamiliar with—but vendors are usually always happy and willing to tell me how to best use them. And if I can't find something, I don't hesitate to ask vendors if they can order it for me. Most are obliging. I suggest you create a similar rapport with your local produce managers and butchers. If you can't find something in a store, it doesn't hurt to ask!

What is Asian BBQ?

People from all regions of Asia, including central Asia, have been experimenting for thousands of years with spices and honing the techniques of cooking on open grills or ovens. When you step into the markets on the streets of Asian cities, be it Bangkok, Beijing, Hanoi, Jakarta, Delhi, Seoul or Tokyo you immediately see numbers of stalls where food is grilled and you can smell the rich flavors and perfumes of the spices that are used. One step from one food stall to the next and you get a different smell of some extraordinary spice or herb. It was the desire to re-create these exciting Asian aromas and flavors on my own backyard grill that generated the recipes in this cookbook.

In Asia grilling is a traditional cooking technique. Until recent years most households were cooking on clay ovens, hearths or open fires. The mother of the house could choose to cook with woks, pans or just directly grill the food over an open fire. You can witness these traditional cooking techniques when you travel through Thailand, Laos, Indonesia, China and India. The

Japanese and Koreans went one step further and brought the grill directly to the dinner table. All these cuisines developed their own grilling techniques and naturally very diverse recipes. The combination of herbs and spices and grilling techniques vary from region to region in Asia. In the central Asian regions, including northern India, fuelwood has been rare since these areas have been traditionally very dry and arid. The tandoor or vertical clay oven was most likely one of the first energy-saving inventions. Many dishes from these areas including meat and bread were cooked in these tandoor ovens. In Southeast and East Asia grilling is done on a small open grill like the hibachi or a clay brazier. The hibachi was the heating source in traditional Japanese houses and was often built into tables. Persons sitting around it would grill small snacks like fish or chicken, and keep warm in the process!

The clay brazier was and often still is the only cooking stove in some Far East households. The charcoal-fired braziers are still often used to cook with a wok or as a small grill. The Chinese wok is virtually a thin metal sheet pan that barely separates the food from the glowing embers. This allowed the cook to prepare food with the least amount of expensive charcoal or fuelwood. Simultaneously, small cuts of meat and skewers are grilled on these small open grills, adding to the diversity of Asian cuisine where you often find curries, stir-fried vegetables and grilled foods combined in a single meal. The exception to this general rule is the roast duck oven in China and the kamado in Japan, which most likely have been introduced by the Mongols from central Asia. And this book addresses not only the Asian grilling techniques but also the exceptionally rich diversity of herbs, spices, rubs, sauces and marinades that make Asian barbecue so delicious and special.

With this book, you will experiment with flavors from India, Thailand, Vietnam, Indonesia, China, Korea and Japan and further afield; yet all of the recipes can be accomplished using a standard kettle-style grill. In some cases I adapted some typical Western grilling fare—such as burgers and steaks—to give them an Asian twist, as is often done nowadays in contemporary restaurants in Asia. This does not mean mixing Western spices with Asian ones or significantly changing the taste of traditional Asian recipes, but rather using Western meat cuts, ways of serving, latest health considerations and so on, which can result in surprising new dishes. Our Western guests often prefer to have larger pieces of meat as compared to the traditional Asian style of cooking with small slices of meat. The serving sizes in this book reflect the Western style of serving meat, yet while maintaining the distinct Asian flavor.

Throwing an Asian BBQ Party

Grilling food is a way of life in Asia, however different from Western culture. Traditionally food is grilled and sold on the streets and serves as snacks throughout the day, whereas in Western countries grilling is a pastime activity. Western methods of grilling, and the Western-style barbecue party, are becoming more and more part of Asian cuisine and an influence of both cultures can be noticed. Asians like to entertain with steaks and burgers, but naturally they will give the barbecue a special local touch. My family loves the American style of potluck backyard barbecue parties. Our barbecue parties are usually a venue where friends

join in. The menu is often improvised because everybody brings a dish along that he or she has prepared in advance. This usually results in a medley of specialties. Whenever I organize parties and events I try to cook something that is unique and a surprise to my guests, and very often my guests reciprocate and surprise me with some new dishes. Most of all, I hope this book encourages you to experiment with new techniques and flavors, and that you enjoy entertaining your friends and guests with new and exotic Asian recipes in the true sense of barbecuing.

Whenever we have a grill party we serve a great variety of drinks, both alcoholic and non-alcoholic. I'll highlight some of the most popular Asian beers, and then give you some general guidelines for matching food with beer or wine.

Singh beer is a popular Thai beer. It has a relatively high alcohol content, so drink with caution. In China, the most famous beer is Tsingtao. It is available in most countries abroad. This beer is quite light and a bit sweet due to being made with rice. Japan has its own brands, such as Asahi or Sapporo, which are also available in the West. They are a light beer and have a pleasant, not too strong taste. The Singaporean Tiger beer is an excellent beer with a nice deep amber color and a relatively strong wheat and hoppy taste. It is available in Vietnam, Thailand and Indonesia.

The wines that have become most popular in Asia are from New Zealand, Australia and Chile. In countries that were once French colonies, such as Vietnam and Laos, you can get a great selection of French wines. There are attempts to cultivate wine in Asia, but these are rarely available in the West.

As a general guideline to drinks to be served with Asian food I would suggest the following: Spicy food such as Thai, south Indian, Indonesian and Malaysian: best served with any kind of beer or light white wine; Chinese, Japanese and Korean seafood and chicken dishes: light white wine or beer; Japanese and Korean beef and pork: red wine, sake or beer; north Indian, Persian and central Asian and Middle Eastern lamb dishes that are mildly spiced: red wine or beer.

Basic Barbecuing Techniques

To make the recipes in this book you will be grilling with either direct or indirect heat. The direct grill method exposes food to much higher temperatures than the indirect method. When applying direct grilling, the food is exposed to the radiant heat of the glowing charcoal that is directly underneath the food—hence only parts of the food which are directly exposed to the radiation (the bottom part of the meat) are heated, whereas the top stays cool. The heat can be controlled by the thickness of the glowing embers and the distance to the grill. This method is usually applied for food which needs quick searing like sirloin or T-bone steaks, beef tenderloin, lamb chops, lamb tenderloin, fish fillet, shrimp, small veggies, burgers, kebabs and small items like chicken breasts and chicken wings, and so on. Indirect grilling can be done with any closed grills, rotisseries, ceramic grills, smokers and fire pits. The charcoal is placed so that it is not directly underneath the food—usually around a drip pan or to one side of the grill. The food is mainly heated by hot smoke that is captured in the closed grill and flows around the food. The temperature is controlled by opening and closing vents, which increases or reduces the temperature. The indirect method bears less risk of burning the food and usually applies for larger pieces like large pieces of chicken, turkey, brisket, porterhouse steaks, stuffed vegetables and so on, which require longer cooking times.

Indirect grilling can be differentiated into two categories: medium to high temperatures of 250 to 400°F (120 to 200°C) and low temperatures of 195 to 250°F (90 to 120°C). The higher temperature range is suited for lean and naturally tender pieces like porterhouse steak, leg of lamb, lamb rack, pork tenderloin, chicken or turkey drumsticks or whole chicken or whole fish in parcels. Typical grilling time for this method is around 20 to 25 minutes per pound (500 g) of meat to reach medium-well doneness. The lower temperature range of 195 to 250°F (90 to 120°C) is usually applied for high-fat and/or naturally tough meats. Pieces of meat under this category are pork or beef ribs, strip loin, brisket, porterhouse steak (can be grilled both ways, either high or low), suckling pig, whole duck or goose, whole turkey, ham with skin and so on. Having said that, other meats like tenderloin can be grilled as well with this method but it will not result in a big difference to the previous method. The grilling times for indirect low-temperature grilling are significantly longer than the high-heat method. You need to calculate about 1 to 1½ hours per pound (500 g) of meat to be medium-well done. In traditional Chinese and Indonesian recipes for duck, free range chicken and beef flank steak, which are naturally very tough to grill, the meat is first steamed for a few hours until it is completely tender. Only then it is placed on the grill over high heat to give it a final crust. They obviously knew that the only way to make these meats tender is through a soft hand approach. The indirect low temperature method works on the same basis but uses smoke instead of steam.

CHARCOAL GRILLS

Lighting a Charcoal Fire Starting a grill with wood is my preferred way to start a fire. The traditional way in Asia to start a charcoal fire is to use eucalyptus wood, which contains a lot of resin and oil and ignites very fast. To start a charcoal grill with wood, cut a few slivers of wood and pile some charcoal on top. Don't pile too densely or the air cannot flow freely to

Using eucalyptus wood to start a charcoal grill

the burning wood. Light the wood and wait for 15 minutes. Add more charcoal until you the sufficient amount. To start an average-size Weber-type grill you will need about 2 to 3 pounds (1 to 1½ kg) maximum of charcoal for direct and indirect grilling to provide 30 to 45 minutes of cooking time with high and medium temperatures.

For low temperature grilling and smoking, you will need only 1 to 1½ pounds (500 to 750 g). For larger grills you will need more fuel. You may also use lighter fuel or newspaper to light the charcoal. You dowse the charcoal with the lighter fuel and toss in a match. Do not use any other type of liquid fuels except ones specifically sold as barbecue lighter fuel. However, this method is not eco-friendly. Also, you must wash your hands before handling food as you may have a residue of fluid on your hands after starting the grill. Once the coals are glowing and covered with ash, which usually takes about 20 minutes, spread the coals out evenly in a single layer for single zone direct grilling. Put your grill rack in place, and let the grilling begin! You will have about 30 to 45 minutes of cooking time before you have to add charcoal to the grill.

Chimney Starters are made of galvanized or stainless steel. To use follow the illustrated sequence at the top of this page. For instructions on how to prepare multiple zones for indirect or indirect and direct grilling, read on!

Left to right For a standard-size Weber grill fill the chimney starter with 2 to 3 pounds (1 to 1½ kg) charcoal or briquettes. For larger grills you will need more charcoal. Place the chimney starter on the charcoal tray of your grill. Place a crumpled newspaper sheet or one to three paraffin or sawdust starters in the bottom of the cylinder. Ignite the newspaper or starter with a long match. As soon as the top charcoal starts to glow, which takes normally 15 to 20 minutes, pour the contents of the starter onto the charcoal tray. Be certain to wear heatproof mitts. Then disperse with a charcoal shovel or rake. Add more charcoal on top. When the coals are glowing and covered with ash, spread the coals out evenly in a single layer for single zone direct grilling with medium or high heat. Put your grill rack in place, and let the grilling begin!
Below For direct grilling with multiple zones, use a rake or charcoal shovel to mound the coals up in two or three different heights for different heat intensities.

Direct Grilling with Multi Zones If you have to grill larger items you will have to prepare the grill for two or even three zones, whereby the coals are piled in a 3-inch (7.5-cm)-thick layer at one side of the grill and approximately a 1½ to 2-inch (3.75 to 5-cm)-layer in the center. The remaining grill area is left without coals. This arrangement allows you to control the heat by moving the food around, as you feel necessary. The area without coals is reserved for food that is cooked and needs to rest and be kept hot. If you grill several pieces and some are finished earlier than others, the area without coals is the parking lot. You can then leave all pieces to rest in that area for a few minutes prior to carving.

Adding Charcoal Depending on the initial amount of fuel you started with, after about 30 to 45 minutes the heat generally becomes too low for grilling. You will need to add more charcoal. If you don't have a chimney starter you need to add the charcoal onto the grill. This will cause the temperature to drop and will release smoke and soot, in particular when you are using briquettes.

The smoke of briquettes and charcoal tends to have an acrid smell. Leave the grill hood open to allow for maximum airflow. I suggest removing the food and waiting for 5 to 10 minutes before you continue to grill in order to avoid exposure to unhealthy soot and acrid smoke. The proven method for adding charcoal is to prepare the chimney starter some 35 to 40 minutes after you started to grill. Place the starter on a metal tray on the floor. In about 15 to 20 minutes, the coals will glow.

Once ready add the glowing coals onto the charcoal tray and rake the coals to make heat zones as you did before. This allows you to continue grilling without major interruption.

Indirect Grilling For closed charcoal grills like the Weber-type grills, heating using the indirect grilling method is mainly via convection and radiation, working much like the oven in your kitchen with combined grill and hot air circulation. The main difference is that we use smoke rather than hot air. The radiation is relatively low and contributes only a little to the cooking process, whereas in direct grilling the radiation is the main source of heat.

The food is placed over a drip pan and the charcoal is arranged around this pan. The hood of the grill needs to be closed to maintain the hot smoke and thus heat the food evenly from all sides. Heat is mainly controlled by the amount of fuel

Top A grill set up for indirect grilling with the drip plan placed to the side. After your embers are covered with ash, rake the coals to one side of the grill and place a drip pan on the other side. For the medium- to high-heat method you can start browning your meat after some 10 to 15 minutes when the grill has cooled down to 400°F (200°C). When the temperature is around 210°F (120°C) add two to three handfuls of additional charcoal. **Above** A grill set up for indirect grilling with a centrally placed drip plan. **Opposite** Goat is grilled on a rotisserie for a traditional Mechui barbecue.

and air. The more air available—the more wide open the vents are—the hotter the coals burn and vice versa. When indirect grilling with the low temperature method or smoking method, start with only 1 to 1½ pounds (500 to 750 g) of charcoal (for an average-size Weber-type grill). Place a drip pan in the middle or to one side and the glowing coals on one side or both sides, close to where you can easily add additional charcoal. You may need to wait almost 20 to 25 minutes after you have poured the charcoal from the chimney starter onto the grill tray until the temperature reaches less than 120°C (250°F) when the grill is closed. Once this temperature is reached place the meat over the drip pan. Browning will occur very slowly. Don't overheat the meat. Add one handful charcoal every 20 to 30 minutes or when the temperature becomes less than 195°F (90°C). Once the core temperature is almost achieved, remove the meat from the grill. Add ½ to 1 pound (250 to 500 g) of additional charcoal. When the charcoal is fully aglow grill the meat over high heat 6 inches above the coals to give a final crust or crispy glazed surface.

Grilling on a Rotisserie Grilling on a rotisserie is the oldest method of grilling large pieces of meat. The rotisserie also belongs to the category of indirect grilling but uses radiant rather than convective heating. To equally expose the entire surface of the meat to radiation, a skewer is rotated over a drip pan either on the open grill, in front of a fire or high above the charcoal in a fire pit. Rotisseries can be operated at medium to high temperatures or at the low temperature range depending on the meat that you intend to grill. If you use a charcoal grill or Weber-type grill, start the grill as described in the previous section. When your starter

chimney is ready pour the glowing coals on one side of the grill tray and rake them alongside the spit on only one side of the grill. Place a drip pan underneath the spit to prevent fat dripping into the coals. Some grills are equipped with vertical charcoal trays that are placed sideways and allow the coals to be piled vertically. The food is placed on a rotating spit in front of a wall of glowing coals. This gives the same effect as direct grilling, since the main heat is transferred by radiation but eliminates the problem of fat dripping into the coals. This method has been applied in old chimneys and ancient kitchen spit ovens, including the traditional shawarma. Fill these charcoal trays with glowing coals from the chimney starter. The fuel needs to be added continuously into these trays.

When replenishing charcoal remove the meat or use a starter chimney to prepare glowing coals before adding them onto the grill. For the medium to high temperature method start with a higher temperature and seal the meat. Once the meat is nicely browned, move the rotisserie up and continue to grill at a lower temperature of 250°F (120°C) until you reach the desired core temperature. When using the low temperature method place the rotating spit sufficiently high over the coals to not exceed 250°F (120°C) at most. Lower temperatures of 210°F (100°C) are even better.

Note that it isn't possible to adjust the height of the rotisserie in most household size charcoal grills and therefore the only way to control the heat in these grills is by the amount of fuel and waiting long enough until the temperature is sufficiently low. Grill the food until you've almost reached the desired core temperature. Then place over high heat for a few minutes to give a final crust.

Ceramic Grills like the Big Green Egg, the tandoor or even the ceramic pizza oven use both radiation and convection and can work as a grill, oven or smoker. The ceramic walls are first heated up. Through radiation from the ceramic walls and convection from the glowing charcoal at the bottom, the food is heated. The ceramic grills are tightly closed to maintain the steam and smoke. Temperatures in ceramic grills can be adjusted between 200 and 750°F (100 and 350°C), making it possible to do all styles of grilling. Temperature is controlled mainly by regulating the airflow and by fuel quantity. Since the ceramic walls store most of the heat, the grill maintains very stable temperatures. Light the charcoal (about 1 to 2 lbs/500 g to 1 kg) with all vents open and wait for about 10 to 15 minutes. Adjust the temperature by damping the vents to reach your required temperature. Place the food on the grill tray and close the grill. For high temperature direct grilling start after about 15 minutes. For medium to high temperature indirect grilling you should wait some 20 minutes

Tips for Grilling Whole Suckling Pig, Sheep or Goat Whole animals, such as a suckling pig weighing 24 pounds (12 kg), will take about 8 to 10 hours to cook when grilled at medium to high temperatures. The skewer is placed at least 3 feet (1 meter) above the glowing embers. I add one or two wood pieces every half hour to the fire. This will result in a well-done hog without having burnt skin. If you grill at lower temperatures the hog will be even better but you need to count on 1½ hours per pound (500 g), which means 24 hours of grilling for a 24-pound (12-kg) hog. If you wish to cook the hog at the lower temperature, I recommend that you split the hog lengthwise and grill each piece for about 12 to 14 hours.

and keep the vents slightly open. For low-temperature grilling keep the vents closed and wait until the temperature is below 250°F (120°C). Add additional charcoal (2 to 3 handfuls) every 30 to 40 minutes. For low temperature grilling add charcoal every 50 to 60 minutes.

Fire Pits and Open Fires The fire pit can be used for indirect or direct grilling. For direct grilling the food is placed on the grill once the wood is covered with ash. The glowing embers should cover the area underneath the grill with a thickness of a maximum 2 inches (5 cm). Adjust the height of the grill between 10 and 15 inches over the glowing embers depending on what you intend to grill.

For indirect grilling on a fire pit or an open fireplace light the wood and wait until the logs are covered with ash. Don't make a too large fire. The glowing embers should be at maximum around 1 to 2 inches (2.5 to 5 cm) thick when spread over the surface of the pit. The biggest mistake that beginners make is to use too much fuel, which results in a too-hot grill. Once the wood is nicely covered with ash, the food is placed on a rotisserie or on a grill. For the medium-to high-heat method, place the grill or rotisserie at the height where you are able to count to 6 to 8 seconds when placing

your hand over the fire. When the food starts to get a nice brown coloring raise the grill or the rotisserie to a higher level where the temperature is medium to low—you should be able to count to 11 to 12 seconds when placing your hand over the fire at this level. Continue to cook slowly, until you reach the desired core temperature. When done set at a level where the temperature is less than 150°F (65°C) to let rest for 10 to 20 minutes or remove from the fire and wrap in aluminum foil. Add wood little by little to the grill to maintain the heat. When grilling a leg of lamb or a pork shoulder on the rotisserie at medium to high heat I allow normally 20 to 25 minutes of cooking time for each pound (500 g) of meat.

For the low temperature heat method, set the grill or rotisserie at a level where the temperature is around 200 to 250°F (100 to 120°C) and place the meat onto the grill or the rotisserie. The grill times for the same leg or shoulder are around 1 to 1½ hours per pound (500 g) of meat. When you almost reach the core temperature, lower the grill or rotisserie and grill at a very high temperature of 400°F (200°C) for a few minutes to give a final crust. When done raise the grill to a level where the temperature is about 150°F (65°C) to keep the meat warm and rest for another 10 to 20 minutes to let the juices distribute.

Smoking The fire in traditional barbecue smokers is burning in a separate firebox, therefore only convection through smoke and no radiant heat cooks the food. Smokers typically use low temperatures from 195 to 300°F (90 to 150°C). The cooking times are longer, resulting in very tender meat. The exposure to the smoke gives a distinctly strong smoke flavor that is sometimes not suitable for the recipes in this book. In addition to the temperature the smoke itself cures the meat.

If you use a standard Weber-type grill, the preparation for smoking is similar to the indirect grilling method for low temperature grilling Once the charcoal is burnt down sufficiently you need to add water-soaked wood chips on to the coals. Whenever the charcoal is replenished you add more soaked wood chips as well. The food is kept in a section of the grill with no coals underneath and the temperature in the closed grill should not exceed 250°F (120°C).

Temperature Control The temperature on a charcoal grill is controlled by three factors: amount of fuel (charcoal or wood); distance between the food and embers and duration of burning fuel. As you can see from the graph below, the temperature on a charcoal grill reaches some 600°F (320°C) after about 20 minutes from starting with a chimney starter. (Keep in mind that everytime you add fresh charcoal, you'll have to wait another 20 minutes for the maximum termperature to be reached.) It then gradually decreases to about 210°F (100°C) after 1 hour. One way to judge the approximate temperature is to use the hand test count. Hold your hand over the grill at the height that the food shall be placed. Then you count how long you can hold the hand in that spot before your hand becomes uncomfortably hot.

The graph below indicates the temperature range in relation to the hand test, measured at one single elevation above the grill with no fuel added. For

example, if you can hold your hand only 1 to 3 seconds, the temperature will be around 520 to 600°F (280 to 320°C). This temperature is good for searing. Accordingly, if you can hold your hand between 8 and 14 seconds, the temperature will be around 195 to 240°F (90 to 120°C). To increase or lower the temperature, you can always change the height of the grill or change the thickness of layer of glowing coals. One method to quickly reduce the temperature is using cold ash. If the temperature is too hot, you can throw some ash over the glowing embers, which reduces the temperature of the grill immediately. This is usually applied by the food vendors who don't have fancy temperature control vents on grills.

Height over Embers When you have lit your grill and embers are just getting covered with ash, another rule of thumb for grilling steaks is: For a 1-inch (2.5-cm)-thick steak, place the grill 2 inches (5 cm) over the embers. For a 2-inch (5-cm)-thick steak, place the grill 3 to 4 inches (7.5 to 10 cm) over the embers. When using the indirect grill method the food should be placed at least 8 inches (20 cm) over the embers. When you roast a suckling pig, whole sheep, or other large pieces of meat on a spit above a fire pit, the spit is usually placed some 30 to 40 inches (75 to 100 cm) over the embers.

GAS GRILLS

Not every gas grill works the same way. So it's important to familiarize yourself with the manufacturer's instructions before you use your grill.

Before you light your gas grill check that you have sufficient fuel. If not, get another gas bottle as a spare. Nothing is worse than having to find out that gas has run out on a Sunday afternoon and you have not finished grilling your food.

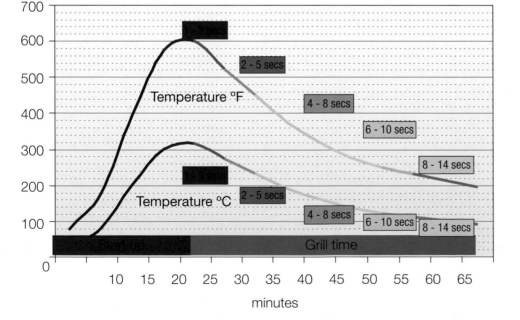

Next open the hood. It is dangerous to light your gas grill with the hood closed since gas can accumulate and may explode when you light it. It happened to me once with a gas oven and it is not fun! I still cook with a gas stove but I no longer use a gas oven in my household.

To light the gas grill first open the gas tank valve, turn the knob to start gas flow into the burner and light the grill using a match, gas lighter or push the ignition button (for those grills that have an electric starter). To start grilling you need to wait 15 to 20 minutes until the grill reaches optimum grilling temperatures. Some grills will take up to 30 minutes.

The temperature gauge should show at least 450 to 480°F (240 to 255°C) with a closed hood before you start placing food onto the grill. If the grill fails to light and you have checked the gas supply and made sure the valve is opened and there is no leakage of gas then you may need to clean the burner nozzles. Use either a metal brush or a small needle to remove soot and grease from the burner holes. If that fails you need to contact the nearest grill shop or the supplier.

Direct Grilling For direct grilling fire up all burners to maximum heat, which is about 450°F (240°C), or you can use the multi-zone method whereby one burner is at maximum and the others are set at medium or one burner is off. When you are cooking larger pieces, start at this high temperature and once the meat is nicely browned and the pores are sealed, move to a medium-heat zone or reduce the heat to between 300 and 400°F (150 and 200°C), depending on the size of meat.

Indirect Grilling It is possible only if you have multiple burners. For indirect grilling, set one burner to maximum heat (about 450°F/240°C) and leave the other burner switched off. For a three-burner grill, set one burner to maximum (about 450°F/240°C), and leave the remaining burners switched off to create a low temperature zone. Place your meat on the grill when this temperature is reached. When you have larger pieces, start at the high temperature and once the meat is slightly browned and the pores are sealed, move the meat to the low temperature zone (where the burners are switched off), close the hood and operate the burners such that the temperature in the closed grill reaches an average of 300°F (150°C). Continue to grill and check regularly for doneness. If you use the grill for both indirect and direct grilling at the same time, you can leave the middle burner at medium heat (300 to 400°F/150 to 200°C) and turn it to low when you do the large piece with indirect grilling.

Some gas grills have vertical burners on the back wall for grilling with a rotisserie, which has the same effect as a vertical charcoal tray. The heat is controlled by the gas valve and in some cases by the horizontal distance to the burner surface.

For indirect, low-temperature grilling and smoking set one burner to medium temperature and check when the hood is closed that the temperature in the grill does not exceed 250°F (120°C). The food is cooked at temperatures just above 190 to 250°F/90 to 120°C (check with a temperature gauge). The meat takes longer to cure (1 to 1½ hours per lb/500 g) but it becomes very tender. To achieve even and low temperatures on a gas grill, it needs to be rather large.

For smoking prepare the grill as you would for indirect grilling. Make a small pouch of aluminum and fill it with soaked wood chips, spices and herbs, such as bay leaves or rosemary, if you wish.

Close the pouch and poke a few holes in the aluminum foil to allow the smoke to escape. Place the pouch directly on the lava stones or ceramic elements. Some high-end grills have a special smoker box with a separate burner that can be loaded with wood chips or spices.

MASTER GRILLING TIPS

Tenderizing Meat In the West meat is typically hung for 14 to 21 days to tenderize. The meat processor or butcher should do this. In most Asian countries, the hanging and storing technique has not been mastered and thus meat is sold fresh. In Asia I often buy meat for a barbecue 1 week in advance to leave time for hanging it to make sure it's tender. Even if you live in the West, where hanging meat is a common practice, you might experiment with hanging meat to make your grilled meats extra tender.

Since most of us don't have large meat hooks installed in our refrigerators, the easiest way to "hang" the meat is to place it on a grill grate or meat rack over a pan in the refrigerator. The grate will ensure that air circulates around the meat and that it remains well drained. Keep it in a cool place between 32 and 40°F (0 to max 5°C), but preferably just below 40°F (5°C) for three to five days. Or you can place the meat in oil and keep it for 2 to 3 days in the refrigerator at the same temperatures as described above, which will have a similar but less strong effect since the oil reduces the access of oxygen to the meat. After hanging for a few days the meat will turn to a dark red, almost brownish in the case of beef and venison, and dark pink in the case of pork. Remove from the refrigerator and keep the meat at room temperature for at least 1 hour before placing onto the grill.

Marinades that contain yogurt, vinegar, wine or fruit juice—in particular green papaya, kiwi or fresh pineapple juice—will tenderize the meat. When marinating meat with these types of tenderizing ingredients don't marinate more than overnight. If tenderized too long, the meat will be come dry and tough.

Avoiding Dry Meat If meat is taken from the deep freezer, it should be taken out early enough to defrost up to room temperature. Don't put frozen or cold meat onto the grill. It will not seal the pores and as a result will become dry and tough. Meat should be removed from the refrigerator 30 minutes before grill time. Large pieces should be removed at least 2 hours prior to grilling. If you grill beef or other large meat pieces by applying the medium- to high-temperature method, initially use a high temperature to seal the surface. Then reduce the temperature by removing the coals from underneath to the outside or raising the grill and let it cook over lower heat. The juices are then trapped in the meat and it will stay moist. If you are using the low-temperature grilling method, you don't seal the meat. Place the meat onto the grill and cook it until you have almost reached the core temperature. Then increase the temperature to give it a final crust. This works for low temperatures since the meat is not exposed to a thermal stress and its moisture and juices are less released. This method is usually applied for meats that contain large amounts of internal fat. To keep small cubes of meat and thinly sliced meat moist, they should be grilled at a high temperature. After reaching the final temperature, the meat should be taken from the grill, wrapped in aluminum foil and let rest for about 10 minutes to allow the juices to be absorbed into the meat. Alternatively you can keep it on the grill at temperatures less than 150°F (65°C). Note however that this is not pos-

sible for most small household-size grills but only on larger grills and fire pits.

Prepping Lean Meat Some meats—such as tenderloin, beef fillets, pork chops, turkey, veal, venison, pheasant or rabbit—become dry very quickly because of their low internal fat content. To keep such meats from becoming dry, I prefer to add very small pieces of cold butter on top of the food while grilling. Alternatively you can wrap meats in lard or very mildly smoked bacon or pancetta, which is the traditional French method called "barding." However, be aware that the smoky taste of bacon will add a distinct flavor to the meat, which is particularly undesirable with subtle foods such as fish and seafood. Lean types of meat should not be marinated with salt because it extracts the water and makes the meat dry. Instead, salt should therefore be added just before placing the meat on the grill.

Aluminum Foil Packet Whether ready-made packets or handmade from sheets of folded heavy foil, these offer the utmost convenience for grilling vegetables, mussels, small shrimps, etc. Handling is easy and you can discard the foil after usage without having to clean woks or pans. However, grill flavors are sacrificed as the foods are insulated from the smoke.

Before You Start Make sure the grates are clean. Just shortly before adding food, the hot grilling grate should be brushed with oil. This will keep food from sticking to it. When applying the oil, use a natural fiber brush, a good-quality paper towel (one that does not leave fibers) or a piece of lard. Never use a synthetic brush. Make sure that you don't leave the oil on the grate too long before you begin grilling. The oil will overheat and burn and

the grate will become even stickier than without any oil. Hence once the grate is oiled be ready to put the food onto it. You can use oil spray (remove rack from the fire to apply the spray), vegetable oil or a piece of lard. Food that falls apart easily, such as vegetable burgers, fish fillets, burgers with fillings, can be placed in special grilling trays made of sheets of nonstick enamel-coated metal. They have small holes to allow heat and smoke to penetrate foods. Before use, oil lightly and place them directly on the grill rack. Use tongs to turn and remove foods. Once you're an experienced and confident grill chef, you will learn to cook even the most fragile hamburger on a normal grill grate without having to fall back on these grill trays.

Cleanup To clean a charcoal grill, simply place the grate directly over the coal to let the remaining bits of food burn off. Brush the grate with a wire brush and scrape off any remaining burnt food with a scraper. When it has cooled down the hood can be cleaned using a special cleaning spray (devised for cold application) and wiping it with a towel. The ash is collected in the ash bin (if available) or with a shovel and is either used as fertilizer or thrown away. However, do not use unburnt remains of briquettes that have been started with lighter fuel. Most gas grills can be easily cleaned by heating up to maximum temperature for a few minutes before shutting it down to burn the fat or remaining bits of food off the grill grate. You don't have to do this after every grill session but it is advisable every once in a while. The dripping pan needs to be removed and cleaned separately. In some super grills this is a bit more difficult. Collect the drippings and fat in an empty container before discarding it into the garbage bag.

DIFFERENT CUTS OF MEAT

It is very important to choose the right type and cut of meat when planning a barbecue as you need to leave yourself enough time to properly cook the meat as well as coordinate the timing of side dishes. You will find a brief table of cooking times at the start of each of the meat chapters to help you get the best results.

How Do I Know When It Is Done?

The best way to test your meat for doneness, and here I am talking about steaks, chicken breasts, tuna and so on, is to poke it quickly with your finger. This test will tell you whether your meat is rare, medium rare or well done. When first learning how to use the poking test, use the ball of your hand as a comparative reference for telling doneness. Here is how it works. When gently pressing together your index finger and your thumb, the ball of your hand close to the thumb is equivalent to the softness of rare meat. Next hold together your middle finger and thumb. The ball will now feel firmer, and is equivalent to medium rare to medium doneness. If you then hold together your ring finger and your thumb, the ball of your hand feels like medium well and, finally, when holding together your pinkie and your thumb the ball of your hand will feel like medium well to well done. When grilling chicken, turkey and pork, in addition to the poking test, you should use the pricking test. Prick the meat with a thin needle or small knife. When the juices run clear with no red color, the meat is done. To test the doneness of fish insert a metal skewer and hold it for a little while. Take it out and hold it to the back of your hand. When it feels warm, the fish is done. If it feels hot the fish is overcooked. Apart from the poking and pricking methods, the best tool to tell doneness is a meat thermometer.

These poking and pricking techniques need experience and I suggest trying them together with the meat thermometer until you get the right feel for it. After some time and experience you will use the meat thermometer for only very large pieces of meat.

Very Rare, Seared Beef, lamb and tuna can be served very rare. It is an alternative to carpaccio and the meat is sliced very thinly. The feel is very soft. The meat is very red in the center and almost cold. Pork, chicken and turkey cannot be served at this stage.

Rare Beef, lamb and tuna are often served rare. When you poke the meat the feel is soft. The meat is still red in the center and the internal temperature is between 125 and 130°F (45 and 55°C). Pork, chicken and turkey are not safe to be served rare.

Medium Rare Beef, lamb and tuna can be served medium rare. When you poke the meat the feel is slightly soft but a bit more firm than rare. The meat is pinkish red in the center and the temperature is around 130 to 135°F (55 to 60°C). Pork, chicken and turkey are not safe to be served medium rare.

Medium Beef, lamb and tuna are often served medium. When you poke the meat, the feel is only slightly yielding. The meat shows traces of pink in the center and has an internal temperature of about 140 to 150°F (60 to 65°C). For large pieces of lamb like leg of lamb or lamb shoulder you should check with the pricking test or with a meat thermometer. When pricking the lamb to the center, the juices will be rose colored and it is ready to be served medium. Pork, chicken and turkey can not safely be served.

Medium Well Poking the meat will feel firm. The meat shows no trace of pink with a touch of gray and the internal temperature is 150 to 160°F (65 to 70°C). For large pieces of lamb, like leg of lamb or lamb shoulder, you should check with the pricking test or with a meat thermometer to confirm that the temperature above has been reached. When pricking the lamb to the center, the juices will be almost clear. For pork you should now switch to the pricking test. Prick the meat with a skewer or a small knife. If the juices run clear, the meat is done and should be served immediately. You can also check with the meat thermometer, which should show 150 to 160°F (65 to 70°C).

For chicken and turkey breasts, if when poking them they feel slightly firm to the touch, you should switch to the prick test. Prick the meat with a skewer or a small knife. The meat is done and ready to serve when the juices run clear with no traces of red. The meat thermometer should indicate 165 to 170°F (75 to 77°C). Chicken and turkey legs should read 175 to 190°F (80 to 88°C) when measured at the bone.

Well Done When poking the meat it will feel almost hard. It will be well cooked inside and hot with an internal temperature of 160 to 170°F (70 to 77°C). The color will be grayish brown. For most people's preference, beef and lamb are overdone at this stage. In addition to the poking test, prick the meat with a thin needle or a small knife. If the juices run clear with no traces of red, the meat is done and should be served immediately. When cooking the whole bird, the meat thermometer, inserted to the bone should show just below 195°F (90°C).

Grills, Tools and Starters

Buying your first grill or upgrading to a new one is a very exciting purchase, but the countless variety of choices can make the decision seem overwhelming. Most types are nowadays readily available online and in specialized grill shops. The choice of grill depends very much on the number of persons you plan to feed, the type of food you want to cook and your budget. Grills are available from under $50 up to several thousand dollars with all possible options.

When I moved to Thailand I could not find a good charcoal grill (that has changed now and many are available). Since I am educated as an engineer, I took up the challenge and designed and built my own grill. I thought of the various grilling techniques that I might like to use and came up with a combination grill-tandoor-smoker. It allowed me to cook virtually any recipe I could get my hands on. But frankly I use the direct and indirect grilling functions the most. To meet most of your grilling needs, and to grill all of the recipes in this book, any type of Western-style grill, including your kitchen oven, which allows direct and indirect grilling, will work.

You don't need to spend a fortune on the grill. The key things to consider are sturdiness, easy maintenance and easy handling, as well as available grilling space to fit your needs. If you cook for only a few people a medium-sized grill will do the job.

Another major factor to consider is whether you want to go for a charcoal or gas grill. I prefer the charcoal grill. I believe it is more fun to light a real fire—there is the aura of connecting to the elements and our much simpler past. In addition to being fun, charcoal burns hotter than gas, which permits better searing.

Charcoal grills also offer greater flexibility with fuel selection since you can burn wood and throw in spices and fragrant leaves to give a smoke flavor. You can place wood chips or pellets wrapped in an aluminum pouch in a gas grill but the flavor is not as rich and smoky as it is when placed directly on a wood- or charcoal-fired grill.

The disadvantage is that you need to handle charcoal and ash, which some people deem messy (I consider it fun!), and you need more time to fire it up compared to a gas grill, which is often started with just a touch of a button. Therefore it's a matter of weighing the advantages and disadvantages to each. I personally enjoy using the charcoal grill for leisurely weekend barbecues and the gas grill for the quick weekday dinners.

In the following section I give a summary of the most important or common grills available on the market. At the end of this chapter you will find descriptions of some specialized Asian grills for the enthusiast who wishes to venture into using some of these specialized grills.

Hibachi Grills The simplest form of grill is the open grill. The hibachi grill, the clay brazier and satay grill as well as the Weber-type kettle grill, when used without its lid, fall into this category. Cleaning of these grill types is done by lowering the grill grate over the coals and letting the fat burn off. The remains are then brushed off with a wire brush. The hibachi is the simplest form of grill. Throughout Asia this grill can be found at many roadside grill shops. Among this type of grill there are two versions available, the simple ceramic or steel vessel or the more modern ventilated grill. The most simple type is a steel or ceramic vessel that is filled almost two-thirds with ash. The live coals are embedded in the ash and fresh coals are added from time to time. There is no vent opening in the bottom of the grill and the burning air accesses the coals through the ash. The limited airflow causes the coals to burn relatively slowly. If more heat is required, the cook will fan air on the coals to increase heat. This type of grill is mostly used for grilling skewers, satays and small slices of fish. You can grill whole fish or chicken legs, however since the heat generation is very low it takes much more time to grill larger pieces of food compared to other grills.

Thai Clay Brazier

In the modern hibachi the charcoal is placed on a rack made of steel or clay, allowing the air to pass through from underneath. These grills allow you to raise or lower either the charcoal tray or the grill. The heat can be regulated by adding or removing live coals under the food, opening a vent for increased air (and thus higher temperature) or raising and lowering the tray. Such grills are used nowadays by street vendors, by individuals with limited space for grilling and in Japanese and Korean restaurants. Gas-fired hibachi grills are often used in Japanese households and restaurants.

The greatest virtue of hibachi grills is their portability and small size, which allows them to fit in every household or be transported to the camp ground. You can even use them to grill on the dinner table. However, if you do place insulation or even better a shallow heat-proof tray with water underneath. If you buy a hibachi make sure that it is designed to raise or lower the grilling grate, which allows you to have more flexibility with your heat control. Hibachi grills are available in stores like Grate Grills & More (www.grategrillsonline.com) or Grill Showroom (www.grillshowroom.com). Eva Solo from Denmark has designed a modern version that fits into your dinner table. It comes in a sleek ceramic vessel design similar to the very original hibachis. The same supplier also manufactures a larger patio version.

Weber Kettle Grill This type of grill is the most popular grill in the United States and I consider it the easiest to use and most versatile. These grills can be used for direct grilling but due to their voluminous shape indirect grilling is easily done. Various copies of the original Weber design are now available on the market. The temperature is controlled by vents in the bottom and in the lid. Some of these grills also come with a set to install a rotisserie on top and charcoal baskets that are placed alongside the food to allow for indirect grilling. When you buy this type of grill it should be of stable construction and equipped with vents at the bottom and the top. Preferably the grill should have an ash-collecting bin and the grill grate should have a hinge to easily add charcoal.

Fire Place Grill In Europe garden equipment suppliers sell ready-made large stone fireplaces with vent hoods for use outside. You can also grill in your fireplace at home, in particular during wintertime. Grilling in the fireplace is done either with the **Fire Place Grill** or

Spit Jack Round Rock Fire Pit

Tuscan Grill or the manual **Rotisserie**. You place the cantilevered Tuscan grill directly onto the embers and grill your meat. This is good for direct grilling only. You can also place a rotisserie with a drip pan placed in front of the glowing wood for indirect grilling. Some high-tech versions of Tuscan grills come in stainless-steel construction and can be completely disassembled and transported in a small pouch. For original fireplace grills, Tuscan grills and rotisseries see Spit Jack Fire Place Grills at www.spitjack.com.

Spit Jack Fire Place Grill

Fire Pit The fire pit is a large open grill that is normally fired with wood kindling and small logs, but charcoal can be used as well. The grate height is adjustable and most of the larger models come with a rotisserle. These grills do not have a hood and therefore they cannot be used for smoking. Indirect grilling is accomplished by placing the food at great distance from the heat—some models allow the food to be placed 4 feet (1.25 meters) over the embers. Other models come with meat hooks that allow you to slowly grill your meat, just like the Native Americans prepared their jerky. These types of grills are excellent for roasting suckling pigs or whole lamb on a rotisserie and to grill large quantities of meat for parties. If you buy one make sure that the structure is stable to carry the weight of the large pieces of meat and the grill tray height is easily adjustable with the weight of food on it.

Thueros Grill System This stainless-steel German designer grill (see **www.thueros.de**) has several options, including a standard open grill with or without a rotisserie kit and optional smoker box module. The charcoal can be lit in a built-in chimney. The shape of the firebox allows for direct and indirect grilling. The temperature is controlled with vents in the bottom and in the lid. A large smoker box module can be placed over the grill. Since it is constructed entirely of stainless steel it is higher priced than a standard kettle grill. This grill is a very popular model in Europe.

Big Green Egg

Big Green Egg and Imperial Kamado This vertical egg-shaped grill (or oven) originates from Japan. It is included here, rather than the "Exotic Grill" section, because it has become very popular in the West and is easy to find. The charcoal fire is lit in the bottom and heats up the ceramic walls, which allows for even cooking. The grill is very suitable for large pieces of meat, poultry, ribs and leg of lamb. The tight lid keeps the moisture inside the grill and leaves the food moist.

A perforated charcoal holder allows the air to enter from below the coals and control the heat. The heat is controlled by modulating the air vents and can be regulated between 200°F (95°C) to above 600°F (315°C). Both direct and indirect grilling can be done in this grill and it is suitable for almost all of the recipes in this book.

The original Japanese version of this ceramic grill is known as the "Imperial Kamado" (**www.kamado.com**).

The American version is known as the "Big Green Egg" (**www.big-greenegg.com**). Both are available at most grill retailers.

Gas Grills Gas grills are the most popular grills worldwide. The main advantage of the gas grill is the quick start-up, no messing around with charcoal and ash, easy temperature control and cleanup. The basic gas grill has two or three burner zones. If you want to grill larger pieces of food you will need at least three burner zones. Most of the recipes in this book can be grilled on gas grills with three burner zones.

The gas burners heat the cooking elements, which are made of lava stones or ceramics. Ceramics have an even surface that allows the dripping fat to evaporate immediately and thus reducing the risk of flare-ups. Other models use ceramic rods. The minimum requirement is three burners, an enameled grate, a large hood, which allows even distribution of heat, and a second tray on a higher level.

The gas super grills have up to four burners or more, a smoker box with a separate burner, rotisseries with vertical burners and side burners for heating sauces and cooking in a wok. These outdoor kitchens are suitable for every recipe mentioned in this book. The smallest gas grills are hibachi-type grills that are fitted over the camping gas. The grills are portable and are very useful when camping. These grills can only be used for small pieces of food and small steaks. Charbroil, Ducane, DCS and SMEG from Italy supply good-quality gas grills.

Barbecue Smokers These are available as horizontal- or vertical-type smokers and some with several smoking chambers. They are useful for smok-ing ribs and other large pieces of meat. The food is cooked in a separate smoking chamber and the fire is lit in the offset firebox.

Some models have a grill installed in the firebox to allow for optional direct grilling of steaks. The classic American barbecue is done at lower temperatures and longer grilling times (1 to 1½ hours per pound/500 g of meat) — "low and slow" is the dictum. They use soaked wood chips to create smoke, which gives the strong smoky flavor. Some recipes in this book may not be suitable for this type of grill because the smoke flavors do not go well with some Asian spices. If you decide to buy this type of grill look for sturdy and heavy construction, including sturdy wheels to support

Spitjack Barbecue Smoker Grill

it. Also, the firebox and smoke chamber should have adjustable vents. There should be an opening to collect the dripping fat. Barbecue smokers have an opening where you can collect the dripping fat with a scraper in a bowl. In my experience a lot of fat collects during smoking and I prefer to do this after every smoking event. Every so often, it's a good idea to clean it with a special cleaning spray and kitchen towels.

Grill Pan This is a pan with a ridged surface. The best grill pans are made of cast iron. Other models are heavy iron or cast aluminum coated with Teflon. If you're using the original cast-iron pan you need to rub the pan with vegetable oil and heat it until the oil starts smoking. Remove from the fire and let cool. Don't wash the pan with soap. After using rinse the pan and scrub with a brush. Or rub with a paper towel. They are useful only for small pieces of meat, skewers, vegetables and steaks. The disadvantage of grill pans is that no smoke flavor can be created.

Electric Grills These use infrared heat to grill. High grilling temperatures can be achieved. With a few exceptions, these grills are normally not suitable for indirect grilling and smoking. Typically electric grills are better for small pieces of food and are often used on the table. Some models have a lid. The thermostat makes temperature regulation easy. If you buy such a grill, look for drip pan that can be easily removed. Large

electric grills are supplied by Charbroil and Weber.

Electric Table Grills These are used for on the table grilling. The benefit of these grills is that they are easy to heat and there is no messing around with charcoal, no ash and little smoke. The disadvantage is that the unique taste of smoke is missing and the general fun factor of charcoal-fired grills. However, if you live in a small apartment and you want to organize a table grill party, this is a great way to go and the results are good as well.

EXOTIC ASIAN GRILLS

The Vertical Ceramic Grill or Oven
This grill/oven can trace its 3,000-year-old origins to Persia, though it is now used in various forms all over Asia. In Punjab it is known as the "tandoor," in Turkey as the "*tandir*," in China it is mostly used for roast duck and thus called "*kao ya lu*" or "roast duck oven," in Thailand it is called the "*ong*" and in Japan it is referred to as the "kamado." The kamado has become very popular in the West, and has even inspired an American-made version known as the "The Big Green Egg" (see page 22). With the exception of the kamado, most of the grills highlighted in this section are far too specialized to serve the needs of the typical Western grill jockey.

Chinese Roast Duck Oven In China the oven for the famous Beijing roast duck is based on the same design principles as an Indian tandoor, includ-ing the stainless steel cladding. Ducks, geese, chicken, pork tenderloins and kebabs are hung by special hooks. This technique is different from the tandoor, which uses skewers. It is not suitable for smaller meat pieces and vegetables.

Korean BBQ Grill In Korean barbecue restaurants you sometimes find an alternative to the hibachi grill. The live coals are placed in a steel vessel that sits in a tray filled with water. In some restaurant models, the air is sucked through a vent in the center of the grill and through a duct underneath the table. The exhaust is led out of the room.

This system works very well and avoids having all the smoke and fumes in the room. However the ducting construction is quite complicated, which makes this type of grill normally only applicable for restaurants. Other restaurants use a normal square or round hibachi-type grill, which is lowered into a specially built table.

Satay Grills The satay grill is an alternative open grill but its shape is uniquely designed to grill skewers. It is used in Indonesia, China and Thailand. The top is not covered with a grill but there are two jagged rails on each side of the grill, which hold the satay skewers. Thueros from Germany produces a satay grill with automatic rotating skewers.

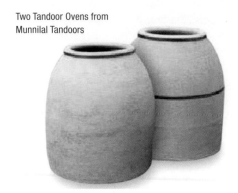

Two Tandoor Ovens from Munnilal Tandoors

Tandoor This is an example of a verticle oven. Originally the tandoor was used to bake flat breads such as roti and naan. Only in the last century did it come to be used for grilling meats and seafood. Tandoors have come into use in most Indian restaurants throughout the world and are available in either charcoal- or gas-fired versions. Breads are cooked by sticking the dough onto the clay walls and letting them bake for a few minutes before scraping them off. Meat, typically kebabs, is inserted on skewers. Chickens are normally grilled at half size. In Turkey large lamb pieces are grilled by hanging them into the tandoor. The tandoor cooks at relatively high temperatures. Therefore this grill type is not suitable for most Western recipes and large pieces of meat. Another disadvantage is the limited lifetime. The ceramic vessel may have to be changed after a few years. I've adapted the tandoori recipes in this book to be successfully cooked in any other type of grill.

Traditional tandoors are available from Nishi Enterprise (**www.nishienterprise.com**). Good modern-day tandoors are available from the Woodstone Corporation in Washington state (**www.woodstone-corp.com**). One of the largest Indian suppliers of tandoors is Munnilal India, Pvt. Ltd. (**www.munnilaltandoors.com**).

Thai Ong The Thai version of the clay grill is a large ceramic vessel that originally was designed for collecting rainwater. The ong is a very specialized and regional grill used for cooking chickens that are dressed, split and skewered onto a bamboo stick, and placed in the ong. Some vendors hang the whole chicken with hooks from the brim. Chicken cooked in this ong (*gai ob ong*) is found mainly in the western part of Thailand but has spread to other provinces as well.

TOOLS

Basting Brushes are available in various sizes and shapes. Some have stiff brush hairs, others have soft heads like mops. Make sure the brush is natural hair, bamboo or cotton. Don't use nylon or similar artificial textiles because when they burn they can emit poisonous components. The basting brushes or mops should be at least 7 inches (18 cm) long but the best brushes have 12-inch (30-cm) or longer handles.

Chicken Sitters Various sizes and shapes are available which hold the chicken in a vertical position while grilling. Some can be filled with beer or other liquids that steam the chicken from inside and grill it from outside. One model combines a sitting beer can with a grill wok—indeed a very good idea. In some areas in Asia a young coconut is used for the same purpose.

Drip Pans are available in various shapes and sizes. Aluminum is the best choice, but make sure the pan is sufficiently thick.

Gloves should be thick and well insulating. Every grill enthusiast should have them to protect his hands from burns.

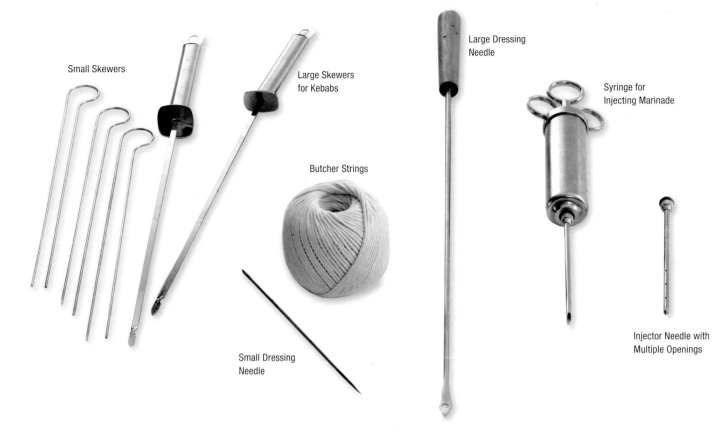

Small Skewers

Large Skewers
for Kebabs

Butcher Strings

Small Dressing
Needle

Large Dressing
Needle

Syringe for
Injecting Marinade

Injector Needle with
Multiple Openings

Grill Baskets Grill baskets are used for fish and fragile food pieces that are difficult to handle. Place the fish into the basket and place it over the charcoal. When food needs to be turned on the grill, the entire basket is turned. Grill baskets with long handles are most practical.

Grill Plates, Woks and Trays Grill plates or trays are made of sheet metal with a nonstick surface. They have either a ridged surface like a grill pan or small holes and slots to allow the smoke to pass through. Grill plates with a ridged surface are used for burgers and steaks.

Grill woks and trays are mainly used for vegetables, fruit and fish pieces. These woks and trays are mainly used for small food pieces that would either easily stick onto the grill or fall through the grill.

The vertical roasting wok allows you to grill a chicken or turkey sitting on a can while cooking vegetables around it. When using nonstick trays and woks, place the tray or wok on the hot grill. Rub with vegetable oil. Wait until the tray or wok gets hot and then place the food on it. Remember to only use wooden or plastic spatulas or tongs. Metal spatulas will damage the nonstick surface.

Grill Thermometers can measure up to 750°F (350°C) and are placed directly onto the grill. They are especially helpful for low-temperature grilling but can be used for normal direct grilling as well.

Metal Grill Brushes and Scrapers These are used to clean the grill. The brush should have a long sturdy handle and a scraper to remove scaling and burnt food remains. The best brushes have wooden handles and a replacement head. Soft heads are difficult to use when the grill is really crusted.

Meat Thermometer Meat thermometers are available with analogue or digital instant read display. The advantage of the analogue display is that you don't need batteries. When buying a meat thermometer make sure the display is large enough and easily readable. Also look for a thermometer that has a sufficiently long needle to stick and measure the core temperature of meat.

Roast Holder A roast holder makes it easy to keep a round piece of meat in place over the grill. These roast holders are also very useful when you grill your food in an electric oven.

Rotisseries are rotating spits and are usually supplied with electric motors that are battery driven. The speed should be adjustable. Some rotisseries are designed for a particular grill model whereas others are generic and can be used for any grill. If you plan to grill

with rotisseries look for a grill that is designed to accommodate one or has a rotisserie feature among its options.

Kettle grills and gas grills need a sufficient high wind screen (some grill suppliers offer this screen together with the rotisserie as a set). Suppliers of larger models and fire pits offer a support that you can fix the rotisserie to that is high enough to grill whole animals such pigs or lamb. If you plan to use a rotisserie for your home fireplace, it should come with a support stand and drip pan.

Skewers are made either of bamboo or metal. They are available in various sizes and thicknesses. Some metal skewers are decorated or have wooden handles.

Metal skewers should preferably be flat or have a square section. Flat or square skewers will help to hold ground meat kebabs in place. Bamboo skewers should be soaked in water for about a half hour prior to grilling to prevent burning. All skewers should be rubbed with oil before threading meat to make it easier to remove the meat when done.

For small pieces, which are difficult to hold in place when turning on the grill, you should preferably use two skewers or double skewers.

Skewer Rack The skewer rack is a rack to hold several skewers in place. There are several models available. Some are placed on a rotisserie. Others are a square frame, which enables you to turn all skewers at once by inverting the rack.

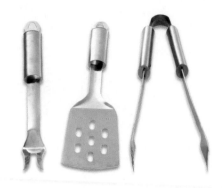

Tongs, Forks and Spatulas are the most important grill tools because they allow you to handle your food without burning your fingers. It is best to have several different-sized tongs starting from a 9-inch (23-cm) length. Grill forks are long forks to hold the food and turn it on the grill.

Grill forks should be at least 12-inches (30-cm) long, stainless steel and be sufficiently strong to handle whole leg of lamb. Spatulas, grill forks and tongs should be sturdy enough to handle small and large pieces like whole chicken. Look for stainless steel with wooden handles. Avoid plastic. If your grill grate has a nonstick surface you need wooden or Teflon spatulas. Don't use metal spatulas because they will damage the nonstick surface.

STARTERS AND STARTER FUEL

Starter Fuel Lighter fuel is the most commonly used starter fuel. Sprinkle the fluid onto the charcoal, set the fluid can aside and close the lid of the can to avoid any accidental spilling and risk of fire. Light the dowsed charcoal by tossing a match. Paraffin blocks are white-colored small blocks that burn for several minutes. Two or three blocks are enough to fire up your grill.

Sawdust starters and impregnated wood chip starters are used in a similar fashion as paraffin starters.

Note: Never use petrol or other chemical fluids. They are volatile and create explosive mixtures.

Charcoal Briquettes It takes ½ hour for briquettes to reach the optimum glowing point. Briquettes burn slow but more regularly than charcoal. The temperature of briquettes can reach 570°F (300°C) to 610°F (320°C) and will last, depending on the thickness of the ember bed, for 30 minutes to 1 hour at a more or less constant high level. If the briquettes are not entirely burnt you can reuse them. Look for briquettes specifically for grilling or barbecue. Some brands may contain waste wood or petrochemicals that give off an acrid smoke and may be dangerous to your health.

Charcoal burns much more quickly than briquettes. It reaches its optimum glowing temperature of approximately 480°F (250°C) to 610°F (320°C) after 15 to 20 minutes. However, the temperature will start to drop after only 20 to 30 minutes. Charcoal usually burns out completely.

Wood Chips or Pellets or Hardwood
Wood pellets are used for smoking rather than fuel. They are enclosed into a pouch and tossed in the glowing embers in a chimney starter, on the grill or onto the gas grill. This will give your food a special smoke flavor. In Europe the main wood for indoor firing is birch but also pine, oak, poplar and wood from fruit tree trimmings. Naturally these woods are used for barbecuing. In the United States the preferred wood is either hickory or mesquite. The wood from grape vines is a very suitable wood for barbecuing and is used in most wine growing areas.

Wood from juniper, orange trees and lemon trees as can be found in the Mediterranean is a very special fuel for barbecuing since it gives a unique taste to the meat. In Asia the preferred fuel is the hard portion of palm leaves, sugar-cane trimmings, casuarina (a kind of pine tree) and cedar (north India and central Asia). Both latter varieties contain resin that makes them not very suitable for smoking. A very special fuel is charcoal of mountain ebony in Thailand. The fibrous shell of coconut is often used for smoking. It is also common to add spices to the charcoal or wood to enhance the flavor, particularly when you use a smoker or closed grill. You may add rosemary, bay leaf, thyme, sage or other spices to the wood. In India it is not uncommon to add cinnamon and cloves to the burning coals. Don't be shy to try your own ideas.

Note: Avoid used wood from construction sites since it may be treated with chemicals that are harmful when burnt. Also do not use any waste material such as plastic or plasticized paper for burning or for lighting the grill. These materials burn very slowly and produce extremely poisonous gases. Thus even when your fire is well developed, these waste materials continue to release poisonous components into the smoke and onto your food.

Chimney Starters are shaped like a vertical tube, which creates a draft and produces glowing charcoal within the shortest period. There is a perforated charcoal tray in the bottom section of the starter with space underneath it for the starter fuel. The starter fuel is lighted and in turn ignites the charcoal above. The cylindrical shape of the chimney starter funnels the hot gas through the coal pile above, which produces glowing charcoal.

Mesquite Wood Chunks

Briquettes

Charcoal

Apple Wood Chips

Coconut milk is made from freshly grated coconut. Fresh coconut milk is made in two grades: thick and thin. The thick coconut milk is made by squeezing the freshly grated coconut pulp. The remaining pulp is then soaked in hot water, which is squeezed out to give thin coconut milk. Coconut milk is sold sweetened or unsweetened in cans. Use unsweetened coconut milk for the recipes in this book. When opening the can you will find that the coconut milk has separated into a thick cream on top and thinner milk. You will need to blend the two together. You can do this by shaking the can vigorously before opening it, or placing the contents in a blender and processing until smooth. Once opened pour the contents into a neutral plastic container and store it in the refrigerator where it will last for about one week.

Coriander leaves (cilantro) I use fresh coriander, often referred to as "cilantro" in the West and sometimes as "Chinese parsley," in many marinades, sauces and salads. If you can find fresh coriander with the root, don't discard it. In Asia the root is very often used as a separate ingredient. It's an important ingredient in Thai curry pastes and stocks. I use the root in marinades for grilled chicken and fish. The root is cleaned and finely chopped. Larger roots should be scraped to remove the outer skin. To scrape the root, cut vertically onto the surface of the root with a sharp knife. Then scrape the surface till the white internal color appears. If you cannot find fresh coriander with the root attached, replace with the lower part of the stems.

Coriander seeds are the dried, ripe seed of the fresh herb coriander. They are sold as seeds or in ground form. I use them in many marinades, sauces and chutneys and they are also used in Western-style dry rubs.

Cumin is sold as dried seeds or as a powder. I use it often in marinades, sauces and spice mixtures. It is a member of the parsley family and is native to central Asia and India. The flavor of cumin plays a major role in Indian, Indonesian, Thai, Vietnamese and Middle Eastern cuisines.

Curry leaves The curry tree is native to India. The leaves are preferably used fresh, though they are available fresh or dried in Asian grocery stores. Their taste is somewhat earthy. If you cannot find fresh or dried curry leaves, you may use half as much fresh coriander leaves instead.

Curry powder is a mixture of various spices and can differ from area to area as well as from dish to dish. With the exception of the original East Indian Company recipe for madras curry, which consists of fenugreek, coriander, turmeric, cumin, mustard seeds, nutmeg, mace, star anise, cinnamon, cloves, pepper and chili, there is no standard curry recipe.

Dashi stock is the basis for most Japanese soups and is also used in many sauces. The easiest method for making dashi stock is to buy dashi stock granules and dissolve them in hot water, following the instructions on the package. One of the key ingredients in dashi are fish flakes made from dried skipjack tuna.

Fennel seeds are sold as whole dried seeds or powder. I prefer to use the whole dried seeds for spice mixtures and in marinades as well as dry rubs. In Asian recipes fennel is often combined with coriander, cumin, cinnamon, cloves, nutmeg and turmeric and is used in curry blends and Chinese five spice powder.

Fenugreek is usually sold as dried seeds in Asian grocery stores. It is often included in curry mixtures available in the West, giving them their distinct "curry" aroma. When used as seeds they need to be toasted or preferably fried in a little oil before being ground.

Fish sauce Known as "nam pla" in Thailand and "nuoc mam" in Vietnam, this key sauce is mostly made of anchovies, salt and water. Some varieties use squid or other kinds of fish. Thai and Vietnamese fish sauce are very similar and each can easily be substituted for the other.

Five spice powder
This Chinese spice mixture of fennel, cinnamon, cloves, star anise, Szechuan pepper and sometimes cardamom, licorice and brown cardamom (grains of paradise) is often used in sauces and marinades together with soy sauce and honey. Here is a simple but fragrant five spice powder recipe:
One 1-in (2.5-cm) piece cinnamon
2 star anise
2 cloves
½ teaspoon fennel
1 teaspoon Szechuan pepper

Heat a skillet and roast the spices slightly until the flavor emerges. Place in a mortar or food processor and grind to a fine powder. Pass through a sieve and grind remaining larger pieces again until they are a fine powder. Keep in an airtight jar.

Garam masala
This Indian spice mixture typically includes coriander, cumin, cinnamon, nutmeg, mace, cloves, cardamom and black pepper. A favorite mixture of mine is:
2 tablespoons green cardamom pods
2 pods grains of paradise (or a heaping ½ teaspoon seeds)
1½ tablespoons cumin seeds
2 teaspoons aniseed
1½ tablespoons black pepper corns
Four 1-in (2.5-cm) cinnamon sticks
½ tablespoon cloves
½ teaspoon ground nutmeg
3 pieces mace
Slightly roast the spices and grind in a food processor. Pass through a sieve, regrinding the larger pieces. Keep in an airtight container.

Cardamom originates from India and is available as dried pods or in ground form. I prefer to use the dried pods, which keep the aroma better. Enclosed in the fruit pods are tiny, brown, aromatic seeds that are slightly pungent to taste. Cardamom pods are generally green but are also available in bleached white pod form. Cardamom is used alone in sweets and is often combined

with cinnamon, cloves, nutmeg, mace and ginger for savory dishes. It is often slightly toasted together with other spices and then ground (any remaining pieces of pod shell are discarded). If you cannot find cardamom pods, you may substitute ground cardamom as follows: pinch of ground cardamom for 2 pods; heaping ¼ teaspoon ground cardamom for 5 pods.

Grains of paradise (brown cardamom) originate from West Africa, and are mainly sold as complete pods or as seeds. This spice is from a plant in the ginger family and is shaped like cardamom seeds, but a bit larger and reddish-brown in color. I love to use this spice, which is spicy and slightly bitter, in several marinade recipes as well as in sauces and chutneys. In some cases the pods are toasted, then the skin of the pod needs to be removed and only the inner seeds are used for cooking. In other cases the seeds themselves are toasted. To remove seeds from a pod, split open the pod and scrape out the seeds. I often call for pods in the recipes in this book, however seeds can be used in place of pods if you can't find them. (One heaping ¼ teaspoon of seeds can be substituted for one pod.) If you cannot find grains of paradise, use allspice instead. This spice is known as "brown cardamom" in Asia.

Green mango powder (amchur) has a tenderizing effect and is often used in marinades for poultry and lamb. It is made from the unripe or green mango fruit that has been sliced and sun-dried. It is mainly used in Indian dishes. It gives a slightly sour taste and can be combined with any spice. If you cannot find it, replace with twice the amount of lime juice to provide sourness.

Green mangoes sold in Asian shops are a particular variety that even when ripe are not too sweet. Their shape is rather elongated compared to the usually sold sweet mango that is rather round and plump. These green mangoes are sold to be eaten raw with some sugar or used in salads or for fish recipes. Raw unripe regular mango can be used instead.

Ground red pepper (cayenne pepper) is sometimes referred to as "cayenne pepper," named after the chilies grown in the vicinity of the Cayenne River in French Guiana. Early Spanish explorers found red pepper pods in the Caribbean. Red pepper is used in Italian, Indian, Mexican and Caribbean cuisines.

Hoisin sauce is a sweet thick Chinese sauce made from soybeans. It is very useful in barbecue recipes.

Kaffir lime (leaves and zest) is a special type of lime and the leaves are sold fresh or dried. In Asia the fresh leaf is used predominantly but in Western countries often times only the dried leaves are available. I use the leaf and zest of the fruit for sauces, marinades and in curry pastes. If you cannot find the fresh kaffir lime for zesting, replace with the same amount of lime zest. If you cannot find fresh leaves, use half as many dried leaves instead.

Kecap manis is a sweetish, thick soy sauce made with palm sugar and seasoned with star anise and garlic. It can be used as a dip or as a substitute for dark soy sauce in Indonesian recipes.

Lavender is the dried flower of the lavender bush. It is native to the Mediterranean region and India. It has a distinctive sweet aroma and combines well with rosemary, thyme and marjoram.

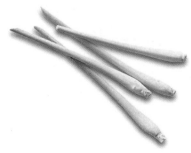

Lemongrass is a tropical grass and is available fresh or as dried slices. I prefer the fresh herb for marinades and dips as well as in curry pastes. The fresh stalks and leaves have a lemonlike flavor. Lemongrass is often combined with ginger, galangal, green coriander, lime, kaffir lime and turmeric. The outer leaf needs to be removed and only the inner lower two-thirds of the stalk is used.

Mace and nutmeg are from the same fruit of a tree that is native in Indonesia. Mace is the thin, bright red lacelike covering over the shell of the nutmeg. It is sold as whole dried pieces or ground. Its flavor is similar to nutmeg but more delicate and is often combined with cardamom, cinnamon and cloves. I prefer to use the whole pieces, which should be slightly toasted before being ground.

Mirin is a sweet Japanese rice wine used for marinades together with soy sauce and sake and sugar.

Miso is a paste made of fermented soybeans. There are several varieties of miso available. Shiro miso, or white miso, has a mild slightly salty taste and is often used in marinades and soups. Hatcho miso, or red miso, has a stronger taste that is reminiscent of malt or dark beer and is widely used for marinades and sauces. Sweet miso, which has a sweet taste, is used less for marinades but rather for sauces and dips.

Mustard seeds come in three kinds: white or yellow, brown and black seeds. The brown and black mustard seeds have a stronger pungent flavor compared to the yellow variety. Mustard is sold as whole seeds or ground. I prefer to use the whole seeds in marinades and sauces as well as dry rubs. It can be combined with most Asian spices.

Nutmeg is the seed of the same fruit as mace. It is sold as a whole nut or ground. I use it preferably as a whole nut and grate it freshly. Nutmeg blends well with mace, cinnamon, cloves and cardamom.

Oyster sauce is a popular Chinese sauce that is widely available. It is used very often in Thai marinades together with soy sauce and other ingredients for grilled chicken, beef and pork.

Palm sugar is normally sold either as brown dried cakes or as a light brown paste in cans. It is made from the juice of the sugar palm, which is indigenous to south India, Thailand, Indonesia and Vietnam. Its leaves are cut off and the juice is collected in large containers. The juice is then dried and shaped into small cakes. Its taste is similar to brown sugar

but a bit more aromatic. It is less sweet than normal cane sugar. If you cannot find palm sugar replace it with equal parts light and dark brown sugar.

Paprika is sold mainly as dried powder. It is mildly flavored and has a brilliant red color. Early Spanish explorers returned from South America with red pepper seeds to Europe, where the plant gradually lost its pungency and became "sweet" paprika. It can be easily combined with Asian spices to create various marinades and sauces, but it can also be used in Western-style dry rubs.

Pomegranate concentrate is sold in bottles in Middle Eastern grocery stores. It is made from pomegranate juice that has been concentrated without sugar. It has a sour very fragrant flavor and is used in marinades and salads in Iranian and Middle Eastern cuisine. To make it yourself you need about three-quarters of a gallon (3 liters) of fresh pomegranate juice to produce 1½ cups (150 to 200 ml) of pomegranate concentrate. The juice is cooked over very low heat for a few hours until the water has evaporated. If you do not have time to make this concentrate use a combination of fresh pomegranate juice and lemon juice—2 tablespoons fresh juice mixed with 1 tablespoon lemon juice to replace one tablespoon concentrate.

Red dates (jujubes) are sold as dried fruit in Western markets and in Asia. They look similar to medjool dates but contain significantly less sugar. They are used in Chinese cuisine in stuffings and desserts such as Eight Treasures glutinous rice (*ba bao fan*). If you cannot find Chinese dates (*hong zao*), replace with half amount medjool dates.

Saffron is the dried yellow stigmas of the flowers of the crocus family. It is sold as entire stigmas or ground. I use saffron mostly in marinades and sauces. It can be combined with many spices like mint, mace, nutmeg, cinnamon and cardamom.

Sake is produced in a multiple fermentation process. In the first step, the mold breaks the starch down into sugar, and then the sugar is fermented with yeast to alcohol. This process is very similar to beer production, except that beer production is carried out in only one step. The highest quality sake is made with polished rice where the starch layer has been partially removed. The more polished the rice, the higher the quality of the sake and it is then labeled "junmai." Junmai sakes are drier and more balanced than the less expensive sakes. For cooking purposes one can use a cheaper sake, which tastes sweeter than high quality sake.

Sambal oelek is a multipurpose condiment that is popular throughout Indonesia. It consists of fresh bird's-eye chilies ground together with vinegar, oil and salt. Some varieties contain garlic as well.

Sawtooth herb, also known as thorny coriander, is a fresh herb used in Vietnamese cuisine. It has elongated leaves with a serrated edge. I use it in sauces and dips, but it can be chopped and added to salads and soups. If you cannot find thorny coriander use the same quantity of fresh coriander.

Sesame oil is used in Chinese and Japanese marinades. This aromatic oil is pressed from roasted sesame seeds, which gives it an amber color and rich flavor. It is referred to in the recipes in this book as "dark" sesame oil to distinguish it from the colorless sesame oil that is pressed from untoasted sesame seeds and is used as a neutral cooking or salad oil.

Sesame paste in Asia is made from toasted sesame seeds. In central Asia, it is made from untoasted sesame seeds, and is known as "tahini." Tahini is easier to find in the West, and can be substituted for Asian sesame paste.

Sesame seeds have a rich nutlike flavor when toasted. I use toasted sesame seeds to add texture and flavor to marinades and sauces and in stuffings. Sesame can be combined with nuts, almonds, pistachio and poppy seeds or with most of the other spices used in this book.

Szechuan peppers are small brownish-red berries that are sold whole or ground. The taste is pungent and biting and leaves a slightly numbing feeling on the tongue. It is used in marinades and sauces in Chinese and Japanese cuisine and often combined with cinnamon and star anise.

Shiso leaves are sold in two varieties: green and purple shiso. The taste of shiso is reminiscent of mild mint with a hint of fresh coriander (cilantro). Shiso leaves are very popular in Japan and are also used in Vietnamese cuisine. They

are mostly used when fresh as a garnish to sashimi, or other fish and chicken dishes. And they are often added to salads. If you cannot find them, replace with equal parts fresh mint and coriander.

Shiitake mushrooms are available fresh or dried. They come in two varieties: one dark brown and one with a brown crackled pattern. When using dried mushrooms they should be soaked in hot water for about one hour. Shiitake mushrooms have been cultivated in China and Japan for over a thousand years and are now also grown in the United States and therefore increasingly available in large supermarkets or Asian grocery stores. If you cannot find fresh shiitake mushrooms replace with small-sized portabello mushrooms.

Soy sauce Chinese light soy sauce (*shen jiang you*) has a light brown color and is slightly saltier than dark soy sauce. **Chinese dark soy sauce** (*lao chou jiang you*) is dark and has a stronger flavor. There are various varieties with mushroom flavor or pure soy flavor. Dark soy sauces are good for marinating. **Thai**

dark soy sauce (*siu dam*) is very thick since it has sugar or molasses added to it. It is sweeter than Chinese dark soy sauce and needs to be used carefully. The same applies to Indonesian **dark soy Sauce**. **Japanese soy sauce** (*shou*) is similar to Chinese dark soy sauce but with less rich flavor and a bit saltier.

Sri racha chili sauce is made of chilies, garlic, salt, sugar, vinegar. There are several varieties. The Sri Racha sauce from Vietnam is less sweet compared to the Thai counterpart.

Star anise has five pods and resembles a small brown star and is sold as the whole dried fruit or ground. It is the fruit of a plant closely related to the magnolia family and has a taste like anise, but stronger and sweeter. The plant originates from southern China and Vietnam and is used in many Asian and Southeast Asian cuisines.

Sumac is sold as a purple-reddish powder, often mixed with salt. It is made from the dried fruits of the cashew family and originates in the Mediterranean and central Asia. I use sumac in marinades, kebabs and salads. Sumac has a tart and sour, and slightly astringent flavor.

Tamarind is an important ingredient in Indian, Southeast Asian and Latin American cuisines. It is available in fresh whole pods, a compressed block, paste or liquid concentrates. I use the whole pods and for ease use the compressed block or paste to prepare marinades and dips. It is sold in most Asian grocery stores, some natural foods stores and even some conventional grocery stores. Ffresh tamarind pulp is brownish black in color and has a sour taste with a hint of sweetness. The dry pulp needs to be soaked before usage. One tablespoon of tamarind pulp should be dissolved in 3 tablespoons of hot water, after which the seeds and veins are discarded. This amount of dissolved and strained pulp can be replaced by 1 tablespoon tamarind concentrate. If you cannot find tamarind in any form, you can replace it with lime juice as follows: 1 tablespoon tamarind pulp dissolved in 3 tablespoons water, or 1 tablespoon tamarind paste or 1 tablespoon tamarind concentrate can be replaced with 1½ teaspoons lime juice.

Thai basil leaves are dark green with purple rims and they hare an anise/licorice flavor to the sweet basil scent. Thai basil is mainly sold fresh in Asian grocery stores, but is increasingly available in conventional grocery stores. Thai basil can be combined both with Western and Asian spices and goes especially well in marinades, Thai dips, Southeast Asian curries and any kind of salad, either Asian or Western.

Turmeric is the root of a plant related to ginger and is well known for its bright yellow color. It is the ingredient that makes curry yellow. It is sold as fresh root or as a dried bright yellow powder. It can be combined with most Asian spices.

Wasabi Japanese horseradish is similar to Western horseradish in taste, but much stronger. Its color is bright green, whereas Western horseradish is white. Wasabi is sold mostly as prepared paste and less often as a fresh root.

Yuzu is a Japanese citrus fruit with a very strong fragrant flavor. It can be replaced with lemon juice and a little lime zest.

Yellow soy bean paste is used in many stir-fried vegetable dishes and can be used for grilling vegetables in vegetable packs. If not available then it can be replaced by Chinese light soy sauce.

Char Siu Marinade

The Char Siu Marinade is the traditional marinade for pork strips in the Canton area of China. Honey and five spice pow-der are the main source of flavor. This marinade is not only suitable for pork but also for duck and chicken, in particular chicken wings.

PREPARATION TIME: **15 minutes**

MAKES ¾ cup **(185 ml)**

1 tablespoon light neutral-flavored oil
1 tablespoon peeled and finely chopped fresh
 ginger
2 small green onions (scallions), finely chopped
1 tablespoon hoisin sauce
1 tablespoon Chinese dark soy sauce
2 tablespoons Chinese light soy sauce
2 tablespoons honey
2 tablespoons Chinese Shaoxing wine or dry
 sherry
2 tablespoons water
½ teaspoon five spice powder (page 31)
Dash of red food color (optional)

In a small skillet, heat the oil over medium-low heat. When hot, add the ginger and green onion and cook briefly. Add the other ingredients and continue to simmer for 3 to 5 minutes. Remove from the heat and let cool before using.

Orange Yogurt Marinade

A mix of orange and saffron is widely used in Persian cuisine. In most tandoor dishes yogurt is used as a marinade base for chicken and lamb. The yogurt helps to tenderize the meat. This marinade is mild and perfumed with orange and saffron. It goes well with chicken, or any other kind of poultry, and lamb. It is a good choice when using either the Rice, Pistachio and Raisin Stuffing (page 43) or the Pine Nut and Herb Stuffing (page 45).

PREPARATION TIME: **10 minutes**

MAKES **1 cup (250 ml)**

Zest of ½ orange
¾ cup (185 ml) plain yogurt
2 tablespoons finely chopped fresh flat-leaf
 parsley or chervil
1 teaspoon Tabasco
Pinch of ground cinnamon
¼ teaspoon saffron dissolved in 2 tablespoons
 warm milk
2 tablespoons finely chopped fresh mint leaves
Salt to taste

In a small bowl, add all the ingredients. Whisk until smooth.

Spicy Soy Marinade

This recipe stems from the most western part of China bordering Pakistan and central Asia. Kebabs marinated with this sauce are sold by street vendors from Europe to Beijing. Try this unique marinade with lamb, beef and chicken skewers.

PREPARATION TIME: **15 minutes**

MAKES ABOUT ½ **cup (125 ml)**

1 tablespoon neutral-flavored oil
3 red chilies, finely chopped
2 tablespoons finely chopped shallot
1 tablespoon finely chopped garlic
1 tablespoon peeled and finely chopped fresh
 ginger
1 tablespoon Chinese soy sauce
1 teaspoon Chinese black vinegar or Worcestershire sauce
2 teaspoons paprika powder
1 tablespoon Chinese Shaoxing wine or dry
 sherry
Pinch of ground cumin
Pinch of five spice powder (page 31)
1 tablespoon sugar
3 tablespoons water

Heat the oil in a small skillet and slightly sauté the chili pepper, shallots and garlic. Add the other ingredients and continue to cook over low heat for 1 to 2 minutes. Set aside to let cool before using.

Ginger Sherry Marinade

This Chinese-inspired marinade gets its flavor from the Chinese rice wine called Shaoxing, which is somewhat similar to dry sherry. The sugar helps to accentuate the wine flavor and gives a nice crispy caramel crust. It is suitable for chicken and pork.

PREPARATION TIME: **10 minutes**

MAKES ABOUT ½ **cup (125 ml)**

1 tablespoon peeled and finely chopped fresh ginger
½ teaspoon black pepper
3 tablespoons Chinese Shaoxing wine or dry sherry
3 tablespoons neutral-flavored oil
2 tablespoons dark Chinese soy sauce
2 teaspoons brown sugar

Peel the ginger and chop coarsely. Place the chopped ginger in a mortar or food processor and grind to a fine paste. Add the remaining ingredients and mix well.

Lemon Marinade

This marinade is similar to the one used for Rack of Lamb with Olive Oil and Fresh Herbs (page 138), yet milder, making it ideal for fish and seafood, as well as chicken and vegetables such as asparagus, Brussels sprouts and zucchini. It originates from the central Asian area and suits both Asian and European dishes.

PREPARATION TIME: **10 minutes**

MAKES ½ **cup (125 ml)**

Zest of ½ lemon
Zest of ½ lime
3 tablespoons lemon juice
4 tablespoons neutral-flavored oil
½ tablespoon Worcestershire sauce
2 tablespoons finely chopped fresh flat-leaf parsley
2 tablespoons finely chopped fresh coriander leaves (cilantro)
Salt to taste

Mix all the ingredients in a small bowl.

Teriyaki Marinade

This is a classic Japanese marinade. Its mild sweet flavor goes great with fish, chicken, tofu and vegetables. This recipe is for a basic all-purpose teriyaki. Variations on this recipe, adjusted for different types of meats, exist throughout the book.

PREPARATION TIME: **5 minutes**

MAKES ¾ **cup (185 ml)**

4 tablespoons Japanese soy sauce
4 tablespoons mirin
2 tablespoons dry sake
3 tablespoons sugar, preferably superfine

Mix all the ingredients in a bowl and stir until all the sugar is dissolved.

Caramelized Lemongrass Marinade

This recipe is widely used by grilled-food vendors in Vietnam. Its sweet lemony flavor greatly enhances the taste of grilled food. It is well suited to chicken, beef and lamb. It is used for Carmelized Soy and Lemongrass Spareribs (page 120).

PREPARATION TIME: **20 minutes**

MAKES ½ **cup (125 ml)**

3 tablespoons sugar
4 tablespoons water, divided
1 lemongrass stalk, outer tougher leaves removed and lower two-thirds finely chopped
3 tablespoons finely chopped shallot
4 cloves garlic, finely chopped
1 tablespoon light soy sauce
1 tablespoon fish sauce, preferably Vietnamese (nuoc mam)
½ teaspoon black pepper

Heat the sugar and 2 tablespoons of the water in a small saucepan over medium heat and simmer until the sugar starts to caramelize (the liquid will turn a slight yellowish color). At this point insert a metal teaspoon into the liquid and remove to let cool. The liquid on the spoon should become sticky and slightly yellow. Add the remaining 2 tablespoons of water and the rest of the ingredients and remove from the heat. Let the marinade cool before applying it to the meat.

2 In a small skillet, heat the sesame oil and vegetable oil over medium heat. Add the ginger and green onion and sauté slightly. Add the other ingredients and simmer for 5 minutes. Remove the marinade from the heat. Set aside to let cool before using.

Fiery Szechuan Pepper Marinade

Szechuan pepper gives this stand-alone marinade a kick. If you wish to add even more zing, add some red chili pepper or red chili oil to it. I recommend using it for duck, chicken and pork as well as glazed ham. Wipe the marinade off the meat before placing it on the grill and brush it on toward the end of the grilling time to give the meat a nice crust.

PREPARATION TIME: **25 minutes**

MAKES ABOUT ¾ **cup (200 ml)**

1 tablespoon sesame seeds, lightly toasted
½ teaspoon Szechuan peppercorns, toasted
1 small piece star anise
One ½-in piece stick cinnamon
1 tablespoon sesame oil
1 tablespoon light neutral-flavored oil
1 tablespoon peeled and finely chopped fresh
    ginger
2 tablespoons finely chopped green onion
    (scallion)
1 tablespoon Hoisin sauce
2 tablespoons Chinese light soy sauce
1 tablespoon Chinese Shaoxing wine or dry
    sherry
1 teaspoon chili flakes
1 tablespoon sugar
4 tablespoons water

1 Combine the toasted sesame seeds and Szechuan peppercorns, star aniseed and cinnamon in a mortar or food processor and grind to a powder.

Chermoula Marinade

This herby paste is suitable for any kind of fish and seafood, and even chicken and lamb. Its fresh and herby flavor gives the meat a very special touch. I added turmeric for an extra Asian touch.

PREPARATION TIME: **15 minutes**

MAKES ¾ **cup (175 ml)**

1 teaspoon cumin seeds, toasted
½ cup (30 g) chopped fresh coriander leaves
    (cilantro)
6 cloves garlic, finely chopped
½ teaspoon ground turmeric
½ teaspoon chili powder
1 teaspoon dried thyme leaves
½ teaspoon black pepper
2 tablespoons extra-virgin olive oil
1 tablespoon fresh lemon juice

In a mortar, grind the toasted cumin seeds to a powder. Add the rest of the ingredients, except the oil and lemon juice, and grind to a coarse paste. During grinding slowly drizzle in the olive oil until all ingredients are ground. Add any remaining olive oil and the lemon juice.

Yogurt Korma Paste

Korma is a preparation of food, either meat or vegetables, that is typical in the northern part of India. The dish was introduced by the Moghuls and shows a distinct Persian background. Korma dishes are usually served cooked in a thick rich sauce. This aromatic stand-alone paste uses classic korma ingredients but has been thickened to the right consistency for the grill. I use cashew nuts and almonds, but you can use any kind of mild tasting nut. The paste should be applied for marinating and then wiped off before placing the food onto the grill. Shortly before the meat is done you should apply the paste to give it a rich creamy crust. Or the remaining paste can be cooked with a little stock and served as a sauce on the side.

PREPARATION TIME: **25 minutes**

MAKES **1 cup (250 ml)**

4 cloves, toasted
4 green cardamom pods, toasted
1 grain of paradise pod, toasted, or a heaping
    ¼ teaspoon grains of paradise seeds
One 1-in (2.5-cm) piece cinnamon, toasted
1 piece mace, toasted
1 piece star anise, toasted
3 tablespoons blanched almonds
3 tablespoons cashew nuts
1 tablespoon finely chopped garlic
1 tablespoon peeled and finely chopped fresh
    ginger
2 tablespoons desiccated coconut, soaked in
    water

1 tablespoon neutral-flavored vegetable oil
4 dried apricots, finely chopped
½ cup (125 ml) plain yogurt
Pinch of ground nutmeg
1 tablespoon finely chopped fresh coriander
    leaves (cilantro)

1 Place the toasted spices in a food processor or mortar and grind to a powder, removing remaining pieces of pod shells.
2 Slightly roast the almonds and cashew nuts until they just start to brown. Remove from the heat and grind to a paste. Add the garlic and ginger and grind together with the nuts. Add the desiccated coconut and oil and grind to a smooth paste. Finally add the chopped apricots and continue to grind. When everything has been ground to a fine paste add the yogurt and spices and at last the coriander leaves. Salt to taste.

Coconut Spice Paste

This was inspired by an Indonesian recipe but was toned down to appeal to Western taste. The original paste contains shrimp paste and a yellow root called *kencur*, both are most definitely an acquired taste. This paste can be used for beef, lamb, chicken and seafood. Note that for fish and seafood the lime juice and zest is added to the paste, and the entire lower half of the lemongrass stalk

is used. Use the paste for marinating meat and remove it before grilling. When the meat is almost done, apply a thick layer of the paste to create a nice crust. A few other coconut-based marinades or pastes are sprinkled throughout the book.

PREPARATION TIME: **20 minutes**
MAKES **1 cup (250 ml)**
2 teaspoons coriander seeds, toasted
1 teaspoon black peppercorns, toasted
½ teaspoon cumin seeds, toasted
1 tablespoon neutral vegetable oil
1 shallot, finely chopped
1 lemongrass stalk, outer tougher leaves
    removed and ½ of lower ⅔ of stalk finely
    chopped (chop the entire lower ⅔ of stalk
    for fish or seafood)
1 fresh or dried kaffir lime leaf
1 tablespoon peeled and finely chopped fresh
    ginger
4 cloves garlic, finely chopped
3 to 6 large mild red chilies
1 tablespoon tamarind pulp dissolved in
    3 tablespoons water or 1 tablespoon tama-
    rind concentrate
½ teaspoon ground turmeric
1 teaspoon lime juice (for fish or seafood only)
1 teaspoon lime zest (for fish or seafood only)
3 tablespoons freshly grated coconut or desic-
    cated coconut soaked in water for half an hour
About 4 tablespoons coconut milk

Grind the toasted spices in a mortar or food processor. In a small skillet, heat the oil over medium heat and fry the shallot until crispy brown. Remove and discard the remaining oil. Grind by adding one after the other the chopped lemongrass, lime leaf, ginger, garlic, chilies, fried shallot, tamarind pulp diluted in water, toasted and ground spices, turmeric and, if using the paste for fish or seafood, the lime juice and zest. Finally add the grated coconut and coconut milk little by little until you get a thick paste.

Orange Zest Glaze

Traditionally, this glaze calls for Chinese dried orange peel, which has a very sweet perfume and is made from a special orange. However, the more widely available fresh orange zest also can be used. This glaze can also be used as a marinade, although, with only a small amount of acid from the zest, its primary funtion is to impart flavor rather than to tenderize. To use a similarly flavored marinade that will tenderize as well as impart flavor, use the marinade for Grilled Duck Breast with Orange Soy Glaze (page 90).

PREPARATION TIME: **20 minutes**
MAKES ⅓ **cup (80 ml)**
2 tablespoons honey
1 tablespoon sugar
1 tablespoon dark Chinese soy sauce
2 tablespoons light Chinese soy sauce
1 tablespoon orange zest or 2 slices dried
    Chinese orange peel soaked in 3 table-
    spoons water for 1 hour
¼ teaspoon black pepper
One ½-in (1.25-cm) piece peeled fresh ginger,
    crushed to a paste in a mortar

In a small saucepan, heat the honey and sugar over low heat until the sugar is dissolved. Add the other ingredients and let simmer for a few minutes. If you use the dried Chinese orange peel, let it simmer until the orange flavor emerges. Set the glaze aside before using to let cool.

Honey Cinnamon Glaze

This glaze was inspired by a classic Chinese roast goose recipe from Nanjing. This glaze is usually applied hot to the skin of the bird (goose, duck, turkey, chicken) and left to cool, which will result in a very crisp skin. This glaze is also excellent for ham. If you're applying the glaze to skinless meat, let the glaze cool before applying it. The marinade for Cinnamon Glazed Duck with Grilled Mangoes (page 84) is similar to this glaze, however, it does not have salt, in keeping with the general rule of salt-free marinades. Here salt is included as the glaze is applied only during grilling.

PREPARATION TIME: **15 minutes**
MAKES **½ cup (125 ml)**
3 tablespoons honey
1 tablespoon sugar
3 cloves garlic, crushed with the side of a knife
One ½-in (1.25-cm) piece fresh ginger, peeled
   and finely chopped
1 tablespoon dark Chinese soy sauce
2 tablespoons light Chinese soy sauce
½ teaspoon salt
½ teaspoon ground cinnamon
1 piece star anise, crushed

Heat the honey and sugar in a saucepan over low heat until the sugar is dissolved. Add the garlic and ginger, and then the rest of the ingredients. Simmer for a few minutes and set aside to cool.

Tandoori Spice Rub

Typically tandoori is made with a paste of yogurt, lemon juice and spices. This stand-alone rub does not use the yogurt and lemon juice but does use similar flavored spices, giving food a nice crispy texture. I recommend using this rub with chicken or lamb.

PREPARATION TIME: **15 minutes**
MAKES **¼ cup (50g)**
2 teaspoons cumin seeds, toasted
3 cloves, toasted
One ½-in (1.25-cm)-piece cinnamon, toasted
4 green cardamom pods, toasted
½ whole mace, toasted
2 teaspoons ground red pepper (cayenne) or
   medium-hot paprika
½ teaspoon ground ginger
2 teaspoons garlic salt

Place the toasted spices in a food processor or mortar and grind to a powder. Remove any remaining pieces of pod shells. Add the remaining ingredients and set aside for usage.

Five Spice Chili Sesame Rub

This stand-alone rub was inspired by Beijing street vendors who use five spice powder and soy sauce to flavor grilled meat skewers and, when the skewers are almost done, dip the skewers into sesame seeds before the final cooking on the grill. Here I combine the spices to prepare a rub. This rub can be used for beef, mutton or pork.

PREPARATION TIME: **10 minutes**
MAKES **3 tablespoons**
2 tablespoons sesame seeds, toasted
1 teaspoon five spice powder (page 31)
1 teaspoon ground red pepper (cayenne)
½ teaspoon ground cumin powder
1 teaspoon garlic salt

Slightly crush the toasted sesame seeds in a mortar or food processor. Don't crush them too fine. Add the remaining ingredients. Store in an airtight container.

Kerala Spice Rub

Rubs are relatively rare in Asia since most spices are combined with oil to extract the flavors of the spice. This kind of rub is used in Kerala for fish but it can be used with beef, chicken or pork as well.

PREPARATION TIME: **10 minutes**
MAKES **¼ cup (40 g)**
3 green cardamom pods, toasted
2 teaspoons coriander seeds, toasted
2 teaspoons black peppercorns, toasted
3 cloves, toasted
1 teaspoon chili flakes
1 teaspoon ground turmeric
1 teaspoon ground ginger

Split open the cardamom pods and scrape out the seeds. Place the cardamom seeds and other toasted spices in a food processor or mortar and grind to a fine powder. Sieve and grind the larger parts once more. Combine with the rest of the ingredients and store in an airtight container.

Fragrant Herb and Bread Stuffing

This stuffing can be used for fish but it also goes well with poultry. It should be combined with the Chermoula Marinade (page 40), the Mint Lemon Marinade (page 40), the Tandoori Spice Rub (page 42) or the Northern Indian Marinade (page 105).

PREPARATION TIME: **20 minutes**

MAKES **1 cup (200 g)**

1 teaspoon coriander seeds, toasted

1 teaspoon black peppercorns, toasted

4 cloves garlic, finely chopped

1 teaspoon ground red pepper (cayenne)

1 tablespoon extra-virgin olive oil

2 tablespoons lemon juice

4 tablespoons bread crumbs

½ cup (30 g) coarsely chopped fresh flat-leaf parsley

½ cup (25 g) coarsely chopped fresh coriander leaves (cilantro)

1 bay leaf

2 teaspoons butter

Salt to taste

Place the toasted coriander seeds and pepper in a food processor or mortar and grind to a powder. Add the garlic, red pepper, olive oil and lemon juice and continue to grind to a paste. In a bowl, add the paste with the rest of the ingredients. Mix thoroughly.

Rice, Pistachio and Raisin Stuffing

This mild-flavored lean stuffing goes well with any kind of meat, but preferably with chicken, turkey, duck, pork shoulder, rolled leg of lamb and vegetables like tomatoes, onion, cabbage or braising greens, such as Swiss chard, and sweet bell peppers. It is best suited to the Lemon Marinade (page 39), Orange Yogurt Marinade (page 39), Teriyaki Marinade (page 39), Chermoula Marinade (page 40) or Ginger Sherry Marinade (page 39).

PREPARATION TIME: **30 minutes**

MAKES **4 cups (750 g)**

½ cup (80 g) unsalted shelled pistachios or sunflower seeds

1 tablespoon neutral-flavored vegetable oil

1 cup (200 g) uncooked basmati rice

1½ cups (350 ml) chicken stock

2 onions, finely chopped

2 tablespoons raisins

2 tablespoons finely chopped fresh mint leaves

1 tablespoon finely chopped dill

2 tablespoons finely chopped flat-leaf parsely

Zest of ½ lemon

Juice of ½ lemon

Salt to taste

Coarsely crush the pistachios. In a medium-size saucepan, heat the oil over medium heat and sauté the basmati rice for a few minutes. Add the stock and boil until soft. Set aside and let cool. In a large bowl, mix all of the ingredients with the cooled boiled rice.

Chinese Chestnut Stuffing

This rich stuffing goes well with duck, turkey and chicken. With this stuffing use soy-based marinades such as Teriyaki Marinade (page 39), Spicy Soy Marinade (page 38) or Fiery Szechuan Pepper Marinade (page 40) and glazes such as Orange Zest Glaze or Honey Cinnamon Glaze (page 42).

PREPARATION TIME: **30 minutes**

MAKES **2½ cups (450 g)**

1 tablespoon neutral-flavored oil

3 green onions (scallions), finely sliced

½ tablespoon peeled and finely chopped fresh ginger

6 dried shiitake mushrooms, soaked in water for 30 minutes and finely chopped

1 cup (150 g) dried shelled chestnuts, soaked in water for 45 minutes, or 1½ cups (220 g) drained canned chestnuts

1½ teaspoons hoisin sauce

1 teaspoon sugar

2 teaspoons sherry

1 tablespoon light Chinese soy sauce

1 cup uncooked Thai fragrant rice, boiled and cooled

In a large skillet, heat the oil over medium heat and sauté the scallions. Add the ginger, and after a few minutes the mushrooms. Then add the soaked and drained or canned chestnuts, hoisin sauce, sugar, sherry and soy sauce. Continue to cook for a few minutes and remove from the heat. Add the precooked rice to the skillet and mix to combine. Set aside to cool.

Sesame Chili Dipping Sauce

This is one of my favorite dips. It is served with Porterhouse Steaks with Szechuan Pepper (page 66). It goes very well with all types of grilled steaks, lamb cutlets and pork. This dip uses fried minced garlic—a popular condiment for many dishes in Asia—and has a generous amount of chili paste, making it very spicy. I suggest you start with 1 teaspoon of the paste and then check the heat level before adding more. Because it's difficult to successfully make a small amount of chili paste, this recipe makes more than is needed for this batch of sauce. However, chili paste will keep for a few months. Chili paste is often found on Asian dinner tables, allowing diners to heat up food to their liking. You might start the tradition in your own home!

PREPARATION TIME: **15 minutes**
MAKES ½ **cup (125 ml)**

3 tablespoons neutral-flavored oil
1 tablespoon minced garlic
1 teaspoon sugar
1 tablespoon light soy sauce
2 tablespoons Chinese black vinegar or
   1 tablespoon Worcestershire sauce
1 tablespoon finely chopped fresh coriander
   leaves (cilantro)
1 tablespoon finely chopped green onion
   (scallion)
1 tablespoon sesame seeds, toasted and lightly
   crushed in a mortar
1 teaspoon dark sesame oil
1 to 2 teaspoons chili paste (start with 1 teaspoon, then taste for heat level)

CHILI PASTE
3 tablespoons chili flakes
3 tablespoons drained and reserved neutral-
   flavored oil

1 In a small skillet, add the oil and place over medium heat. Add the garlic and fry until it's slightly brown. Remove from the heat and drain the oil, reserving both the oil and browned garlic.
2 To make the chili paste, place the chili flakes in a small heatproof bowl. Add the drained oil to the same skillet used to fry the garlic and place over high heat. When the oil is smoking hot add the oil to the chili flakes while stirring. The hot oil roasts the chili flakes, which will absorb the oil and become a thick dry paste. Set aside to let cool.
3 In a small bowl dissolve the sugar in the soy sauce and vinegar. Add the coriander, green onion, sesame seeds, fried garlic, sesame oil and 1 to 2 teaspoons of the chili paste. The sauce should be served immediately while the sesame seeds are still crunchy. If you'd like to make this dipping sauce a day or two before serving it, for best results, add the toasted sesame seeds just before serving.

Mint and Coriander Yogurt Sauce

This sauce can be made either very spicy or mild, but in both versions it is a very good supplement to grilled dishes. The coriander and mint give a very refreshing aroma that goes well with most Indian-type dishes. It is the perfect accompaniment for Chicken Tikka (page 82).

PREPARATION TIME: **15 minutes**
MAKES ¾ **cup (185 ml)**

1 cup (50 g) fresh coriander leaves (cilantro),
   coarsely chopped
½ cup (6 g) fresh mint leaves, coarsely
   chopped
2 green and red chilies (optional)
1 tablespoon lime juice
½ cup (125 ml) plain yogurt
½ teaspoon salt or to taste
½ teaspoon sugar (optional)

Place the chopped coriander and mint leaves, chilies and lime juice in a food processor. Blend to a fine paste, pushing down the herbs regularly with a spatula. In a bowl whisk the yogurt until it is creamy. Fold in the blended herbs, salt and sugar, if using.

Green Onion Sesame Sauce

This Korean sauce is often served with lamb. It is one of the suggested sauces for Lamb Steaks with Three Asian Sauces (page 130). It also can be served with Korean-Style Kalbi Ribs with Garlic Sesame Paste (page 65).

PREPARATION TIME: **10 minutes**

MAKES ⅓ **cup (80 ml)**

10 cloves garlic, coarsely chopped
2 green onions (scallions), finely chopped
Salt and black pepper, to taste
¼ cup (65 ml) dark sesame oil

In a mortar or food processor, crush the garlic, green onions and salt to a smooth paste. Drizzle in the sesame oil while stirring (or running the food processor) to make a smooth mayonnaise-like sauce.

Wasabi Tartare Sauce

This spicy version of tartare sauce goes great with deep-fried and grilled seafood as well as with grilled vegetables. I use it on Grilled Salmon Burgers (page 98).

PREPARATION TIME: **20 minutes**

MAKES **2 cups (500 ml)**

Egg yolks of 4 hard-boiled eggs
1 raw egg yolk
1 teaspoon wasabi paste
2 tablespoons lemon juice
1 tablespoon water
1 cup (250 ml) olive oil
2 tablespoons capers, finely chopped
2 tablespoons finely chopped pickled cucumber (sour, not sweet), preferably cornichons
1 tablespoon finely chopped fresh flat-leaf parsley
¼ teaspoon dried tarragon
Pinch of salt and pepper
6 tablespoons sour cream (optional)

In a bowl, crush the hard-boiled egg yolks. Whisk in the raw egg yolk until a creamy consistency is achieved. Slowly add the wasabi, lemon juice and water. Add the olive oil, initially drop by drop and then in a thin drizzle, while continuously whisking. Add the rest of the ingredients. For a lighter sauce, the some sour cream.

Satay Sauce

Variations on this sauce are served all over Southeast Asia to accompany satay—small grilled skewers of meat, chicken or seafood. It combines sweet and spiciness in a smooth blend of crushed peanuts. I serve this sauce with Thai Chicken Satays (page 78).

PREPARATION TIME: **25 minutes**

MAKES **2 cups (500 ml)**

1 teaspoon chili flakes
6 cloves garlic, finely chopped
1 lemongrass stalk, outer tougher leaves removed and lower two third of stalk finely chopped
2 tablespoons minced shallot
1 cup roasted peanuts
1 tablespoon neutral-flavored oil
½ teaspoon ground coriander
½ teaspoon ground turmeric
½ tablespoon tamarind pulp dissolved in 2 tablespoons water or ½ tablespoon tamarind concentrate
1 teaspoon shrimp paste (Thai *kapi*) (optional)
1 fresh or dried kaffir lime leaf, finely chopped
2½ tablespoons sugar
3 tablespoons water
Salt to taste

1 In a mortar or food processor, grind the chili flakes, garlic, lemongrass and shallot to a smooth paste. Grind the peanuts separately to a fine paste. Set aside.
2 In a medium-size skillet, add the oil and place over medium heat. Add the lemongrass paste and sauté until soft.
3 Add the coriander, turmeric, tamarind, shrimp paste, if using, kaffir lime leaf,

sugar and water and cook for a few minutes. Remove from the heat and add the peanut paste immediately. Mix to combine. If the sauce is too thick, add small amounts of water little by little. Taste for seasoning and add salt if needed. Let cool and serve with satay.

Soy Bean Paste Sauce

With a balance of sweet-and-sour flavor, this Japanese-inspired sauce makes an excellent side dish for grilled foods. Depending on the brand, bean paste is sometimes either salty or more sweet. Before you add sugar try the sauce and use sugar according to your taste. This sauce is good with grilled beef, chicken or duck. I enjoy serving it with Grilled Miso Teriyaki Tenderloin (page 68).

PREPARATION TIME: **10 minutes**

MAKES ⅓ **cup (80 ml)**

3 tablespoons Japanese soy sauce
1 tablespoon lemon juice
1 teaspoon bean paste (dou ban jiang)
1 tablespoon chopped fresh coriander leaves (cilantro) (optional)
1 tablespoon sugar or to taste

In a small bowl, mix all of the ingredients. This sauce should be served cold.

Spicy Tomato Sauce

This sauce is served in India with deep-fried or grilled dishes and is very similar to tomato ketchup as its known in the West. Tamarind provides a slight sourness, which is balanced with palm sugar, or jaggery as it is called in India. This is a sauce that goes well with all Asian grilled and deep-fried foods. I serve this sauce with Indian-Style Beef Burgers (page 69) and Barbecued Ribs with Indian Spice Rub (page 72).

PREPARATION TIME: **15 minutes**

MAKES **2 cups (500 ml)**

One 1-in (2.5-cm) piece fresh ginger, peeled and finely chopped
4 cloves garlic, finely chopped
1 tablespoon neutral-flavored oil
½ teaspoon mustard seeds
Pinch of asafetida powder (optional)
¼ teaspoon ground turmeric
1 teaspoon ground red pepper (cayenne)
½ cup (85 g) finely chopped onion
1 lb (500 g) large ripe tomatoes, peeled, deseeded and diced
2 tablespoons tamarind pulp soaked in ½ cup (100 ml) hot water
4 tablespoons palm sugar or light brown sugar
½ teaspoon salt or to taste

SPICES
3 fenugreek seeds
¼ teaspoon cumin seeds
One ½-in (1.25-cm)-piece cinnamon
2 cloves
6 coriander seeds
¼ piece mace
Small pinch of ground nutmeg
Pinch of grain of paradise seeds
5 black peppercorns

1 Heat a skillet and toast the spices for 1 to 2 minutes until an aroma emerges. Set aside and crush the spices in a large mortar or food processor. Add the ginger and garlic and crush to a paste.
2 Heat the oil in a large saucepan. Add the mustard seeds and asafetida, if using. When the mustard seeds crackle, add the turmeric, ground red pepper and chopped onion and sauté until soft. Add the spice paste. Continue to fry for a few minutes. Add a little water if necessary to avoid scorching the spices.
3 Add the diced tomatoes and the tamarind. Boil for about half an hour until the sauce gets thick. Add the sugar and salt and continue to cook for 15 to 20 minutes. Let cool. Store in a glass jar or bottle with a sealed lid in the refrigerator. It will keep for a few weeks.

Tomato Pomegranate Dip

My introduction to pomegranate concentrate was in a salad made by my sister-in-law Mouna. I was caught off guard by its delicate aroma. This sauce, which is widely popular from Iran to Turkey, also uses pomegranate concentrate but combines it with tomatoes and fresh herbs. It works wonderfully as a dipping sauce or relish for grilled lamb or beef. Pomegranate concentrate is used from Iran to the Middle East in salads, marinades and as an ingredient in koftas. Pomegranate concentrate should not be substituted with pomegranate syrup. If you can't find pomegranate concentrate, you can make your own or, in a pinch, substitute a combination of fresh pomegranate and lemon juice (see page 33). I serve this dip with Rack of Lamb with Olive Oil and Fresh Herbs (page 139).

PREPARATION TIME: **20 minutes**

MAKES **2 cups (500 ml)**

1 small red or white onion, minced
2 teaspoons sumac
Pinch of salt
1 teaspoon sugar
4 tomatoes, deseeded and minced
½ cup (60 g) finely chopped fresh flat-leaf parsley
2 tablespoons finely chopped fresh mint leaves
3 tablespoons extra virgin-olive oil
1 tablespoon pomegranate concentrate
3 tablespoons lemon juice
1 teaspoon chili flakes

Lightly crush the onion with the sumac and salt in a mortar or food processor. Place the crushed onion in a large bowl. Add the remaining ingredients and stir to combine. Keep the sauce in the fridge for at least an hour before serving.

Sambal Oelek

This multi-purpose Indonesian condiment is used both as a dipping sauce and as a marinade. Sambal oelek also is used as an ingredient in other sauces and marinades. You can buy sambal oelek in grocery stores but this fresh, homemade version not only tastes better but is free of preservatives.

PREPARATION TIME: **15 minutes**

MAKES **1 cup (250 ml)**

1 cup (150 g) finely chopped fresh red or green chilies
1 tablespoon tamarind pulp dissolved in 3 tablespoons water, 1 tablespoon tamarind concentrate, or ½ tablespoon lime juice
1 teaspoon salt
4 to 6 tablespoons neutral-flavored oil
½ teaspoon finely grated lime zest

Combine everything but the lime zest in a mortar or food processor and grind to a fine paste. If you use a food processor, blend for a few seconds. Stop and push down the chilies, add a little of the oil and then continue blending until the chilies are completely ground to a fine paste. Add the lime zest to the chili paste and mix to combine. Transfer the paste to a glass jar. Heat the remaining oil and pour the hot oil on top of the paste until the paste is completely covered. This will keep in the refrigerator for several months.

Tamarind Chili Dip

This sauce is served with grilled pork and beef in Thailand. It is also eaten with sticky rice and herbs, such as holy basil, coriander, cilantro and raw vegetables. I serve it with Sweet Soy Glazed Pork Kebabs (page 113).

PREPARATION TIME: **15 minutes**

MAKES **1 cup (250 ml)**

1½ tablespoons uncooked sticky rice
1 tablespoon tamarind pulp
½ shallot, finely chopped
3 tablespoons fish sauce
2 teaspoons palm sugar
1 tablespoon chili flakes
2 fresh thorny coriander leaves, finely chopped, or 1 tablespoon chopped fresh coriander leaves (cilantro)
1 tablespoon chopped fresh mint leaves
2 small green onions (scallions), chopped

1 Place a small skillet over medium heat. When hot add the sticky rice and roast until light brown. Remove from the heat and lightly crush in a mortar.Place the tamarind in ½ cup (125 ml) of hot water and let rest for ten minutes. Squeeze the pulp and remove fibers and seeds.
2 Return the skillet to medium heat. Add the shallot and roast without oil until light brown. Add the fish sauce, prepared tamarind pulp, palm sugar and chili flakes. Add the rice powder, coriander leaves, mint leaves and green onion.

Vietnamese Chili and Lime Dip

This chili and lime dip is served with many types of grilled or fried foods in Vietnam. You can use this dip for a variety of dishes with Southeast Asian flavors. I enjoy it with Lemongrass Curry Burgers (page 75).

PREPARATION TIME: **15 minutes**

MAKES **1 cup (250 ml)**

3 fresh green Thai bird's-eye chilies or 3 serrano chilies
½ teaspoon finely chopped lime zest
2 cloves garlic
3 tablespoons sugar
½ cup (125 ml) warm water
2 tablespoons lime juice
3 tablespoons fish sauce
Salt to taste

Grind the chilies, lime zest and garlic in a mortar or food processor to a fine paste. In a small bowl, dissolve the sugar in the warm water. Add the chili paste, lime juice, fish sauce and salt to the sugar water. Mix thoroughly.

Lemon Chutney

Lemon chutneys exist in various versions from Turkey to India. Lemon gives a refreshing sourness to grilled food, be it meat or vegetables. Here is a mild version that I like to serve with grilled lamb, chicken or fish. I serve this chutney with Stuffed Lamb Roast (page 135).

PREPARATION TIME: **45 minutes**

MAKES **1 cup (250 ml)**

1 tablespoon olive oil

1 small onion, finely chopped

Zest of 3 lemons, finely chopped

Flesh of ½ lemon (with skin, seeds and inner membranes removed), coarsely chopped

¼ cup (65 ml) white wine

3 tablespoons sugar

Pinch of cumin seeds, toasted and ground

Pinch of black pepper

Salt to taste

In a medium-size skillet, add the olive oil and place over medium heat. Add onion and sauté until soft but not browned. Add the remaining ingredients and cook for about 30 minutes or until most of the liquid has evaporated and the mixture has a syrupy consistency. Remove from the heat and let cool. Serve cold.

Sweet and Sour Tomato Chutney

Mango and tomato chutneys are very common sides in India and can be served with any grilled meat or vegetable. If you wish you can add a teaspoon of ground red pepper (cayenne) to this recipe to make it spicier. I serve this chutney with Saffron Lamb Loin Chops (page 131).

PREPARATION TIME: **40 minutes**

MAKES **2 cups (500 ml)**

½ tablespoon finely chopped garlic

½ tablespoon peeled and finely chopped fresh ginger

1¼ lb (600 g) tomatoes, peeled, deseeded and finely chopped (see Tip, below)

½ cup (125 ml) white vinegar

½ cup (80 g) sugar

Spices

¼ teaspoon fennel seeds, toasted

Pinch of fenugreek seeds, toasted

¼ piece mace, toasted

One ½-in (1.25-cm)-piece cinnamon, toasted

2 cloves, toasted

2 green cardamom pods, toasted

Heaping ¼ teaspoon grain of paradise seeds, toasted

¼ teaspoon coriander seeds, toasted

5 black peppercorns, toasted

3 dried red chili peppers

1 In a mortar or food processor, grind the toasted spices and the dried red chili peppers to a powder. Pass through a fine sieve and regrind the larger parts. Discard any remaining unground pieces of cardamom pod. Add the garlic and ginger to the ground spices and chili peppers and grind to a paste.

2 Place a large saucepan over medium heat. When hot add the chopped tomatoes and spice paste. Stir-fry for a few minutes. Add the vinegar and sugar and simmer over low heat for about 25 minutes. Let cool. Store in a glass jar in the refrigerator for up to 3 weeks.

Filipino Salsa

This recipe clearly reflects the Spanish influence on Filipino cuisine. The combination of tomatoes, chilies, green onions and flavor from the green celery and cilantro makes it a very refreshing sauce for any kind of grilled meat. I sometimes serve this salsa with Grilled Pork Shoulder with Tangy Orange Sauce (page 122) in lieu of the orange sauce or along with it, for variety.

PREPARATION TIME: **20 minutes**

MAKES **2½ cups (650 ml)**

1 lb (500 g) large ripe tomatoes, peeled, deseeded and diced

1 cup (100 g) finely sliced celery

2 cloves garlic, crushed to a paste

½ cup (60 g) finely chopped green onions (scallions)

3 green finger-length chilies, deseeded and finely chopped

⅓ cup (10 g) fresh coriander leaves (cilantro), finely chopped

2 tablespoons lime juice

1 to 2 tablespoons white vinegar

Salt and pepper to taste

In a large bowl, add all of the ingredients and mix well to combine. Serve immediately.

Tip for Peeling and Deseeding Whole Tomatoes Bring a large pot of water to a boil. Add the tomatoes and boil until the skin cracks. Plunge the tomatoes into cold water and drain. When the tomatoes have cooled sufficiently that you can hold them in your hands, remove the skin. Cut the peeled tomatoes in quarters and remove the seeds.

Curry Herb Butter

Herb butter originates from French cuisine but has been readily adopted in Asia where it has been transformed to suit the local flavor. It can be served with a simple grilled steak to give it an Asian touch. I serve it with Porterhouse Steaks with Szechuan Pepper (page 66).

PREPARATION TIME: **10 minutes**

MAKES ¾ **cup (150 g)**

2 cloves garlic, finely chopped
Pinch of salt
½ cup (125 g) unsalted butter, softened
2 tablespoons finely chopped fresh mint leaves
2 tablespoons finely chopped fresh coriander leaves (cilantro)
1 teaspoon hot curry powder heated in 1 teaspoon melted butter
1 teaspoon ground red pepper (cayenne)

In a small mortar, grind the garlic and salt to a paste. In a bowl, mix together the garlic paste and the remaining ingredients. Refrigerate for 20 minutes before serving to allow the butter to set.

Roasted Pepper Herb Butter

The combination of fresh herbs in this delicious flavored butter was inspired by the Middle Eastern salad called "fatoush." This butter goes particularly well with lamb and seafood. I serve it with grilled lobster (page 94).

PREPARATION TIME: **15 minutes**

MAKES ¾ **cup (150 g)**

½ cup (125 g) unsalted butter, softened
1 tablespoon finely chopped roasted and peeled red bell pepper
1 tablespoon finely chopped fresh flat-leaf parsley
1 tablespoon finely chopped fresh basil leaves
1 tablespoon finely chopped fresh mint leaves
2 teaspoons sumac

In a bowl, mix the ingredients until combined. Refrigerate for 20 minutes before serving to allow the butter to set.

Tips for Making and Serving Flavored Butters To sufficiently soften butter, remove it from the refrigerator 30 minutes before making flavored butters. If you've chilled the flavored butter for more than 20 minutes, remove the butter from the refrigerator to allow it to soften and warm slightly prior to serving. Flavored butters shouldn't be served ice-cold as they will cool down grilled food.

Cilantro Chili Butter

This butter was designed for those who love spice. This red pepper butter goes well with vegetables—especially mashed potatoes or corn on the cob—and any kind of meat. Add a little more or less Tabasco, depending on how much spice you like.

PREPARATION TIME: **10 minutes**

MAKES ½ **cup (135 g)**

½ cup (125 g) unsalted butter, softened
1 to 2 teaspoons Tabasco sauce
1 teaspoon sweet paprika powder
1 tablespoon finely chopped fresh coriander leaves (cilantro)
Salt to taste

In a bowl, mix together the ingredients until combined. Refrigerate for 20 minutes before serving to allow the butter to set.

Lime Butter

This butter goes best with seafood. I serve it with grilled lobster (page 94).

PREPARATION TIME: **10 minutes**

MAKES ½ **cup (120 g)**

¼ lb (100 g) unsalted butter, softened

1 lemongrass stalk, outer tougher leaves removed and lower two third of stalk finely chopped

2 tablespoons lime juice

1 clove garlic, minced

Zest of ½ lime, finely chopped

2 tablespoons finely chopped fresh coriander leaves (cilantro)

Salt to taste

In a bowl, mix together the ingredients until combined. Refrigerate for 20 minutes before serving to allow the butter to set.

Basic Mayonnaise

A good mayonnaise is an excellent dip for for grilled foods. This basic recipe serves as the base for all the flavored mayonnaise recipes in this book. Mayonnaise will keep in the refridgerator for 2 days.

PREPARATION TIME: **20 minutes**

MAKES 2½ **cups (350 ml)**

2 raw egg yolks

2 cups (500 ml) neutral-flavored oil

Juice of 1 lemon

Salt and pepper to taste

In a bowl, thoroughly whisk the egg yolks. Slowly add the oil; first drop by drop, then in a thin stream. If the mayonnaise separates, add 2 tablespoons of hot water or 1 mashed cooked egg yolk to stabilize the mayonnaise. When the mayonnaise is firm, slowly pour in the lemon juice while stirring. Add the salt and pepper and whisk until the salt is dissolved.

Chive and Garlic Mayonnaise

Chinese chives have a stronger garlic flavor than Western chives. You can serve this mayonnaise with grilled pork or beef.

PREPARATION TIME: **5 minutes**

MAKES ½ **cup (120 g)**

1 clove garlic

1 cup (200 g) Basic Mayonnaise (left)

1 tablespoon finely chopped Chinese or regular chives

In a mortar crush the garlic to a fine paste. In a small bowl, combine the ingredients until well blended.

Chili and Curry Mayonnaise

This mayonnaise is suitable for grilled beef, chicken, lamb and vegetables.

PREPARATION TIME: **5 minutes**

MAKES ½ **cup (120 g)**

1 cup (200 g) Basic Mayonnaise (left)

1 teaspoon ground red pepper (cayenne)

1 teaspoon curry powder

In a small bowl, combine the ingredients until well blended.

Wasabi Mayonnaise

This wasabi mayonnaise goes well with Japanese-style grilled beef or fish. I serve this mayonnaise with grilled lobster (page 94) and Grilled Salmon Burgers (page 98).

PREPARATION TIME: **5 minutes**

MAKES **½ cup (120 g)**

1 cup (200 g) Basic Mayonnaise
  (page opposite)
1 tablespoon wasabi paste

In a small bowl, combine the ingredients until well blended.

Sri Racha Chili Sauce Mayonnaise

This mildly spiced mayonnaise is suitable for many different dishes such as steaks or grilled pork or as a dip for raw vegetables. I use it for the Grilled Chicken Crostini (page 158).

PREPARATION TIME: **5 minutes**

MAKES **½ cup (120 g)**

½ cup (200 g) Basic Mayonnaise
  (page opposite)
2 tablespoons Vietnamese chili sauce or Sri
  Racha Chili Sauce

In a small bowl, combine the ingredients until well blended.

Yellow Mixed Pickles

This yellow pickle receives its color from turmeric, which also gives this dish a special taste. This pickle goes great with satay or as a side dish for other meat dishes. These pickles are a particularly good match for Flank Steaks with Tropical Sambal Spice Paste (page 70).

PREPARATION TIME: **30 minutes**

MAKES **3 cups (750 ml)**

¼ small cabbage, cut into 1-in (2.5-cm)
  squares
1 lb (500 g) green beans, cut into ½-in
  (1.25-cm) pieces
1 large carrot, diced
½ cup (125 ml) rice vinegar
⅔ cup (160 ml) water
1 tablespoon sugar
1 teaspoon ground turmeric
Salt to taste

1 In a large pot, bring water to a boil and blanch the vegetables. Pour the blanched vegetables into ice water to stop the boiling process and keep them crisp. Drain well. Place the vegetables in a large glass container with a tight-fitting lid.
2 In a small saucepan, add the vinegar, water, sugar and turmeric and bring to a boil.
3 Pour the hot liquid over the vegetables and set aside for a few hours to marinate. Add the salt. When the pickles have cooled, serve or seal the jar and store in the refrigerator. These pickles will keep for a few weeks.

Carrot and Radish Pickle

This quick-to-make pickle is served in every Vietnamese restaurant as a side dish. The crunchy carrot and radish in the sweet and sour sauce taste delicious and refreshing. I enjoy this side dish with a number of dishes, including Beef Lemongrass Satay (page 61) and the Vietnamese-inspired Grilled Chicken Crostini (page 159).

PREPARATION TIME: **20 minutes**

MAKES **2 cups (400 g)**

5 tablespoons sugar
1 teaspoon salt
¾ cup (185 ml) rice vinegar
1 carrot, cut into matchstick strips
½ medium-size daikon radish, cut into matchstick strips

1 In a small bowl, combine the sugar, salt and vinegar. Stir until the sugar is dissolved.
2 Place the vegetables in a glass jar with a lid and add the vinegar mixture.
3 Mix well and keep in the refrigerator for at least 30 minutes.
4 Serve cold. This pickle keeps for a few weeks in the fridge.

Chapter 1

Beef Barbecue Recipes

With the exception of Korea and Indonesia, beef is not traditional fare in Asia. In India the cow is a holy animal and most Indians are devout vegetarians. In Southeast Asia the cow and the water buffalo traditionally provided milk and served as working animals and therefore were not eaten.

The consumption of beef came to Asia with Westerners. The French introduced beef into Vietnamese cuisine and the Americans introduced it in Thailand and Laos during the Vietnam War.

Some of the recipes in this chapter are authentic Asian recipes—such as T-bone Steak (page 71) served with Thai Glass Noodle Salad or "Steak Lao," which was introduced in Bangkok after the Vietnam War. Others combine classic Asian flavors with favorite BBQ fare in the West—such as the Lemongrass Curry Burger (page 75). Until recently it was very difficult if not impossible to find a restaurant in the countryside that serves steaks. The consumption of steaks and grilled beef is limited to the large cities where the cultures are merging. Asians are increasingly indulging in Western food and wine. By serving the client's preferences the chefs combine the flavors of the native country with the techniques of cooking tender steaks.

I have had one of my best grilled beef ever in a small restaurant in Tokyo. The food is famous and many renowned Western guests have visited it. The meat is Kobe beef and it is grilled in small cubes to absolute perfection. The beef virtually melts on your tongue. Tataki Seared Beef (page 64) and Tenderloin in Miso Marinade (page 68) are typical representatives of grilled Japanese beef dishes. Another Japanese-style recipe featured in this chapter is the Beef Short Ribs with Teriyaki Glazing Sauce (page 67).

Korea as I indicated above is an exception in that beef is part of the indigenous cuisine. Koreans love beef and prepare excellent grilled dishes out of almost every part of the cow. Korean-Style Barbecued Sirloin Steaks (page 62) and Kalbi Ribs with Garlic Sesame Paste (page 65) are delicious examples of the Korean barbecue tradition.

Since traditionally beef in Asia is not cured as it is in Europe, including the beef in Korea, the meat is thinly sliced against the grain and either grilled as slivers or skewered. Thus meat that is usually quite tough can be grilled and becomes tender. I have added some recipes using brisket and flank steak in this manner.

India does not usually barbecue beef and I have taken the freedom to adapt some Indian recipes to suit grilling, such as Beef Brisket Kerala Style (page 74) and Barbecued Ribs with Indian Spice Rub (page 72). Also an Indian seasoned hamburger is presented in this chapter. I have included a Chinese marinated porterhouse steak (page 66) and a Malaysian satay-style whole flank steak (page 70) to give you a taste of the large variety of flavors that has been developed in this region.

Beef Cooking Times mentioned in the table refer to direct grilling and indirect grilling at medium to high heat temperatures. For low temperature grilling the time needs to be adjusted by multiplying by 3 to 3.5. For example, if I state in the table a grilling time of 20 to 25 minutes, then for low temperature grilling you will have to calculate 60 to 90 minutes. Most of the cooking times in the recipes are based on cooking to medium rare or medium. Simply increase or decrease the time according to your preference for doneness.

State	Internal Temperature			Pressing Test	Pricking Test	Meat Internal Color	Steak ¾ inch thick	T-Bone Steak 1 inch thick	Porterhouse 1½ inches thick
Rare (Bleu)	125°F 45°C	to to	130°F 55°C	soft touch	red juice	red	5 to 8 minutes	10 to 12 minutes	10 to 14 minutes
Medium Rare	130°F 55°C	to to	135°F 60°C	soft to firm	dark pink juice	pinkish red	6 to 10 minutes	12 to 14 minutes	14 to 20 minutcs
Medium	140°F 60°C	to to	150°F 65°C	slighty yielding	pink juice	traces of pink	8 to 14 minutes	13 to 17 minutes	16 to 22 minutes
Medium Well	150°F 65°C	to to	160°F 70°C	firm	pinkish juice	no traces	12 to 15 minutes	15 to 20 minutes	20 to 25 minutes
Well Done	160°F 70°C	to to	170°F 75°C	firm and hard	clear colorless juice	grayish brown	14 to 20 minutes	17 to 25 minutes	25 to 30 minutes

Beef Tenderloin or Filet Mignon For some beef lovers this is the most tender and valuable cut of beef. It has very little fat and therefore has a tendency to dry out. If it is grilled on a rotisserie as a whole piece, it should be wrapped in bacon. You may cut the whole tenderloin into slices, referred to "filet mignons" or "medallions," and place them on the grill. In some cases medallions may be too small for grilling whole and may be better suited for skewers.

Brisket is from the lower chest. It has a high fat content, making it suitable for longer cooking times with lower temperatures—for example, indirect grilling with low heat or smoking.

Sirloin Steak This is taken from the larger part of the fillet and cut into ¾ to 1-inch (2 to 2.5-cm)-thick slices. This steak is the most flavorful of the beefsteaks though sometimes it can be a bit tough. It is often served thinly sliced, which makes it seem more tender.

Porterhouse Steak is similar to the T-bone steak with a strip steak and a tenderloin on one bone. It is cut 1 to 2 inches (2.5 to 5 cm) thick and can weigh up to 2 pounds (1 kg). This steak needs to be first seared over high heat to seal the surface and then cooked over medium heat until done. One porterhouse normally serves two to three persons.

T-Bone Steak is from the section next to the center of the beef. It is cut up to 1 inch (2.5 cm) thick and weighs between ½ and 1 pound (250 to 500 g). The biggest part of this steak is the strip steak portion, whereas the tenderloin portion of this steak is normally quite small. It is intended for a single serving.

Short Ribs and Ribs are the crosscut of the rib section of the beef. This piece is most often used for Korean barbecue.

Flank Steak and Skirt Steak are from the underbelly of the beef cow. It is very flavorful but usually quite tough. In Asia it is used for kebabs.

Ground Beef is usually made from chuck steak or shoulder but round steak is also used. Generally about 10 to 20% of fat is added to ground beef. The hamburgers in this book are made from very lean, pure ground beef and hence some bread and milk are added for moisture.

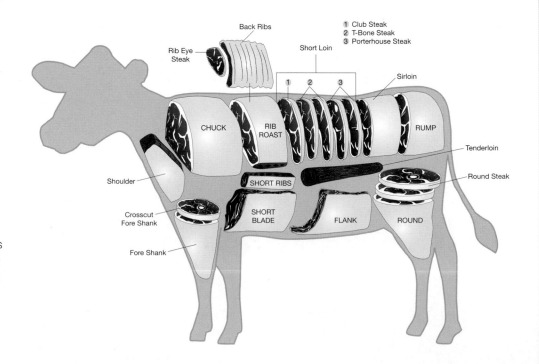

Beef Lemongrass Satay

This delicious beef satay is usually served in Vietnamese roadside shops. The Vietnamese have developed a caramelized marinade, which gives the meat a nice sweet and herb-flavored crust. Flank steak is best suited for this satay because of its strong flavor. Serve with Vietnamese Chili and Lime Dip (page 51), fresh lettuce leaves, mint leaves, coriander leaves and Carrot and Radish Pickle (page 57). For a complete meal, serve with any other kind of salad and rice.

SERVES **2 to 3 as a main course/4 to 6 as an appetizer**
PREPARATION TIME: **30 minutes**
GRILL TIME: **4 to 6 minutes for medium well**

1 lb (500 g) beef flank steak
12 bamboo skewers, soaked in water for
    30 minutes prior to grilling, or metal skewers

CURRIED LEMONGRASS MARINADE
⅓ cup (80 ml) Caramelized Lemongrass
    Marinade (page 39)
¼ teaspoon curry powder

1 Cut the flank steak into strips 1 inch (2.5 cm) long, ½ inch (1.25 cm) wide and between ¼ and ⅛ inch (4.5 mm) thick. Thread each strip of meat lengthwise on a metal or bamboo skewer, weaving it in and out.

2 In a large bowl, combine the marinade ingredients. Add the beef strips and toss to evenly coat them with the marinade. Marinate for 1 hour in the refrigerator.

3 Prepare the grill for direct grilling with two heat zones (medium and high). (See page 13 for charcoal and page 17 for gas.)

4 Remove the beef strips from the marinade, scrape off excess marinade.

5 In a saucepan, add the leftover marinade and bring to boil. Lower the heat and simmer for a few minutes and set the marinade aside to cool. It is now ready to be used as a basting sauce.

6 Just before you begin to grill, oil the hot grate. Place the skewers on the grate over the high heat zone and grill each side for 2 to 3 minutes. Continue grilling for 1 to 2 minutes over the medium heat zone until done. Baste a few times with the basting sauce.

KOREAN STEAK MARINADE

5 tablespoons finely chopped green onions
  (scallions)
2 tablespoons chopped garlic
1 tablespoon peeled and finely chopped fresh
  ginger
5 tablespoons soy sauce
2 tablespoons toasted sesame seeds
1 tablespoon dark sesame oil
1 to 2 tablespoons sugar
2 tablespoons rice wine or sherry
1 to 2 teaspoons chili flakes

1 Sprinkle the steak with the fresh kiwi or pineapple juice and leave for 30 minutes. This will make the meat very tender. Remove the steaks from the juice and wipe it dry with a paper towel.

2 In a bowl, combine the ingredients for the marinade. Add the meat to the marinade, turning the steaks to evenly coat them. Marinate in the refrigerator for 1 to 2 hours.

3 Remove the meat from the marinade (do not discard the marinade!). In a saucepan, add the leftover marinade and place over high heat. Boil for a few minutes. If it becomes too dry add up to ½ cup (125 ml) of water. Set the cooked marinade aside to use as a basting sauce and dipping sauce.

4 Prepare the grill for direct grilling with two heat zones (medium and high). (See page 13 for charcoal and page 17 for gas.)

5 Just before you begin grilling, oil the hot grate. Place the steaks over the high heat zone and grill each side for about 2 to 3 minutes. Move the steaks to the low-heat zone and continue to grill each side for 1 to 2 minutes for medium rare, basting each side once with the cooked marinade. Test for doneness by poking the meat with your finger (see page 19).

6 When done remove from the fire and let rest for a few minutes. Cut into thin slices and serve with lettuce leaves, fresh herbs and the leftover basting sauce or Sesame Miso Sauce (page 47) . You can either pour the sauce over the slices or serve separately as a dipping sauce.

Korean-Style Barbecued Sirloin Steaks

While the Koreans normally cut the meat in thin slices and place it on the grill, I like to grill the whole piece of sirloin and then slice it. This leaves the meat juicier and you can control its doneness more to your taste. Serve the steak slices with a variety of lettuce leaves, fresh herbs and a dipping sauce. Diners place a couple of meat slices and some fresh herbs in the center of a lettuce leaf and then wrap it up into a neat bundle, which is picked up, dipped in a sauce and eaten out of hand. Green onion strips or a green salad and Sesame Miso Sauce (page 47) are a nice accompaniment.

SERVES **4**
COOKING TIME: **30 minutes**
GRILL TIME: **6 to 10 minutes for medium rare**

4 sirloin steaks, about 7 to 8 oz (200 to 240 g) each
1 tablespoon fresh kiwi juice or pineapple juice
Several lettuce leaves
Fresh herbs, such as coriander (cilantro), mint, shiso, Thai or Vietnamese basil

Beef Satay with Ginger Hoisin Marinade

The combination of ginger and hoisin is very popular in Vietnam and China. Satays with hoisin sauce are served throughout Southeast Asia including the roadside shops in Hong Kong. An aromatic thickened marinade covers the satays and keeps them juicy. For a complete meal, serve with sliced onions, rice and Asian Celery Salad (page 164).

SERVES **2 to 3 as a main course/4 to 6 as an appetizer**
PREPARATION TIME: **30 minutes**
GRILL TIME: **5 to 7 minutes for medium well**

1 lb (500 g) flank steak, cut into strips that are 1 inch (2.5 cm) long, ½ inch (1.25 cm) wide and between ¼ and ⅛ inch (4.5 mm) thick.
Bamboo skewers, soaked in water for 30 minutes prior to grilling, or metal skewers
Heaping ½ teaspoon cornstarch mixed with a little cold water to create a slurry

GINGER HOISIN MARINADE
2 tablespoons Chinese light soy sauce
2 teaspoons Chinese dark soy sauce
1 tablespoon plus 1 teaspoon sugar
1 tablespoon hoisin sauce
2 teaspoons peeled and finely chopped fresh ginger
2 teaspoons finely chopped garlic

1 To make the marinade, bring the soy sauces and sugar to a boil in a small skillet while stirring. When the sugar has dissolved add the rest of the marinade ingredients and stir to combine. Remove from the heat and let cool.

2 In a bowl, add the cooled marinade and beef strips. Toss the beef to evenly coat and marinate overnight in the refrigerator.

3 Remove the meat from the marinade. Thread each strip of meat lengthwise on a metal or bamboo skewer, weaving it in and out.

4 In a small saucepan, bring the leftover marinade to a boil. Add the cornstarch slurry and stir until the sauce slightly thickens. Set aside as a basting sauce. Prepare the grill for direct grilling and preheat two heat zones (medium and high). (See page 13 for charcoal and page 17 for gas.)

5 Place the satays on the hot grate over the high heat zone and grill each side for 2 to 3 minutes. Continue grilling for 1 to 2 minutes over the medium heat zone until done. Baste with the basting sauce a few times until the satays are well covered with sauce.

Tataki Seared Beef on a Bed of Onion and Daikon

In this Japanese style of preparing beef, the steak is seared over high temperature leaving the inner part raw. Traditionally this is achieved by grilling the meat over high temperature and then dropping it into cold water to immediately kill the heat. I don't throw it directly into cold water but wrap the meat tightly in cling wrap before immersing it in ice water. This method keeps the flavor and the crust. After being thoroughly chilled in the refrigerator, the meat is then sliced and served over Onion Daikon Salad with either Soy Wasabi Dipping Sauce or Tataki Dipping Sauce (or both sauces if you like variety!). Both the meat and Onion Daikon Salad are dipped into the sauce of your choice. If you don't care for the spicy heat of wasabi, try the mild Tataki Dipping Sauce.

SERVES **4**
PREPARATION TIME: **30 minutes, plus a few hours to chill after grilling**
GRILL TIME: **3 to 5 minutes maximum for rare**

1¼ lbs (600 g) tenderloin
1 teaspoon salt
1 to 2 tablespoons neutral-flavored oil

ONION DAIKON SALAD
1 onion, thinly sliced
Salt
2 fresh shiso leaves or a combination of
 ½ tablespoon chopped fresh mint leaves
 and ½ tablespoon chopped coriander leaves
 (cilantro)
2 small green onions (scallions), cut into slivers
2 small daikon radishes (about 5 oz/150 g each),
 cut into very thin matchsticks

SOY WASABI DIPPING SAUCE
2 teaspoons wasabi paste
2½ tablespoons Japanese soy sauce

TATAKI DIPPING SAUCE
4 tablespoons Japanese soy sauce
2 tablespoons mirin
½ tablespoon sugar
Pinch of dashi stock granules dissolved in
 4 tablespoons hot water or chicken stock
2 teaspoons bonito fish flakes (optional)

1 Prepare the grill for direct grilling with very high heat). (See page 13 for charcoal and page 17 for gas.)

2 If the tenderloin is larger than 2 inches (5 cm) in diameter, cut along the grain in half. This will result in two pieces about 6 to 8 inches (15 to 20 cm) in length. Just before placing the meat on the grill rub it with the salt and oil and oil the hot grate. Place the meat over the high heat zone and grill for 1 to 2 minutes on each side until it just becomes browned. To grill the edges you will have to hold it with tongs. The meat remains raw in the center and only the outer ¹⁄₁₆ to ⅛ inch (2 mm) is cooked. As soon as it is sufficiently browned on all sides, tightly wrap the meat in cling wrap and toss it into ice water. This will stop the cooking process without letting the meat come into contact with the water and dilute the taste.

3 When cold remove the meat from the ice water and place it in the refrigerator for a few hours to completely chill.

4 To make the Onion Daikon Salad, rub the onion slices with a little salt. Set aside for 20 minutes. Drain off any water that has accumulated from the onions. Roll up the

shiso leaves like a cigar and cut into very thin slices. If you're substituting mint and coriander leaves for the shiso, coarsely chop them. Mix the shiso leaves, or chopped mint and coriander leaves, green onions and daikon in a bowl, toss well and arrange on a plate.

5 To serve the Soy Wasabi Dipping Sauce, place a small ball (about ½ teaspoon) of the wasabi paste in a small serving bowl and pour 2 teaspoons of the soy sauce into the bowl. Place the wasabi paste off to the side of the bowl rather than in its center. Do not mix the wasabi paste and soy sauce together. Instead let your guests mix them according to their preference. Repeat with three additional serving bowls.

6 To make the Tataki Dipping Sauce, combine the ingredients for the dip in a bowl and then transfer to 4 small serving bowls.

7 Cut the thoroughly chilled meat on the diagonal into thin slices and place across the top of the Onion Daikon Salad. Serve with the Soy Wasabi Dipping Sauce or Tataki Dipping Sauce.

Korean-Style Kalbi Ribs with Garlic Sesame Paste

Crosscut ribs are often served in Korean BBQ restaurants. The ribs are grilled very quickly and because they contain more fat than other parts of beef, they absorb the flavor of the marinade more readily. If you can't find crosscut ribs beef back ribs can be substituted. The flavor of this paste is full of garlic and green onions and softened by the rice wine and sesame. It's a very delicious combination. Serve with a fresh green salad and Salt and Szechuan Pepper Dip. Alternatively, you may also serve Green Onion Sesame Sauce (page 48).

SERVES **4**
PREPARATION TIME: **30 minutes**
GRILL TIME: **25 to 30 minutes for medium**

2 tablespoons sugar
3 tablespoons rice wine
2 lbs (1 kg) crosscut beef ribs or beef back ribs, cut into individual ribs
3 tablespoons Salt and Szechuan Pepper Dip (page 52)

GARLIC SESAME PASTE
2 tablespoons Japanese soy sauce
2 tablespoons chopped green onions (scallions)
2 tablespoons finely chopped garlic
2 tablespoons dark sesame oil
3 tablespoons toasted sesame seeds
Pinch of salt

1 In a small bowl, add the sugar and rice wine and stir until the sugar is dissolved. Rub the sugar and rice wine mixture onto the ribs.

2 In a small bowl, combine the ingredients for the paste.

3 Rub the paste onto the beef ribs. Set aside for at least 1 hour. (If you have time to marinate them for more than 1 hour, place them in the refrigerator.)

4 Prepare the grill for direct grilling with two heat zones (high and medium). (See page 13 for charcoal and page 17 for gas.)

5 Remove the ribs from the paste. Scrape excess paste off the ribs. Do not discard the paste. Just before you begin grilling, oil the hot grate. Place the ribs on the grate over the high heat zone and grill each side for about 2 to 3 minutes. Move to the medium heat zone when the meat is browned. Continue to grill each side over medium heat for 10 to 15 minutes for medium done. Apply the leftover paste to the ribs after about 6 to 10 minutes just before they are done to give them a nice juicy covering. To be sure test the meat by poking it with your finger (see page 19). Serve with the Salt and Szechuan Pepper Dip.

Porterhouse Steaks with Szechuan Pepper

Porterhouse steak is an excellent cut for grilling and its large size makes it a perfect choice for a party. This recipe uses only little marinade but combines it with a Sesame Chili Dipping Sauce (page 48). In China's Szechuan Province this spicy dip is usually served with boiled meats but it goes great with grilled food too. Feel free to use other dipping sauces and butters such as Sesame Miso Sauce (page 47), Curry Herb Butter (page 55) or Salt and Szechuan Pepper Dip (page 52). This recipe is quite suited to smoking since the smoke flavor will not interfere with the spices and in fact goes very well with the Sesame Chili Dipping Sauce. For a complete meal serve with Arugula Salad (page 162) and Grilled Potato Salad (page 154) or Curried Potato Wedges (page 148).

SERVES **4**
PREPARATION TIME: **15 minutes**
GRILL TIME: **14 to 20 minutes for medium rare; or 30 to 45 minutes if smoking the meat**

2 porterhouse steaks, 1 to 1½ lbs (500 to 750 g) each
2 teaspoons Szechuan pepper or black peppercorns, lightly crushed in a mortar
2 tablespoons light Chinese soy sauce
2 tablespoons sugar
Salt to taste
½ cup (125 ml) Sesame Chili Dipping Sauce (page 48)

1 Rub the steak with Szechuan pepper, soy sauce and sugar shortly before you prepare to place the meat onto the grill.

2 Prepare the grill for indirect grilling with two heat zones (high and medium). (See page 14 for charcoal and page 17 for gas.) If you're using charcoal, place a drip pan in the middle and with live coals around the drip pan.

3 Just before you begin grilling, oil the hot grate. Place the meat over the high heat zone and grill each side for about 2 to 3 minutes. Move the meat over the drip pan or, if you're using a gas grill, over the medium heat zone and continue grilling each side for 5 to 7 minutes for medium rare doneness. When one side is nicely browned, turn and sprinkle with salt.

Check the doneness by poking the meat with your finger (see page 19) or pricking the meat.

4 When done wrap the steak in foil and set aside for 5 to 7 minutes to allow the juices to settle. Cut into ½-inch (1.25-cm) slices and serve with the Sesame Chili Dipping Sauce or another dipping sauce of your choice.

Beef Short Ribs with Teriyaki Glazing Sauce

The Teriyaki Sauce gives the ribs a nice sweet flavorful crust. The ribs in this recipe can either be grilled or smoked. The flavor of smoke combined with the sweet teriyaki sauce gives it a special East-West touch. I like to serve them with Curried Potato Wedges (page 148), a green salad and Special Barbecue Sauce (page 47).

SERVES **4**
PREPARATION TIME: **20 minutes**
GRILL TIME: **25 to 30 minutes for medium**

2 racks beef ribs, about 3 lbs/1.5 kg each
½ cup (125 ml) Special Barbecue Sauce (page 47) (optional)

TERIYAKI SAUCE
1½ cups (375 ml) Japanese soy sauce
3 tablespoons sugar
4 tablespoons mirin
3 tablespoons sake
1 green onion (scallion), finely chopped
2 teaspoons ground ginger
2 teaspoons chopped garlic

1 To make the teriyaki sauce, combine the soy sauce and sugar in a saucepan and place over medium heat. When the sugar is dissolved remove the pan from the heat. Add the mirin and sake and let cool. Then add the green onion, ginger and garlic.

2 Marinate the ribs in the teriyaki sauce for about 1 hour. Remove the ribs from the sauce and place the remaining sauce in a small saucepan over high heat. Boil for a few minutes until the sauce slightly thickens and remove from the heat. Set aside for use as a basting sauce.

3 Prepare the grill for indirect grilling with a low temperature. (See page 14 for charcoal and page 17 for gas.) If you're using charcoal, place a drip pan in the middle and with live coals around the drip pan.

4 Just before you begin grilling, oil the hot grate. Place the ribs above the drip pan or, if you're using a gas grill, over the low heat zone and grill at medium low temperature with the hood closed for 25 to 30 minutes. Baste the meat with the cooked teriyaki sauce every so often and test for doneness by poking the meat with your finger (see page 19) and, if necessary, by pricking the meat.

5 Serve with Special Barbecue Sauce, if using.

SERVES **4**
PREPARATION TIME: **40 minutes**
GRILL TIME: **5 to 8 minutes for medium rare**

4 tenderloin steaks, about ⅓ lb each (140 g) each

MISO MARINADE
2 tablespoons white miso
1 tablespoon red miso (if unavailable use an additional tablespoon of white miso)
1 tablespoon Japanese soy sauce
1½ tablespoons sake
1½ tablespoons mirin
1 tablespoon neutral-flavored oil
1 tablespoon sugar

1 In a small bowl, combine the ingredients for the marinade. Place the beef and marinade in a shallow bowl and set in the refrigerator to marinate for a few hours. Remove from the refrigerator 1 hour before you begin grilling.

2 Prepare the grill for direct grilling with two heat zones (medium and high). (See page 13 for charcoal and page 17 for gas.)

3 Oil the grate and place the steaks over the high heat zone and grill each side for about 2 to 3 minutes. Move the steaks to the medium heat zone and continue to grill each side for another 1 to 2 minutes for medium rare doneness. Baste with the leftover marinade from time to time. Test for doneness by poking the meat with your finger (see page 19).

Grilled Miso Teriyaki Tenderlion

Miso is made of soybeans and is very healthy. The Japanese use miso to marinate beef, fish and vegetables. White miso is not only used as marinade but also in soups and many other dishes. It has a mild earthy aroma and taste, which makes me hungry just when opening the packaging. Dark or red miso is stronger in flavor and has a slightly yeasty or maltlike taste. It provides a very special note but is used in lesser amounts because its strong flavor can easily overwhelm other flavors. The subtle tenderloin goes wonderfully with grilled pouches of asparagus and snow peas (page 155). This tenderloin is delicous enjoyed as is but can also be served with Soy Bean Paste Sauce (page 49) as a dipping sauce, if you prefer.

Indian-Style Beef Burgers

These delicious burgers—called "kofta" in India—include chopped raisins, an ingredient often used by the maharajahs. Instead of raisins you can also use coarsely chopped prunes or dried apricots. Note: Prunes don't have to be rehydrated since they are usually soft. The use of cognac is optional—and it certainly is not authentically Indian. But it does add a delicious flavor to the burgers. Serve with pita bread, with Pesto Zucchini (page 145), and Yogurt Cucumber Raita (page 166). Spicy Tomato Sauce (page 50) is a particularly well suited condiment for these burgers.

MAKES **approximately six ⅓-lb (150-g) burgers**
PREPARATION TIME: **40 minutes**
GRILL TIME: **7 to 10 minutes for medium doneness**

¼ cup (65 ml) cognac (optional) or water
½ cup (80 g) soaked, drained and finely chopped raisins
2 lbs (1 kg) ground beef
1 egg
1 cup (150 g) chopped onion
3 tablespoons chopped fresh coriander leaves (cilantro)
1 teaspoon cumin seeds, roasted and ground
4 teaspoons Garam Masala (see page 31)
1 teaspoon chili flakes or ground red pepper (cayenne)
1 tablespoon bread crumbs
Pinch of salt

1 Combine the cognac or water and the raisins in a small bowl. Cover and let stand for 20 minutes or until the raisins become soft.

2 In a large bowl, combine the ground beef, egg, onions, raisins, coriander leaves, cumin, garam masala, chili flakes, bread crumbs and salt. Set aside for 1 hour to marinate.

3 Prepare the patties and let rest for about a half hour in the refrigerator.

4 Prepare the grill for direct grilling with two heat zones (medium and high). (See page 13 for charcoal and page 17 for gas.)

5 Just before you begin grilling, oil the hot grate. Place the patties over the high heat zone and grill each side for about 2 to 4 minutes. When they are browned move them to the medium heat zone and continue to grill each side for another 2 to 3 minutes for medium doneness.

> **Tip** If you use a particularly lean ground beef, for best results, baste occasionally with a neutral-flavored oil.

Flank Steaks with Tropical Sambal Spice Paste

In Asia, this cut of meat is done as kebabs on skewers. I prefer to marinate the meat whole and then, after it's been grilled, cut it into thin slices and serve with dips. Flank steak is best grilled over medium to low heat for a long period to become tender. If you use another cut of beef—such as sirloin or tenderloin—use the direct grill method and begin grilling over medium to high heat. This dish is also well suited for smoking because the smoke flavor will not interfere negatively with the spices. Before serving cut into thin slices and serve with toasted bread, leftover basting sauce, Yellow Mixed Pickles (page 57) and a salad of your choice. If you wish to give your guests a choice of two dipping sauces, Satay Sauce (page 49) is a great option.

SERVES **4**
PREPARATION TIME: **1 hour**
GRILL TIME: **1 to 1¼ hours for medium well**

2 lbs (1 kg) beef flank steak
⅓ cup (80 ml) beef or chicken stock
Pinch of salt
Fresh coriander leaves (cilantro), for garnish
   (optional)

SAMBAL SPICE PASTE
½ teaspoon black peppercorns, toasted
1 teaspoon coriander seeds, toasted
½ teaspoon fennel seeds, toasted
½ teaspoon cumin seeds, toasted
½ teaspoon turmeric powder
1 teaspoon chili flakes
2 medium shallots, finely chopped
4 cloves garlic, finely chopped
3 candlenuts or macadamia nuts
1 tablespoon tamarind pulp dissolved in
   3 tablespoons hot water and seeds discarded
   or 1 tablespoon tamarind concentrate
2 tablespoons sugar
1 tablespoon fish sauce
½ cup (125 ml) coconut milk
Salt to taste

1 To make the spice paste, grind the toasted spices to powder in a food processor or mortar. Mix in the turmeric and chili flakes. Add the rest of the ingredients one by one, grinding the mixture to a paste.

2 Smear the paste over the meat and let marinate in the refrigerator for a few hours or, for best results, overnight.

3 Wipe the excess paste off the meat. In a small saucepan, add the leftover paste, stock and salt and place over medium heat. Simmer for a few minutes. Set aside for use as a basting sauce.

4 Prepare the grill for indirect grilling with a low temperature. (See page 13 for charcoal and page 17 for gas.) If you're using charcoal, after about 20 minutes when all the charcoal is glowing, spread the live coals and make two zones, one medium heat zone and one without coals, and place a drip pan in the middle and with live coals around the drip pan.

5 Just before you begin grilling, oil the hot grate. Place the steak above the drip pan or, if you're using a gas grill, over the low heat zone and grill while turning frequently for about 60 to 70 minutes. After about 40 minutes, when a nice brown color has developed, begin basting with the basting sauce to give it a thick layer of creamy sauce. Don't begin basting too early because the spices will burn and create a bitter taste.

6 Test for doneness by poking with your finger or pricking the meat (see page 19). If you're not sure, use a meat thermometer. Remove from the fire and wrap in aluminum foil to rest for about 10 minutes. Garnish the remaining basting sauce with a few coriander leaves, if using, and serve on the side.

Thai T-bone Steaks

T-bone steak is not a traditional cut in Asia. The Thais adopted it from Americans during the Vietnam War and it has become very popular in Bangkok and surrounding areas. The marinade is very simple and the steak is complimented with a variety of dips and sauces such as Tamarind Chili Dip (*Nam Jin Jaew*) (page 51) or Vietnamese Chili and Lime Dip (page 51) and the famous spicy Thai Glass Noodle Salad (page 165).

SERVES **4**
PREPARATION TIME: **10 minutes**
GRILL TIME: **12 to 14 minutes for medium rare**

4 tablespoons fish sauce
2 tablespoons sugar
Pinch of salt and pepper
2 T-bone steaks, about 1 lb (500 g) each

1 Prepare the grill for direct grilling with two heat zones (medium and high). (See page 13 for charcoal and page 17 for gas.)
2 In a small bowl, combine the fish sauce, sugar, salt and pepper. Just before placing the steaks on the grill, rub the meat with the marinade.

3 Just before you begin grilling, oil the hot grate. Place the meat on the grate over the high heat zone and grill each side for about 3 to 4 minutes. Move the meat to the medium heat zone and continue grilling for 3 to 4 minutes. When one side is nicely browned, turn and continue to grill another 2 to 3 minutes for medium rare. For medium doneness continue to grill over medium heat for another 2 to 4 minutes. Test for doneness by poking the meat with your finger (see page 19).

4 When the steaks are done, wrap in aluminum foil, set them aside to rest for 5 to 10 minutes to allow the juices to distribute. Cut into ½-inch (2.5-cm) slices and serve with the Thai Glass Noodle Salad.

Barbecued Ribs with Indian Spice Rub

This recipe uses an Indian-style spice rub that works well for indirect grilling or smoking. I recommend using your own homemade Garam Masala (page 31) for the spice rub. These short ribs go great with Grilled Potato Salad (page 154) and either Spicy Tomato Sauce (page 50) or Special Barbecue Sauce (page 47).

SERVES **4**
PREPARATION TIME: **20 minutes**
GRILL TIME: **25 to 30 minutes for medium doneness**

4 lbs (1.75 kg) beef short ribs, cut into segments of 3 to 4 ribs each
Coarse sea salt or kosher salt to season ribs

INDIAN SPICE RUB
3 tablespoons finely chopped garlic
1 tablespoon Garam Masala (page 31)
1 teaspoon black peppercorns, crushed
2 teaspoons chili flakes

BASTING SAUCE
2 tablespoons extra virgin olive oil
1½ teaspoons lime juice
2 tablespoons finely chopped fresh coriander leaves (cilantro)
Pinch of salt

1 In a small bowl, combine the ingredients for the spice rub.

2 Rub the ribs with the coarse salt and then with the spice rub. Set aside for 30 minutes.

3 In a small bowl, combine the ingredients for the basting sauce.

4 Prepare the grill for indirect grilling with a low temperature. (See page 13 for charcoal and page 17 for gas.) If you're using charcoal, place a drip pan in the middle and with live coals around the drip pan.

5 Just before you begin grilling, oil the hot grate. Place the meat on the grate above the drip pan or, if you're using a gas grill, over the low heat zone and grill while turning over once in a while and basting with the basting sauce. If you're smoking the meat, add soaked wood chips from time to time. Test for doneness by poking with your finger or pricking the meat (see page 19). If you are not sure use a meat thermometer.

Spicy Asian Burgers

The burger has found its way to Asia and many Asian versions have been created. These spicy burgers combine the distinctive flavor of Chinese black vinegar and fresh coriander. The amount of spice is up to you. I suggest starting with 1 teaspoon of ground red pepper. If you tend to like food with very little heat, start with 1/2 teaspoon of the ground red pepper. To check the spice level, cook 1 tablespoon of the Spicy Asian Burger mixture in a small skillet and taste. If you want more heat, add up to 1 teaspoon more of the ground red pepper to the mixture. Serve with a sesame bun and your favorite burger toppings and condiments.

MAKES **approximately six 1/3-lb (150-g) burgers**
PREPARATION TIME: **30 minutes**
GRILL TIME: **7 to 10 minutes for medium**

2 lbs (1 kg) ground beef
2 red onions, finely chopped
1 slice toasted bread, soaked in water or milk
1 egg
2 tablespoons ketchup
1 tablespoon Chinese black vinegar or Worcestershire sauce
1 tablespoon finely chopped garlic
1 tablespoon peeled and finely grated fresh ginger
1 teaspoon ground coriander
1 to 2 teaspoons ground red pepper (cayenne)
2 teaspoons dried oregano
1/4 cup (12 g) finely chopped fresh coriander leaves (cilantro)
Pinch of salt and pepper
4 sesame seed buns

1 In a large bowl, add all of the ingredients and mix until combined. Form the mixture into four patties.

2 Prepare the grill for direct grilling with two heat zones (medium and high). (See page 13 for charcoal and page 17 for gas.)

3 Just before you begin grilling, oil the hot grate. Place the burgers over the high heat zone and grill each side for about 2 to 4 minutes. Move the burgers to the medium heat zone and continue to grill for another 2 to 3 minutes for medium doneness. Cut the sesame buns in half and place the cut side down onto the grill. When the meat is ready place the grilled sesame bun on a plate and top with the hamburger.

One 1-inch (2.5-cm) piece cinnamon, toasted
8 pods green cardamom, toasted
2 teaspoons turmeric powder
1½ teaspoons chili flakes

KERALA BASTING SAUCE
1 tablespoon neutral-flavored oil
2 teaspoons black mustard seeds
1 large onion, finely chopped
2 tablespoons finely chopped garlic
1 tablespoon peeled and finely chopped fresh
   ginger
Six fresh or dried curry leaves
Reserved ½ portion of Kerala Spice Rub
1 cup (250 ml) water
6 tablespoons coconut milk
Salt to taste

1 To make the spice rub, place the toasted spices in a food processor or mortar and grind to powder. Remove any remaining unground pieces of the cardamom pods. Mix in the turmeric and chili flakes. Divide the spice rub into two equal portions.

2 Remove excess fat from the brisket and rub with some salt and half of the spice rub. Set aside for 30 minutes.

3 To make the basting sauce, place the oil and mustard seeds in a small saucepan and place over medium-low heat. Fry the seeds until they crackle. Add the onion, garlic, ginger, curry leaves and sauté. Add the remaining half of the reserved spice rub and fry for a few minutes. Add up to 1 cup (250 ml) of the water little by little to prevent the spices from burning. The sauce should be thick so only add water as needed. Add the coconut milk and cook for about 5 minutes. Set aside to cool.

4 Prepare the grill for indirect grilling with a low temperature. (See page 13 for charcoal and page 17 for gas.) If you're using charcoal, place a drip pan in the middle and with live coals around the drip pan.

5 Just before you begin grilling, oil the hot grate. Place the meat above the drip pan or, if you're using a gas grill, over the low heat zone and grill for about 50 to 75 minutes while turning over once in a while and regularly basting with the basting sauce.

Beef Brisket Kerala Style

This beef brisket is inspired by Kerala-style curries, which are often cooked to almost dry. The beef is then covered in a thick rich spicy and very aromatic sauce. I used a similar spice mixture but modified the recipe to use a whole brisket that is slowly grilled and mopped with a rich sauce. The result is a very tender brisket covered in a creamy aromatic sauce. The strong flavor of this marinade does not combine well with smoke flavor. Serve the brisket with rice, any kind of grilled vegetables and Yogurt Cucumber Raita (page 166).

SERVES **6**   PREPARATION TIME: **40 minutes**   GRILL TIME: **50 to 75 minutes for medium**

3 lbs (1.5 kg) beef brisket
Salt to season brisket

KERALA SPICE RUB
2 teaspoons coriander seeds, toasted
2 teaspoons cumin seeds, toasted
10 fenugreek seeds, toasted
6 cloves, toasted
1 teaspoon black peppercorns, toasted

Add water to the drip pan and make sure the drippings don't burn. Test for doneness by pricking the meat. (*Note:* It is difficult to sense the doneness of large pieces of meat when using the poking test so you may want to use a meat thermometer.) When the meat is medium done, collect the drippings and skim off the fat. Add the drippings to the saucepan with the basting sauce. Simmer over medium-low heat for a few minutes and serve hot with the brisket.

Lemongrass Curry Burgers

In Asia ground meat is traditionally served as a kebab on skewers or even wrapped in betel leaves. This mixture of beef and spices works great as a burger too. I modified the recipe to make larger patties that can be eaten either on a bun or served as is with Vietnamese Chili and Lime Dip (page 51) and a salad of your choice.

MAKES **approximately eight ¼-lb (100-g) burgers**
PREPARATION TIME: **40 minutes**
GRILL TIME: **7 to 10 minutes for medium**

2 lbs (1 kg) ground beef
2 tablespoons chopped lemongrass (from lower two third of stalk with tough outer leaves removed)
2 shallots, minced
4 cloves garlic, minced
1½ teaspoons peeled and finely chopped fresh ginger
1 egg
2 teaspoons curry powder
2 tablespoons light Chinese soy sauce
1 tablespoon black Chinese vinegar or Worcestershire sauce
2 tablespoons finely chopped fresh coriander leaves (cilantro)
2 teaspoons sugar
¼ teaspoon black pepper
Pinch of salt
Vietnamese Chili and Lime Dip (page 51), for drizzling over burger or dipping

1 In a large bowl, add the ground beef and lemongrass and mix together. Add the remaining ingredients and knead well with your hands until all is evenly mixed. Prepare the patties.

2 Prepare the grill for direct grilling with two heat zones (medium and high). (See page 13 for charcoal and page 17 for gas.)

3 Just before you begin grilling, oil the hot grate. Place the burgers over the high heat zone and grill each side for about 2 to 3 minutes. Move the burgers to the medium heat zone and continue to grill for another 2 to 3 minutes for medium done.

Chapter 2

Poultry Barbecue Recipes

Apart from pork, poultry is the most widely consumed meat in Asia. In India, apart from the various chicken curries and kormas, the best-known chicken dishes are tandoori chicken and chicken tikka. In this chapter, in addition to these two famous dishes, you will find a recipe inspired by south Indian Kerala cuisine and one inspired by the cuisine of the ancient Moghuls, who lived in what is now northern India.

In Southeast Asia chicken is very popular. Notably one of the biggest chicken producers in the world is located in Thailand. Take a glimpse at one of the many food stalls on a Bangkok roadside and you will find that almost every part of the chicken is grilled, including the whole chicken, chicken gizzards on skewers, chicken feet, chicken wings and so forth. Grilled chicken is usually combined with fresh lettuce leaves, Green Papaya Salad (page 165) and a selection of two dips, the spicy Tamarind Chili Dip (page 51) or the Thai Sweet Chili Dip (page 52). In Southeast Asia, grilled chicken is sometimes eaten as a main course but more often as a snack between meals. As a Thai friend of mine once said, "We Thais don't eat dinner, we normally have a pre-dinner snack, a dinner snack and an after dinner or supper snack."

In Japan chicken is mainly served as grilled chicken on skewers, and some restaurants specialize in this popular dish known as chicken yakitori. It is served with yakitori sauce—a delicious condiment made with soy sauce, sake, mirin and a little sugar.

In China duck is the preferred poultry for both eggs and meat but chicken is very popular as well. When traveling through southern China and Vietnam one can still find farmers herding their ducks, hundreds of them, in the rice fields. Traditionally duck is braised or steamed to make it tender. Nowadays ducks are sold very young and tender and one can grill them without adhering to this tedious procedure. In this book I have included two recipes for duck breast, which are easier to grill than whole ducks. The delicious Cinnamon Glazed Duck with Mangoes (page 84) was inspired by an authentic recipe I received from a Chinese friend whereas Duck Breast with Orange Soy Glaze (page 90), flavored with soy sauce, cinnamon, nutmeg and ginger, is an Asian twist on a classic combination.

Thai Chicken Satays

This Thai specialty originates from the southern part of the country and is influenced by Malaysian cuisine. It is always risky to grill chicken meat because it turns dry very easily. The best way to prepare this satay is to grill it over medium-low heat and let the coconut spice marinade thicken to give a nice juicy cover. The satay is then served with slices of grilled bread and Satay Sauce (see page 49).

SERVES **3 to 4 as a main course/5 to 6 as a starter**
TIME TO PREPARE: **1 hour**
GRILL TIME: **7 to 9 minutes**

1 lb (500 g) chicken breast, cut lengthwise into ½-in (1.25-cm)-wide strips
20 bamboo skewers, soaked in water for 30 minutes prior to grilling, or metal skewers

THAI SATAY MARINADE
½ teaspoon coriander seeds, toasted
Heaping ¼ teaspoon cumin seeds, toasted
1 teaspoon peeled and finely chopped fresh ginger
3 cloves garlic
½ teaspoon ground turmeric
1 fresh kaffir lime leaf (optional)
Lower half of 1 lemongrass stalk, outer tough leaves removed and finely chopped
1 tablespoon minced shallots
1½ teaspoons tamarind pulp dissolved in 1½ tablespoons hot water or 1½ table-spoons tamarind concentrate

1 tablespoon palm sugar or light brown sugar
3 tablespoons coconut milk
1½ teaspoons fish sauce

1 To make the marinade, grind the toasted coriander and cumin seeds in a large mortar or food processor. Add the remaining ingredients, except for the fish sauce, one by one and grind to a fine paste. Add the fish sauce and mix to combine.

2 In a large bowl, add the chicken strips and marinade. Toss to thoroughly coat the chicken and place in the refrigerator to marinate overnight.

3 Remove the satays from the marinade and wipe excess marinade off. Thread the chicken strips lengthwise onto the bamboo skewers, one strip per skewer. (Do not discard the remaining marinade!)

4 In a saucepan, add the leftover marinade and bring to a boil. Lower the heat and simmer for a few minutes and set the marinade aside to cool. It is now ready to be used as a basting sauce.

5 Prepare the grill for direct grilling and preheat two heat zones (medium and high). (See page 13 for charcoal and page 17 for gas.)

6 Place the satays on the hot grate over the high heat zone for 2 to 3 minutes and, when becoming browned, move to the medium heat zone and grill for another 3 to 4 minutes, turning frequently. Baste with the cooked marinade a few times while grilling. Check for doneness by pressing the meat (see page 19).

POULTRY COOKING TIPS Wings and legs are most suitable for grilling since the skin contains a lot of fat and prevents the meat from getting dry. Grilling a whole bird can be challenging, though much depends on the type of poultry and its size. Chicken is relatively easy, and I've included a recipe for grilling a whole bird (see Coconut Roast Chicken with Soy Honey Glaze, page 86). Turkey is more challenging because of its size and tendency to become dry. Duck and pheasant are more difficult because they need longer cooking times to become tender and need to be barded with bacon to avoid becoming dry. Breast meat is one of the best parts of the chicken but it requires special attention. It was named by the French Suprême the Volaille ("most valuable of poultry") not without reason. However, it is has a tendency to become dry. It normally has to be grilled on high heat very quickly or covered with lard. It helps if the skin is not removed since the skin contains fat, which prevents the meat from drying too quickly. Chicken breasts can be stuffed, which also helps to retain moisture.

State	Internal Temperature	Feeling	Pricking Test	Meat Internal Color	Wings	Whole	Breast with bone	Breast without bone	Drumsticks
Chicken	175°F to 185°F 75°C to 85°C	firm	clear colorless juice	white/brown	12 to 15 minutes	25 to 30 minutes per lb	15 to 25 minutes per lb	7 to 9 minutes	20 to 30 minutes
Duck	175°F to 185°F 75°C to 85°C	soft to firm	clear colorless juice	brown with red traces		25 to 30 minutes per lb		7 to 9 minutes	

Hoisin Honey Glazed Chicken Wings

My wife shared this recipe with me when we threw our first BBQ party on a riverside in Brig, Switzerland. I still use it often at home when we have guests. These chicken wings make a great simple starter on their own or make a meal when served with a salad and chili sauce or bean sauce. The marinade used for this recipe is well suited to smoking. The smoke flavor will not interfere with the aroma of the marinade but enhance the overall flavor.

SERVES **3 to 4**
PREPARATION TIME: **30 minutes**
GRILL TIME: **12 to 15 minutes**

2 tablespoons Chinese light soy sauce
2 tablespoons honey
2 tablespoons hoisin sauce
One 1-in (2.5-cm)-piece fresh ginger, peeled and minced
4 cloves garlic, crushed with the back of a knife
1 teaspoon ground cinnamon
2 pieces star anise, crushed
10 Szechuan peppercorns, crushed
12 chicken wings

1 In a small saucepan, add the soy sauce and honey and place over medium heat. When the honey is dissolved add the hoisin sauce, minced ginger, crushed garlic cloves and the spices. Lower the heat and gently simmer for 5 minutes. Remove from the heat and let cool.

2 Rub the chicken wings with the hoisin-honey mixture and let marinate 1 hour before grilling. Remove the chicken wings from the marinade. Wipe off any excess marinade.

3 To make the glaze, put the leftover marinade in a saucepan and place over medium-low heat. Simmer for a few minutes or until it becomes slightly thick.

4 Prepare the grill for direct grilling and preheat two heat zones (medium and high). (See page 13 for charcoal and page 17 for gas.)

5 Place the chicken on the hot grate and grill over the medium heat zone for 5 to 7 minutes on each side. Shortly before the chicken wings are done move to the high heat zone. Turn the chicken wings a few times and baste regularly with the hoisin honey glaze until both sides are evenly done and the skin becomes crispy.

Tandoori Chicken

This is possibly the most well-known grilled chicken dish in Asia. The ways to prepare and serve this dish are perhaps as various as the number of restaurants and families cooking it. Traditionally tandoori chicken is served with naan (page 160), but you can use pita bread (page 160) instead, and served with shredded cabbage and grilled onion rings—the latter is included in this recipe. As an alternative to shredded cabbage, I like to serve a fresh Tomato and Pepper Salad (page 163). Usually tandoori chicken has a distinct red color, which is achieved by adding food color. I normally try to avoid adding artificial coloring to my food and so have made this optional. If you don't care for spicy food, you can substitute the ground red pepper with paprika, which will give a similar appearance. Or for a little less spice use $^1/_2$ teaspoon each.

SERVES **4**
PREPARATION TIME: **40 minutes**
GRILL TIME: **1 to 1½ hours**

1 chicken, about 3 lbs (1.5 kg)
Salt
4 tablespoons lime juice
1 teaspoon ground red pepper (cayenne) or paprika or ½ teaspoon each
2 tablespoons butter
1 onion, sliced into thin rings

TANDOORI MARINADE
2 teaspoons cumin seeds, toasted
4 cloves, toasted
4 green cardamom pods, toasted
1 piece mace, toasted
1 teaspoon coriander seeds, toasted
1 tablespoon peeled and finely chopped fresh ginger
5 cloves garlic, finely chopped
1 cup (250 ml) plain yogurt
Dash of orange food coloring (optional)

1 Rinse the chicken and make a few ¼-inch (6-mm)-deep gashes into the skin. Rub the bird with salt, lime juice and ground red pepper. Set aside for 20 minutes.

2 To make the marinade, grind the toasted spices and to a powder in a mortar or food processor. Add the ginger and the garlic and crush to a paste. In a bowl, whisk the yogurt. Add to the spice paste and add the food coloring, if using, and stir to combine.

3 Rub the chicken with the yogurt mixture and let marinate overnight in the refrigerator.

4 Prepare the charcoal grill for indirect grilling (see page 13). Place a drip pan in the middle and live coals around the drip pan.

5 If you're using a gas grill, prepare the grill for indirect grilling. (See page 17.)

6 Remove the chicken from the marinade. In a skillet, melt the butter over medium heat. Add the leftover marinade and simmer for a few minutes. Set aside to use as a basting sauce.

7 Just before you begin grilling, oil the hot grate. Place the chicken on the grate above the drip pan or, if you're using a gas grill, over the low heat zone and grill at medium temperature with the hood closed for about 1 to 1½ hours. Regularly baste the chicken with the cooked marinade. To crisp the skin,

move the chicken over the coals about 5 to 10 minutes before the chicken is finished cooking. Place the onion rings in a grill tray and set on the grill to brown slightly. Test the chicken for doneness by inserting a thin needle under the wings. When done the juices should run clear.

Chicken Yakitori

The first time I had these chicken skewers was with fellow students when we threw a hibachi party for a Japanese professor. We even used an original Japanese charcoal hibachi grill. The recipe is very simple but the outcome is nonetheless excellent. Yakitori is usually cooked on small table grills placed directly onto the dining table. However, it can also be prepared on a large BBQ grill. Serve with Soy Sesame Vegetables (page 152), Grilled Rice Cakes (page 167) or plain rice, preferably short grain.

SERVES **4**
PREPARATION TIME: **20 minutes**
GRILL TIME: **6 to 8 minutes**

8 boneless chicken thighs with skin left on
2 small leeks (no more than ½ to 1 in/1.25 to 2.5 cm in diameter)
15 bamboo skewers, soaked in water for 30 minutes prior to grilling, or metal skewers

YAKITORI SAUCE
4 tablespoons sake
5 tablespoons Japanese soy sauce
1 tablespoon mirin
1 tablespoon sugar

1 In a small saucepan, combine all the ingredients for the yakitori sauce and bring to a boil. Gently boil for about 5 to 10 minutes until all the sugar is dissolved and the sauce has slightly thickened, stirring occasionally. Set aside to cool.
2 Cut the chicken into 1-inch (2.5-cm) cubes. Using only the white and light green

parts of the leeks, cut them into eight 1-inch (2.5-cm) pieces. Thread the chicken and leek pieces onto the skewers. Rub with the yakitori sauce.
3 Prepare the grill for direct grilling with two heat zones (medium and high). (See page 13 for charcoal and page 17 for gas.)
4 Just before you begin grilling oil the hot grate. Place the chicken skewers on the grate over the high heat. When the meat starts to get brown move the skewers to the

medium heat zone and continue to grill for about 6 to 8 minutes. Turn the skewers a few times and baste with the yakitori sauce until both sides are evenly done.

Chicken Tikka

Chicken tikka has become famous all over the world, and the varieties of recipes are endless. Usually chicken tikka is served as pieces of chicken breast skewered and grilled in the tandoor. I prefer to use whole chicken breast instead because working with the whole piece makes it easier to maintain tenderness and moisture. Chicken tikka is served with any kind of green salad, slices of raw onion and Mint and Coriander Yogurt Sauce (page 53).

SERVES **4**
PREPARATION TIME: **40 minutes**
GRILL TIME: **7 to 9 minutes**

2 lbs (1 kg) boneless, skinless chicken breast
2 tablespoons lime juice
Generous pinch of salt
2 tablespoons melted butter for basting

CHICKEN TIKKA MARINADE
1 teaspoon cumin seeds, toasted
1 piece mace, toasted
4 green cardamom pods, toasted
3 cloves, toasted
One ¾-in (2-cm) piece fresh ginger, peeled and chopped
5 cloves garlic, chopped
1 tablespoon neutral-flavored oil
1 to 2 teaspoons ground red pepper (cayenne)
Pinch of ground nutmeg
½ teaspoon ground white pepper
½ cup (125 ml) plain yogurt
½ teaspoon ground turmeric

1 Place the chicken breast and lime juice in a shallow bowl. Sprinkle on the salt. Turn the chicken to evenly coat and let marinate in the refrigerator for 20 minutes.

2 To make the marinade, place the toasted spices in a mortar or food processor and grind to a powder. Add the ginger, garlic and oil and crush to a paste. Add the ground red pepper, nutmeg, white pepper and turmeric and mix well.

3 In a bowl, whisk the yogurt. Add the ground spice paste and stir to combine.

4 Pour the yogurt marinade over the chicken breasts, rubbing the marinade into the chicken. Let marinate for a least 4 hours or overnight in the refrigerator.

5 Prepare the grill for direct grilling with two heat zones (medium and high). (See page 13 for charcoal and page 17 for gas.)

6 Just before you begin grilling, oil the hot grate. Place the chicken breasts on the grate over the high heat zone and grill each side for 2 to 3 minutes. Move over to the medium heat zone and continue to grill for another 3 to 4 minutes. Keep basting with butter. Test for doneness by poking with your finger. The meat should feel firm. In case of doubt make the pricking test. The juices should run clear.

4 medium-hot green chilies (such as the Thai chee fah chile or serrano chile), deseeded and coarsely chopped
½ teaspoon chopped kaffir lime zest or ordinary lime zest
Lower one half lemongrass stalk, tough outer leaves removed and chopped
2 tablespoons neutral-flavored oil
½ cup (12 g) fresh coriander leaves (cilantro), finely chopped
Salt to taste

COCONUT BASTING SAUCE
4 tablespoons coconut milk
1 tablespoon palm sugar or light brown sugar
2 teaspoons reserved Green Curry Paste

1 To make the curry paste, grind the toasted cumin seeds to a powder in a mortar or food processor. Add the garlic, coriander roots, chilies, lime zest and lemongrass and crush to a paste. Add the oil and mix well. Add the finely chopped coriander leaves and stir to combine.
Do not crush the coriander leaves. Reserve 2 teaspoons of the curry paste for the basting sauce.

2 To allow the paste to penetrate the chicken, slash the skin without cutting into the meat.

3 Rub the chicken breasts with the lime juice and set aside for 10 minutes. Then rub the breasts with the paste and let marinate for 1 hour in the refrigerator.

4 In a saucepan, add the ingredients for the basting sauce and place over medium heat. Stir until the sugar and green curry paste are dissolved. Set aside to cool.

5 Prepare the grill for direct grilling with medium-high heat). (See page 13 for charcoal and page 17 for gas.)

6 Just before you begin grilling, oil the hot grate. Place the chicken breasts on the grate and baste with the cooled coconut milk mixture. After 3 to 4 minutes turn the chicken breasts and continue grilling for about 4 to 5 minutes.

7 Test for doneness by poking with your finger (see page 19). When done it should feel firm, but not hard.

Grilled Chicken Breast with Green Curry Paste

Most people are familiar with green curry served as, well, a curry. What is less well known is that this spice paste is also used for dry-frying and grilling meat. Because the spices are sensitive to burning, it's key to remove the marinade from the chicken breasts before placing them on the grill. In the final few minutes of grilling the chicken is basted with the spice paste to give it a creamy curry covering. As a bonus the paste also helps to keep the chicken moist. Serve with jasmine rice and Grilled Vegetable Skewers (page 142) or alternatively with any kind of green or mixed salad.

SERVES **4**
PREPARATION TIME: **40 minutes**
GRILL TIME: **7 to 9 minutes**

4 boneless chicken breast halves, preferably with skin on
1 tablespoon lime juice
1 tablespoon green curry paste ready made or as per following recipe:

GREEN CURRY PASTE
1½ teaspoons cumin seeds, toasted
6 cloves garlic, coarsely chopped
2 fresh coriander (cilantro) roots, cleaned, or coriander stems, coarsely chopped

Cinnamon Glazed Duck with Grilled Mangoes

The original version of this recipe, which I received from my Chinese friend Zhang Da De, calls for a whole goose that is marinated and stuffed with leeks and ginger and a cinnamon stick. This recipe uses the same marinade but instead of a whole goose I use duck breasts, which are easier to handle and are better suited to serving a typical family of four. I like to serve each duck breast with a grilled mango and a lettuce or arugula salad.

SERVES **4**
PREPARATION TIME: **30 minutes**
GRILL TIME: **7 to 9 minutes**

4 boneless duck breast halves, preferably with
    skin on
1 teaspoon lemon juice
Salt
1 tablespoon oil
2 ripe mangoes

HONEY-CINNAMON MARINADE
1½ teaspoons peeled and chopped fresh
    ginger
1 green onion (scallion), finely chopped
1 tablespoon Chinese dark soy sauce
1 tablespoon Chinese light soy sauce
2 tablespoons honey
½ teaspoon ground cinnamon

1 Rub the duck breasts with the lemon juice and salt and set aside for 10 minutes.
2 In a small mortar, crush the ginger to a paste.
3 To make the marinade, combine the ginger, green onion, light and dark soy sauce, honey and cinnamon in a saucepan. Place over medium-low heat and let simmer for a few minutes. Set aside to cool.
4 Place the duck breasts in a shallow dish and pour the marinade over the top. Turn to evenly coat the duck and let marinate for 1 hour in the refrigerator.
5 Remove the skin from the mangos, cut in

half lengthwise and remove the pits.

6 Remove the duck breasts from the marinade and wipe off any excess marinade. In a saucepan, bring the leftover marinade to a simmer and cook for a few minutes. Set aside for use as a basting sauce.

7 Prepare the grill for direct grilling with two heat zones (medium and high). (See page 13 for charcoal and page 17 for gas.)

8 Just before you begin grilling, oil the hot grate. Place the meat skin side up on the grate over the medium heat zone and grill for 3 to 4 minutes. Baste the skin with the reserved marinade and place the duck breasts skin side down over the high heat zone. Grill for another 4 to 5 minutes or until the skin becomes crisp. Baste shortly before the meat is done on both sides and heat to give a nice glazing. Test for doneness by poking with your finger or pricking. When the juices run clear, the duck breasts are done. Wrap in aluminum foil and let rest for a few minutes before serving.

9 Place the mangoes into a grill tray and grill each side for a few minutes. The mangoes are very tender and need to be handled with care. Serve the mangoes with the duck breasts.

Barbecue Spice Rub Chicken Wings

This recipe is very simple and can be done very quickly. Cumin and paprika give the wings a zesty aroma. Serve with either Mint and Coriander Yogurt Sauce (page 48) or Garlic Sauce (page 47). This dish is an excellent starter with a glass of cold beer.

SERVES **4 as a main course/6 to 8 as a starter**
PREPARATION TIME: **30 minutes**
GRILL TIME: **12 to 15 minutes**

2 lbs (1 kg) chicken wings
2 teaspoons lime juice

CHICKEN WING SPICE RUB
1 teaspoon cumin seeds, toasted
6 cloves garlic, finely chopped
2 teaspoons ground paprika
Heaping ¼ teaspoon salt
½ teaspoon black pepper

LEMON BASTING SAUCE
2 tablespoons lemon juice
2 tablespoons olive oil

1 Rub the chicken wings with the lime juice and set aside for 20 minutes.

2 To make the spice rub, place the toasted cumin seeds in a mortar or food processor and grind to a powder. In a small bowl, combine the ground cumin seeds, garlic, paprika, salt and pepper.

3 Rub the chicken wings with the spices and let marinate in the refrigerator for at least 3 hours and preferably overnight.

4 Prepare the charcoal grill for indirect grilling (see page 14). Place a drip pan in the middle and live coals around the drip pan.

5 If you're using a gas grill, prepare the grill for indirect grilling. (See page 17.)

6 In a small bowl, combine the ingredients for the basting sauce and set aside.

7 Just before you begin grilling, oil the hot grate. Place the chicken wings on the grate above the drip pan or, if you're using a gas grill, over the low heat zone and grill at medium temperature with the hood closed for about 12 to 15 minutes, regularly basting the meat with the olive oil and lemon mixture. A few minutes before the wings are finished cooking, move them to the high heat zone or above the coals and continue to grill until the skin becomes crisp, basting every so often.

Thai Rotisserie Chicken

The combination of garlic, black pepper and distinctive coriander root, which is used in this dish, is a very traditional base ingredient in Thai cuisine equivalent to the bouquet garni in Western cuisine. This rotisserie chicken is traditionally eaten with Green Papaya Salad (page 165) and Thai Sweet Chili Dip (page 52).

SERVES **4**
PREPARATION TIME: **30 minutes**
GRILL TIME: **50 to 60 minutes**

One 2-lb (1-kg) chicken
Salt
1 fresh or dried pandan leaf (optional)

THAI SPICE PASTE

10 black peppercorns
5 cloves garlic, coarsely chopped
1 tablespoon coarsely chopped fresh coriander (cilantro) root or stems
1 tablespoon chopped lemongrass (from inner and lower two third of stalk)
½ teaspoon ground turmeric
1½ tablespoons fish sauce
1 tablespoon sugar

1 To make the spice paste, crush the peppercorns and garlic in a mortar or food processor. Add the coriander root or stems and lemongrass and crush. Add the turmeric, fish sauce and sugar and mix to combine.

2 Generously rub the chicken on the inside and outside with the salt and then with the spice paste. Place the pandan leaf, if using, in the cavity of the chicken. Set aside to marinate in the refrigerator for 2 to 3 hours.

3 Prepare the charcoal grill for indirect grilling (see page 13). Place a drip pan in the middle and live coals around the drip pan.

4 If you're using a gas grill, prepare the grill for indirect grilling (See page 17.)

5 Scrape the spice paste from the chicken. In a saucepan, heat the spice paste and simmer for a few minutes. Set aside for basting.

6 Place the chicken on a rotisserie and place above the drip pan or, if you're using a gas grill, over the low heat zone and grill at medium temperature with the hood closed for about 50 to 60 minutes. During the later stages of grilling, regularly baste the meat with the marinade. Prick the chicken with a thin needle underneath the wings. If the juices run clear, the chicken is done.

Coconut Roast Chicken with Soy Honey Glaze

This dish is something really special and exotic. The chicken is placed over a fresh coconut—a Southeast Asian variation on "beer can chicken"! The coconut water steams the chicken from the inside while the exterior becomes nice and crispy. The chicken is served with the coconut water as a side dish. This aromatic and slightly sweet chicken dish is best served with stir-fried steamed rice or Japanese Grilled Eggplant (page 151).

SERVES **4**
PREPARATION TIME: **50 minutes**
GRILL TIME: **1 to 1½ hours**

1 fresh coconut or 1 can unsweetened coconut water (not coconut milk!) (reserve 3 tablespoons for the marinade)
1 small onion, thinly sliced into rings
2 green onions (scallions)
1 red jalapeno pepper or 2 green jalapeno peppers, deseeded and cut into thin slivers
1 chicken, about 3 to 4 lbs (1.5 to 2 kg)
Salt to taste

SOY HONEY MARINADE

2 tablespoons Chinese light soy sauce
3 tablespoons honey
1 teaspoon sugar
3 tablespoons coconut water
3 cloves garlic, finely chopped
1 tablespoon peeled and finely chopped fresh ginger
½ teaspoon black pepper
Pinch of curry powder (optional)

1 Prepare the chicken support. If you're using a fresh coconut, follow the steps shown to the right.

2 If you wish to use fresh coconut water with a chicken sitter or empty beer can, collect the coconut water from the freshly opened coconut and pour into a chicken sitter or an empty beer can with the top cut off. Add the onion rings, green onions and jalapeno pepper slivers to the sitter or can. Place the marinated chicken over the top of the sitter or can.

3 If you're using canned coconut water, pour it into a chicken sitter or an empty beer can with the top cut off. Add the onion rings, green onions and jalapeno pepper slivers to the sitter or can. Place the marinated chicken over the top of the sitter or can.

4 To make the marinade, place the soy sauce, honey and sugar in a saucepan and set over medium heat. When the sugar is dissolved add the coconut water, garlic, ginger, black pepper and curry powder, if using, and simmer for a few minutes. Set aside and let cool.

5 Rub the chicken inside and outside with the marinade and keep in the refrigerator for 30 minutes.

6 Prepare the grill for indirect grilling (see page 13 for charcoal and page 17 for gas). Place a drip pan in the middle and live coals around the drip pan.

7 Remove the chicken from the marinade and reserve any leftover marinade. In a saucepan, bring the leftover marinade to a simmer and cook for a few minutes. Set aside for basting.

8 Set the chicken resting on its support (can, coconut or sitter) on the hot grate above the drip pan or, if you're using a gas grill, over the low heat zone and grill at medium temperature with the hood closed for about 1 to 1½ hours. During the last 10 to 15 minutes of cooking, regularly baste the chicken with the leftover marinade. Check for doneness by pricking the bird underneath the wings. If the juices run clear, the chicken is done. Check for the meat for seasoning and sprinkle on salt if needed.

1 Remove the bottom husk.
2 Remove the top husk.
3 Cut the top into a cone.
4 Remove the husk from the sides of the coconut.
5 Slice off the top of the coconut.
6 Remove 3 tablespoons of the water and set aside for use in the marinade. The coconut is now ready to be filled with the onion rings, green onions and jalapeno slivers.
7 Place the marinated chicken firmly on top of the coconut.
8 The chicken is now ready to be grilled!

Bombay Chicken Burgers

The first time I had this dish was in the famous restaurant named "Copper Chimney" in Bombay. I have long searched for a similar recipe to replicate this excellent dish. The texture is quite soft and creamy with a scent of mace and nutmeg. Though not traditional, I added yogurt-soaked bread to make the burgers moister and to give them a mild flavor and soft creamy texture. These burgers are best served with Tandoori Naan or Quick Pita Bread (page 160), some Yogurt Cucumber Raita (page 166) and Spicy Tomato Sauce (page 50).

SERVES **4**
PREPARATION TIME: **30 minutes**
GRILL TIME: **6 to 8 minutes**

2 eggs
2 lbs (1 kg) ground chicken
½ cup (12 g) fresh coriander leaves (cilantro), finely chopped
2 slices white bread soaked in ½ cup (125 ml) plain yogurt
2 tablespoons neutral-flavored oil
Pinch of salt
2 tablespoons melted butter for basting

BOMBAY SPICE PASTE
1 piece mace, toasted
3 green cardamom pods, toasted
½ cup (80 g) cashew nuts
One ½-in (1.25-cm) piece fresh ginger, peeled and chopped
1 teaspoon chili flakes
1 teaspoon ground white pepper
¼ teaspoon ground nutmeg
1 small onion, finely chopped

1 To make the spice paste, place the toasted spices in a mortar or food processor and grind them to a powder. Pass through a fine sieve and regrind the larger parts. Remove any remaining unground pieces of cardamom pod. Add the cashew nuts and grind to a paste. Then add the ginger and crush to a paste. Add the chili flakes, white pepper, nutmeg, and onion and continue to grind.

2 Break the eggs in a large bowl and whisk. Add the ground chicken, ground spice paste, coriander, soaked bread with yogurt, oil and salt, and mix well with your hands. Keep the mixture in the refrigerator for 15 minutes. Moisten your hands and prepare patties that are 2½ inches (6 cm) in diameter.

3 Prepare the grill for direct grilling with medium heat. (See page 13 for charcoal and page 17 for gas.)

4 Just before you begin grilling, oil the hot grate. Place the burgers on the grate over medium heat and grill each side for about 3 to 6 minutes while basting with the butter.

Stuffed Saffron Chicken

Traditionally this rich stuffing of two types of nuts, raisins and poppy seeds is stuffed into a whole chicken basted with saffron. To make this a quick-grilling dish, boneless chicken breasts are used in place of the whole bird, which is equally delicious. For a delicious combination, serve with Saffron Rice (page 167) and a Yogurt Cucumber Raita (page 166).

SERVES **4**
PREPARATION TIME: **1 hour**
GRILL TIME: **7 to 9 minutes**

4 boneless, skinless chicken breast halves

GARLIC GINGER PASTE
One 1-in (2.5-cm) piece ginger, peeled, chopped and crushed to a paste
6 cloves garlic, crushed to a paste
1 teaspoon ground red pepper (cayenne)
Pinch of salt

NUT STUFFING
3 tablespoons slivered almonds, lightly toasted
3 tablespoons shelled pistachios, lightly toasted
1 tablespoon butter
1 onion, finely chopped
1 tablespoon peeled and finely chopped fresh ginger
1 tablespoon chopped garlic
2 teaspoons Garam Masala (page 31)
¼ lb (100 g) chicken liver, minced
3 tablespoons poppy seeds soaked in ½ cup (125 ml) milk until slightly softened, then drained
⅓ cup (10 g) fresh coriander leaves (cilantro), coarsely chopped
1 tablespoon raisins
Salt to taste

SAFFRON BASTING SAUCE
⅔ cup (160 ml) plain yogurt
2 teaspoons saffron dissolved in ¼ cup
  (65 ml) milk

1 To make the ginger and garlic paste, combine the ginger and garlic paste, ground red pepper (cayenne) and salt.

2 Create a pouch in the chicken breasts, following the steps shown to the right. Rub the chicken breasts all over with the paste, including inside the pouch, and let marinate in the refrigerator for 30 minutes.

3 To make the stuffing, place the toasted almonds and pistachios in a small mortar or food processor and crush to a coarse paste.

4 In a skillet, add the butter. Fry the onion until slightly glassy. Add the ginger, garlic and garam masla and sauté for a few minutes. Add the minced chicken liver and fry for 2 to 3 minutes or until done. Remove from the heat and add the nut paste,

drained poppy seeds, coriander leaves and raisins. Mix well and add the salt.

5 In a bowl, combine the ingredients for the basting sauce. Whisk until smooth and set aside.

6 Remove the marinated chicken breasts from the refrigerator. Fill each pouch with the stuffing, following the illusrated steps shown to the right.

7 Prepare the charcoal grill for direct grilling with two zones (see page 13).

8 If you're using a gas grill, prepare the grill for direct grilling with two zones (high and medium). (See page 17.)

9 Just before you begin grilling, oil the hot grate. Place the chicken breasts on the grate over the high heat zone and grill for 2 to 3 minutes on each side. Move to the medium heat zone and continue grilling till done. Baste regularly with the yogurt saffron sauce.

1 Using the tip of a sharp knife, make a small deep incision into the chicken breast. **2** While holding the chicken breast with your hand pressed flat on top, continue to make a deep incision along the breast being careful not to cut through to the other side. The tip of the knife should be about ½ inch (1.25 cm) from the other side. **3** Open the pouch and deepen the cut where necessary. **4** Stuff the breast with one-quarter of the filling. **5** Close the pouch and secure with a toothpick or short skewer.

ORANGE SAUCE

Segments from ½ large orange, cut into ⅛-in
  (3-mm)-thick slices
2 tablespoons chicken stock or water
⅓ cup (80 ml) Grand Marnier liqueur
½ teaspoon cornstarch dissolved in a little
  water

1 To make the marinade, combine the orange juice, orange zest, oil, soy sauce, cinnamon, nutmeg, ginger and sugar in a bowl. Stir until the sugar dissolves.

2 Place the duck breasts and marinade in a shallow tray and turn the breasts to evenly coat them with the marinade. Let marinate in the refrigerator for 2 to 3 hours.

3 Remove the duck breasts from the marinade, wipe off excess marinade and generously rub with some salt and pepper. Reserve the leftover marinade.

4 Prepare the grill for direct grilling with two heat zones (medium and high). (See page 13 for charcoal and page 17 for gas.)

5 To make the orange sauce, oil the hot grate of the preheated grill. Place the orange slices on the grate over medium heat and grill for a few minutes. Remove the orange slices when they turn brown and just become soft and place in a saucepan with the leftover marinade. Bring to a boil and add the chicken stock or water and the Grand Marnier. Reduce the heat to medium-low and add the cornstarch slurry. Continue to simmer the sauce until it slightly thickens. Set aside and keep warm to serve with the duck breasts.

6 In the preheated grill, place the duck breasts on the hot oiled grated skin side up over the medium heat zone. Grill for 3 to 4 minutes and baste with the oil. Turn the duck breasts skin side down over the high heat zone and continue to grill for another 4 to 6 minutes to let the skin become crisp. Baste with the oil a few times shortly before the dusk breasts are done. Check for doneness by poking with your finger (page 19). When done they should feel firm, but not hard. If in doubt you can prick the meat. If the juices run clear, the meat is done.

Grilled Duck Breast with Orange Soy Glaze

The classic combination of duck and orange is not new. What makes this version different is the addition of soy sauce, cinnamon, nutmeg and ginger, which gives this dish a distinct Asian touch and wonderful aroma. Serve this duck breast with rice or with Arugula Salad with Ginger Soy Dressing or Chinese Vegetable Salad (page 161).

SERVES **4**
PREPARATION TIME: **45 minutes**
GRILL TIME: **7 to 9 minutes**

4 boneless duck breasts, preferably with skin
  on (about 2 lb/1 kg total)
Salt and pepper to season the duck breasts
2 tablespoons oil for basting

ORANGE SOY MARINADE
¼ cup (65 ml) freshly squeezed orange juice
  (about ½ orange)
Zest of 1 orange, finely chopped
1 tablespoon neutral-flavored oil
1 tablespoon Chinese light soy sauce
½ teaspoon ground cinnamon
Pinch of ground nutmeg
1½ teaspoons peeled and minced fresh ginger
1 tablespoon sugar

Spicy Masala Drumsticks

This chicken recipe uses a mixture of spices with desiccated coconut or fresh ground coconut to give it a nice crunchy and spicy crust. The spice combination is inspired by south Indian cuisine, which is generally tangier than northern Indian dishes. Serve this dish with Mint and Coriander Yogurt Sauce (page 48) and plain rice or Pistachio Rice Salad (page 166).

SERVES **4**
PREPARATION TIME: **30 minutes**
GRILL TIME: **20 to 30 minutes**

8 chicken drumsticks
1 tablespoon lime juice
Salt to season drumsticks
2 tablespoons oil for basting

MASALA SPICE RUB
4 tablespoons desiccated coconut
1 teaspoon coriander seeds, toasted
1 teaspoon ground cumin, toasted
1 teaspoon black peppercorns, toasted
½ teaspoon ground turmeric
1 teaspoon brown sugar
1 tablespoon finely chopped garlic
1 tablespoon peeled and finely chopped fresh
    ginger
1 teaspoon chili flakes
Pinch of salt

1 Soak the desiccated coconut in warm water for about 30 minutes then drain and squeeze out excess water. While the coconut is soaking, rub the chicken drumsticks with the lime juice and some salt and set in the refrigerator for 20 minutes.

2 To make the spice rub, grind the toasted spices to a powder in a mortar or food processor. In a small bowl, combine the toasted and ground spices, turmeric, sugar, garlic, ginger, chili flakes, salt and drained desiccated coconut.

3 Rub the spice rub onto the drumsticks and set aside to marinate for 30 minutes.

4 Prepare the charcoal grill for indirect grilling (see page 13). Place a drip pan in the middle and live coals around the drip pan.

5 If you're using a gas grill, prepare the grill indirect grilling. (See page 17.)

6 Just before you begin grilling, oil the hot grate. Place the chicken on the grate above the drip pan or, if you're using a gas grill, over the low heat zone and grill at medium temperature with the hood closed for 20 to 30 minutes. Regularly baste the chicken with a little oil. When the drumsticks are almost done move them to the high heat zone (directly over the charcoal) and continue to grill until the skin becomes crisp and the chicken is done. Test by pricking to the bone. If the juices run clear, the chicken is done.

Chapter 3

Fish and Seafood Barbecue Recipes

Asia is the world's largest seafood consumer, with Japan ranking number one. In Japan seafood is mainly consumed as sushi and sashimi but there are excellent grilled specialties as well. Whole fish are woven in and out on thin very sharp and long (some are more than 15 inches/38 cm) metal skewers—a method uniquely found in Japan that develops a wonderfully crispy skin. Salmon Fillet with Miso (page 94) makes use of this special Japanese grilling technique. Seared Teriyaki Tuna (page 106), Fish and Scallop Kebabs (page 103) and Grilled Salmon Burgers (page 98) are all based on classic Japanese-inspired recipes using traditional Western grilling techniques.

Whereas saltwater fish are preferred in Japan, the Chinese tend to like freshwater fish. However, in all regions seafood like shrimp, octopus and crab is highly appreciated and is available almost everywhere from coastal Shanghai to Beijing to mountainous Szechuan. Grilled Shrimp with Black Bean Sauce (page 102) is inspired by a recipe from Gansu province that is usually stir-fried and adapted here for grilling.

In Thailand and Vietnam both fresh- and saltwater fish are equally popular. Vietnam is located along the Pacific Ocean with a very long coastline hence seafood is easily available throughout the country. In Thailand, traditionally the cuisine of the central plains, including Bangkok, relied on freshwater fish rather than saltwater fish and seafood, which used to be limited to the coastal provinces. Grilled Garlic Pepper Jumbo Shrimp (page 99) and the Grilled Seafood Platter with Thai Dipping Sauces (page 104) are typical coastal cuisine recipes whereas Lemongrass Ginger Trout (page 107) is a typical central plains recipe.

In India the best fish and seafood are found on the Malabar Coast starting from Mumbai (Bombay) in the central region to the southern regions of Goa and Kerala. Barbecued Snapper with Coconut and Green Mango (page 109) is from this region of India. The coastal areas in Persia, nowadays Iran along the Arabian Sea and Turkey and Lebanon along the Mediterranean Sea, have a rich tradition of fish and seafood recipes that bridge Asia and Europe. It is not unusual to find aromatic combinations of thyme, mint, parsley, olive oil and Asian spices in the same recipe. Mint and Coriander Salmon (page 101), Grilled Fish Steaks with Mint and Saffron (page 105) and Pepper and Pistachio Crusted Snapper (page 100) are all from this region.

Grilled Lobster with Flavored Butters

Lobster is associated with leisure time, boating and summer vacations at the seaside, and coastal areas are traditionally where you can find the best lobsters. Nowadays you can find lobster in many shops but often they are precooked. Live lobsters are always the best choice. I like to serve grilled lobster with Roasted Pepper Herb Butter (page 55), Lime Butter (page 56) or Wasabi Mayonnaise (page 57).

SERVES **2**
PREPARATION TIME: **30 minutes**
GRILL TIME: **10 to 13 minutes**

Two ½-lb (250-g) live lobsters
Extra-virgin olive oil for basting
Salt

1 Prepare the lobster for grilling by following the illustrated steps below.
2 Prepare the grill for direct grilling with two heat zones (medium and high). (See page 13 for charcoal and page 17 for gas.)
3 Just before you begin grilling, oil the hot grate. Place the lobsters cut side up on the grate over the medium heat and baste with the olive oil. If the shell starts burning move over to low heat. Sprinkle with salt. Grill for 10 to 13 minutes. Test by inserting a steel needle. If it feels warm on the back of your hand, the lobsters are done.

1 With the protective rubber bands around its claws, set the lobster on a cutting board with its head facing toward you.
2 Tightly hold the lobster firmly behind its head. Place the point of a sharp chef's knife at the back of his head—this will be at the "X," the place between the head and the body.
3 Quickly and firmly press the tip of the knife down and continue to cut toward the front until the head is split. This will kill the lobster immediately.
4 Cut the lobster in half lengthwise.
5 Cut the claws off the lobster. The lobster will now be in four sections.
6 Remove the stomach pouch but leave the coral (ovaries) and the liver.

Salmon Fillet with Miso

The mild flavor of miso makes it an excellent marinade base for fish. I prefer to use white miso with only a little of the darker more strongly flavored red miso. Instead of salmon you can also use swordfish or tuna. The fish is traditionally skewered with three metal skewers and placed on a rack above the grill grate. Bamboo skewers can be used instead but tend to tear the fish meat slightly and they are not as long as the metal skewers. This ensures that the skin stays intact and becomes nicely browned and crisp. However, using a normal grill works just as well. Chinese chives and Szechuan pepper give this dish some spice, which is nicely offset with Ginger-Soy Dipping Sauce (below) and Grilled Rice Cakes (page 167).

SERVES **4**
PREPARATION TIME: **40 minutes**
GRILL TIME: **7 to 9 minutes**

4 salmon fillets, about 6 to 7 oz (175 to 200 g) each

TWO-MISO MARINADE
1 tablespoon white miso
1 teaspoon red miso
1 tablespoon Japanese soy sauce
1 tablespoon mirin
1 tablespoon sugar
1 tablespoon finely chopped Chinese chives or regular chives
1 teaspoon Szechuan pepper or pink peppercorns

GINGER-SOY DIPPING SAUCE
1 teaspoon peeled and chopped fresh ginger, crushed to a paste
½ cup Japanese soy sauce
2 tablespoons mirin
2 tablespoons sake
1 teaspoon yuzu juice or lemon juice
1 teaspoon dark sesame oil
Finely grated zest of ½ lime

1 In a small bowl, combine the ingredients for the marinade. Place the fish fillets in a shallow tray. Pour the marinade over and turn the fish to evenly coat. Let marinate in the refrigerator for about 1 hour.

2 In a small bowl, combine the ingredients for the dipping sauce.

3 Prepare the grill for direct grilling with one medium heat zone. (See page 13 for charcoal and page 17 for gas.) (To grill the fish using the traditional Japanese method, see below.)

4 Just before you begin grilling, oil the hot grate. Place the fillets on the grate over the medium heat zone and grill each side for 3 to 5 minutes while basting with the leftover marinade. Check for doneness by inserting a needle. The fish is done when the needle feels warm when holding it on the back of your hand. Another method is to hold a skewer between your thumb and index finger and twist it back and forth. If the skewers move easily, the fish is done. The latter test works less easily with bamboo skewers. Serve with the Ginger-Soy Dipping Sauce.

TRADITIONAL JAPANESE BARBECUE Skewer each fillet onto 4 thin metal skewers or thin bamboo skewers, placing the fillets about 1 inch (2.5 cm) apart. Prepare a rack of 2 pieces of solid wood about 2 inches (5 cm) diameter wrapped in two layers aluminum foil and long enough to hold the four fillets, about 15 inches (40 cm) long. Place the two pieces of wood onto each side of the grill to create a base for laying the skewers. Place the skewer ends on top of the wood such that the fillets do not touch the grate and grill over direct heat and with a medium temperature. Grill for 5 to 7 minutes on each side while basting with leftover marinade. Serve with the Ginger-Soy Dipping Sauce.

Fish and Seafood Barbecue Recipes   95

Bombay-Style Swordfish Steaks

In Bombay, pomfret—an excellent saltwater fish—is the fish of choice for tandoori. I use the more universally available swordfish, which is meatier than pomfret and has fewer bones— something that some fish eaters will appreciate. Serve with lightly grilled red onions and Indian Tomato and Pepper Salad (page 163) and Tandoori Naan (page 160).

SERVES **4**
PREPARATION TIME: **30 minutes**
GRILL TIME: **7 to 9 minutes**

4 swordfish steaks, about 6 to 7 oz (175 to 200 g) each

BOMBAY SPICE PASTE
2 teaspoons cumin seeds, toasted
1 teaspoon coriander seeds, toasted
1 teaspoon ajwain seeds, toasted, or
  ½ teaspoon dried thyme leaves
One 1-in (2.5-cm) piece fresh ginger, peeled and chopped
6 cloves garlic, chopped
½ teaspoon ground turmeric
½ teaspoon ground white pepper
1 to 2 teaspoons chili flakes
2 tablespoons lemon juice
¼ cup (65 ml) plain yogurt

1 To make the spice paste, place the toasted spices and thyme leaves, if using, in a mortar or food processor and grind to a powder. Add the ginger and garlic and grind to a paste. Add the turmeric, white pepper, chili flakes, and a little of the lemon juice, if needed, to make the grinding easier. In a bowl, combine the spice paste with the remaining lemon juice and yogurt.

2 Rub the swordfish steaks on both sides with the spice paste and let marinate in the refrigerator for 1 hour. Remove the fish from the spice paste and scrape most of the paste off the fish, leaving some on the fish. In a saucepan, bring the remaining spice paste to a simmer. Cook for a few minutes and set aside for use as a basting sauce.

3 Prepare the grill for direct grilling with two heat zones (medium and high). (See page 13 for charcoal and page 17 for gas.)

4 Just before you begin grilling, oil the hot grate. Place the fish on the grate over the high heat zone and grill for 2 to 3 minutes while turning once. Move to the medium heat zone and continue grilling for 5 to 7 minutes while basting with the spice paste to give it a thick coating. To test for doneness insert a needle. If it turns easily when twisted between your fingers and it feels warm when holding the needle to the back of your hand, the fish is done.

Shrimp Satays

Prawns are used for this popular satay, which is served all over Southeast Asia in many varieties. Prawns can be difficult to find in the U.S, so I substituted jumbo shrimp. This recipe is inspired by a Thai version that uses herbs, curry powder and coconut milk to make a spicy creamy coating for the shrimp. The shrimp satays are served with Vietnamese Garlic Bread (page 160) and Satay Sauce (page 49).

SERVES **4 as a main course/6 to 8 as a starter**
PREPARATION TIME: **30 minutes**
GRILL TIME: **6 to 10 minutes**

1½ lbs (750 g) jumbo shrimp or prawns, peeled
Bamboo skewers, soaked in water for 30 minutes prior to grilling
2 tablespoons coconut milk plus extra to help grind spice paste, if needed
1 tablespoon neutral-flavored oil plus extra for basting

SAMBAL SPICE PASTE
1 teaspoon coriander seeds, toasted
½ teaspoon cumin seeds, toasted
1 teaspoon ground turmeric
1 teaspoon curry powder
1 fresh kaffir lime leaf (optional)
3 cloves garlic, chopped
Lower half of 1 lemongrass stalk, bruised
2 red or green chilies, deseeded and chopped
1 shallot, chopped
2 teaspoons lime juice
1 tablespoon palm sugar or light brown sugar
Salt to taste

1 To make the spice paste, place the toasted coriander and cumin seeds in a mortar or food processor and grind to a powder. Add the turmeric and curry powder.

2 One by one, add the fresh kaffir lime leaf, if using, garlic, lemongrass, chilies, shallot and lime juice, grinding after each ingredient is added. If the paste becomes too dry drizzle in a little coconut milk to make the grinding easier. Add the sugar and salt and mix until completely combined.

3 In a small saucepan, add 1 tablespoon of the oil and place over medium heat. When hot add the spice paste and fry for a few minutes. Add the coconut milk and cook for another 3 to 5 minutes. Remove from the heat and let cool completely.

4 In a bowl, add the cooled spice paste and the shrimp, tossing to coat the shrimp, and marinate for about 30 minutes.

5 Prepare the grill for direct grilling and preheat two heat zones (medium and high). (See page 13 for charcoal and page 17 for gas.)

6 Thread 3 shrimp on a skewer.

7 Place the skewers on the hot grate over the high heat zone and grill for 6 to 10 minutes, turning frequently and basting with the oil. Move to the medium heat zone if the shrimp become browned too quickly.

Grilled Shrimp with Black Bean Sauce

This sweet and tangy dish is based on a stir-fried shrimp dish that is popular in and around Shanghai. I modified the recipe to a grilled version that is served with rice.

SERVES **4**
PREPARATION TIME: **30 minutes**
GRILL TIME: **6 to 9 minutes**

2 lbs (1 kg) jumbo shrimp with tails, peeled and cleaned
6 bamboo skewers, soaked in water for
   30 minutes, or metal skewers
2 tablespoons sesame seeds, toasted

SHANGHAI MARINADE
1 tablespoon neutral-flavored oil
1 tablespoon finely chopped green onion (scallion)
1 tablespoon peeled and finely chopped fresh ginger
1 tablespoon black bean sauce (dou ban jiang)
2 tablespoons light soy sauce
1 tablespoon Shaoxing rice wine or dry sherry
2 tablespoons sugar

1 To make the marinade, place the oil in a small skillet and set over medium heat. Add the green onion and ginger and sauté for a few minutes or until glassy. Add the rest of the marinade ingredients and simmer for 2 to 3 minutes. Remove from the heat and set aside to let cool.

2 Cut the shrimp in half lengthwise but leave the halves together at the tail end. In a bowl, combine the cooled marinade and shrimp and let marinate for 30 minutes.

3 Thread the shrimp onto skewers. In a saucepan, bring the remaining marinade to a simmer and set aside for use as a basting sauce.

4 Prepare the grill for direct grilling with two heat zones (high and medium). (See page 13 for charcoal and page 17 for gas.)

5 Just before you begin grilling, oil the hot grate. Place the shrimp skewers on the grate over the medium heat zone and grill for about 6 to 9 minutes, basting with the leftover marinade. Move to the low heat zone if the shrimp begin to cook too quickly and continue basting with leftover marinade. Watch the color of the shrimp to gauge when the shrimp are done. When done the flesh should turn from semi-opaque to white and the black lines become bright orange. When poking they should feel firm.

6 Just before they are done sprinkle on the sesame seeds by rubbing the seeds between your thumb and your index finger directly over the skewers. Grill for only a short while more because the seeds will burn if left on the grill too long.

Fish and Scallop Kebabs

Fish kebabs are served all along the Asian coastal regions. Some are spicier, others are more fragrant. This recipe is of Indian origin but adapted for the grill. You can choose any kind of fish you like; just make sure that the fish you use have similar cooking times. These kebabs are best served with a Yogurt Cucumber Raita (page 166), Tandoori Vegetables (page 150) and Curried Potato Wedges (page 148) or rice.

SERVES **6**
PREPARATION TIME: **30 minutes**
GRILL TIME: **5 to 7 minutes**

1 lb (500 g) monkfish fillet
1 lb (500 g) salmon fillet
½ lb (250 g) scallops
2 onions, quartered
2 small zucchini, cut into 1-in (2.5-cm) cubes
12 cherry tomatoes
20 bamboo skewers, soaked in water for
    30 minutes, or metal skewers

KEBAB MARINADE
2 teaspoons cumin seeds, toasted
1 tablespoon chopped garlic
1 teaspoon ground turmeric
½ teaspoon ground black pepper
1 tablespoon lemon juice
2 tablespoons neutral-flavored oil

1 To make the marinade, place the toasted cumin seeds in a mortar or food processor and grind to a powder. Add the garlic and grind to a paste. Add the turmeric, pepper, and lemon juice and oil.

2 Cut the fish fillets into 1-inch (2.5-cm) cubes. Combine with the marinade and toss well. Thread the fish pieces, scallops, cubed zucchini, cherry tomatoes and onion quarters on the skewers, and set aside for 30 minutes. In a saucepan, bring the remaining marinade to a simmer and cook for a few minutes. Set aside for use as a basting sauce.

3 Prepare the grill for direct grilling with two heat zones (high and medium). (See page 13 for charcoal and page 17 for gas.)

4 Just before you begin grilling, oil the hot grate. Place the skewers on the grate over the high heat zone for about 5 to 7 minutes. If they begin to cook too quickly, move to the medium heat zone. Turn and baste with the leftover marinade a few times until done.

Test for doneness by inserting a needle. If the needle turns easily when twisted between your thumb and index finger, and feels warm when placed on the back of your hand, the fish and scallops are done.

Grilled Seafood Platter with Thai Dipping Sauces

Delicious variations of grilled fish platters are available almost everywhere in Thailand at the seaside. They are usually served with three dips, the distinct Thai Seafood Dip (page 52), Sri Racha chili sauce, and fish sauce with sliced green chilies. The variety of seafood you can use is endless and depends rather on the catch of the day than anything else. Since the cooking time of each variety is different, you need to start with the ones taking longest first. You can show off your mastery when all the different types are finished at the same time, which is really a challenge. However your guests will not fret if they have to wait a little for some items to arrive later. Green Mango Salad (page 161) is a nice side dish choice for this seafood platter.

SERVES **6**
PREPARATION TIME: **40 minutes**
GRILL TIME: **25 to 30 minutes**

1 lb (500 g) cod fillet
4 swordfish or tuna steaks, about ½ lb (250 g) each
Salt
Pepper
Neutral-flavored oil
4 jumbo shrimp with shells
4 small calamari
6 mussels

1 Lightly rub the cod and swordfish with some salt and pepper and a little oil.

2 Cut the shrimp lengthwise but leave the shells on. Clean the calamari by separating the head and body and removing the inner ink sack. Rinse with water. Soak the mussels in cold water for 20 minutes to release sand. Rinse, brush and debeard the mussels.

3 Prepare the grill for direct grilling with two heat zones (medium and low). (See page 13 for charcoal and page 17 for gas.)

4 Just before you begin grilling, oil the hot grate. Place the cod on the grate over the medium heat zone and baste with the oil. After about 20 minutes add the swordfish steaks and jumbo shrimp halves and, after another 3 to 5 minutes, add the mussels and the small calamari. Test for doneness by inserting a needle. If the needle turns easily when twisted or feels warm on the back of your hand the fish and shrimp are done. Mussels are done when they open. Any that did not open during cooking should be discarded. Calamari takes the least amount of time and should be added to the grill last. They cook within a few minutes and thus need to be watched carefully. They are done when the arms stretch out after first recoiling and feel firm.

Grilled Fish Steaks with Mint and Saffron

The combination of fish with mint and saffron is found throughout central Asia, including northern India and even in Vietnam. This subtle combination of herbs and spices inspired me to use it on a fish with very delicate flesh—such as the very popular snow fish, which is prized in Asia and in Japan in particular. Commonly known as sablefish or black cod in the West, snow fish can be replaced with any firm white fish. Swordfish, Chilean sea bass, orange roughy, John Dory (Peter's fish), or halibut are good substitutes. Serve together with Pistachio Rice Salad (page 166), Tabbouleh Salad (page 161) and either yellow saffron rice or plain rice.

SERVES **5 to 6**
PREPARATION TIME: **20 minutes**
GRILL TIME: **7 to 9 minutes**

2 lbs (1 kg) swordfish or other firm white fish fillets, cut into 5 or 6 portions
¼ cup (65 ml) white wine
Salt to taste
2 tablespoons olive oil for basting

NORTHERN INDIAN MARINADE
3 tablespoons finely chopped fresh coriander leaves (cilantro)
3 tablespoons finely chopped fresh flat-leaf parsley
3 tablespoons finely chopped fresh mint leaves .
1 tablespoon lime juice
2 tablespoons extra-virgin olive oil
½ teaspoon saffron, dissolved in ¼ cup (65 ml) milk or water
Pinch of salt and black pepper
2 small green chilies, finely chopped (optional)

1 In a bowl, combine the ingredients for the marinade. Place the fish fillets in a shallow tray. Pour the marinade over the fish, and gently turn them once. Let the fish marinate in the refrigerator for 1 to 2 hours. Remove the fish from the marinade. In a saucepan, bring the leftover marinade to a simmer. Add the white wine and salt and continue to simmer for a few minutes. Set aside for use as a serving sauce.

2 Prepare the grill for direct grilling with two heat zones (medium and low). (See page 13 for charcoal and page 17 for gas.)

3 Just before you begin grilling, oil the hot grate. Place the fish on the grate over the medium heat zone and grill for 7 to 9 minutes while basting with the oil. Before serving drizzle the marinade over the fish.

Seared Teriyaki Tuna

Tuna is an excellent fish for grilling because you can eat it in almost every cooking stage, from very rare to well done. Here is a very simple tuna recipe that is best served with a Wasabi Mayonnaise (page 57) or Wasabi Tartare Sauce (page 48) or simply soy sauce with some wasabi and a Grilled Vegetable Pack (page 152). Mahi mahi is similar in taste and texture to a mild tuna and can also be used for this recipe.

SERVES **5 to 6**
PREPARATION TIME: **30 minutes**
GRILL TIME: **4 to 6 minutes for medium**

2 lbs (1 kg) tuna or mahi mahi steaks, cut into
   5 to 6 portions

TERIYAKI MARINADE
3 tablespoons Japanese soy sauce
3 tablespoons mirin
3 tablespoons sugar, preferably superfine

1 To make the marinade, combine the ingredients for the marinade in a small bowl. Stir until the sugar has dissolved.
2 Place the tuna steaks in a shallow tray and pour the marinade over top. Turn the steaks to evenly coat. Let the tuna marinate for about 1 hour in the refrigerator.
3 Remove the tuna steaks from the marinade. Reserve the leftover marinade for use as basting sauce. In a saucepan, bring the leftover marinade to a simmer and cook for a few minutes. Set aside for use as basting sauce.
4 Prepare the grill for direct grilling with heat high. (See page 13 for charcoal and page 17 for gas.)
5 Just before you begin grilling, oil the hot grate. Place the tuna on the grate over the high heat zone and baste with the leftover marinade. Grill for 2 to 3 minutes on each side for medium rare doneness. Poke the tuna with your finger. If it feels soft to firm in touch it is ready.

Tuna Cooking Guide

State	Internal Temperature			Pressing Test	Pricking Test	Meat Internal Color	Tuna Steaks 1 inch thick	Tuna Strips 1 inch by 1 inch by 10 inches
Rare (Bleu)	115°F 40°C	to to	120°F 45°C	soft touch	needle feels cold	red	2 to 3	1 to 3
Medium Rare	120°F 45°C	to to	125°F 50°C	soft to firm	needle feels cold	pinkish red	3 to 5	2 to 4
Medium	125°F 50°C	to to	130°F 55°C	slightly yielding	needle feels warm	traces of pink	4 to 6	3 to 5
Done	130°F 55°C	to to	135°F 60°C	firm	needle feels warm	white, opaque	5 to 8	4 to 7

Lemongrass Ginger Trout

This subtle Thai-inspired recipe enhances the flavor of trout. Traditionally the fish is cooked in a banana leaf but foil also works. Serve the trout with Thai Seafood Dip (page 52) and rice.

SERVES **4**
PREPARATION TIME: **40 minutes**
GRILL TIME: **35 to 45 minutes**

1 whole large trout or 2 to 3 smaller trouts (3 lbs/1.5 kg total), gutted and split
1 tablespoon fish sauce
1 tablespoon lime juice
Salt to season the trout
3 cloves garlic, crushed with the side of a knife
2 lemongrass stalks, top one-third and outer tough leaves removed, and crushed with the side of a knife
2 fresh or dried kaffir lime leaves
One 1-in (2.5-cm) piece fresh ginger
2 tablespoons chopped fresh coriander leaves (cilantro)
1 large banana leaf or sheet of aluminum foil large enough to wrap fish

1 Rub the fish with the fish sauce, lime juice and some salt.

2 Place the garlic, lemongrass, kaffir lime leaves, ginger, and 1 tablespoon of the coriander leaves in the cavity of the fish.

3 Place each fish in a banana leaf or sheet of aluminum foil. Wrap the banana leaf or aluminum foil around the fish to form a pouch. Prepare the grill for direct grilling with medium heat. (See page 13 for charcoal and page 17 for gas.)

4 When the grill is hot place this package on the grate over medium heat for approximately 35 to 45 minutes, depending on the size of the fish. Test for doneness by opening the pouch after about 25 minutes and inserting a needle. If the needle feels warm at the back of your hand the fish is done. Or, insert the needle and twist it between your fingers. If it turns easily the fish is done. If the fish isn't done, close the pouch and continue to grill, rechecking periodically. When done open the pouch and sprinkle on the remaining tablespoon of coriander leaves.

Grilled Mixed Seafood with Herbs

This dish is easy to prepare and can be made on a very hot grill.

SERVES **2 as a main course/4 as a starter**
PREPARATION TIME: **30 minutes**
GRILL TIME: **5 to 7 minutes**

¼ lb (125 g) shrimp
¼ lb (125 g) small octopus
¼ lb (125 g) scallops
1 tablespoon lime juice
¾ cup (185 ml) Chermoula Marinade (page 40)
Bamboo skewers, soaked in water for 30 minutes, metal skewers, or a grill tray

1 In a bowl, add the seafood, lime juice and ¼ cup (65 ml) of the Chermoula Marinade. Toss to evenly coat the seafood. Marinate for 30 minutes.

2 Prepare the grill for direct grilling and preheat two heat zones (medium and high). (See page 13 for charcoal and page 17 for gas.)

3 Remove the seafood from the marinade and wipe off the excess marinade. Place the seafood in a grill tray or on skewers. To allow you to better control the grill time, do not combine different types of seafood on the same skewer.

4 Place the seafood on the hot grate and grill over high heat for 2 to 3 minutes. When the seafood starts to brown move it to the medium heat zone and grill for another 3 to 4 minutes, turning frequently. When done remove the grilled seafood from the skewers and place on a large platter. Serve immediately with the remaining ½ cup (125 ml) of the Chermoula Marinade.

CILANTRO GINGER BUTTER SAUCE
6 tablespoons butter
1 teaspoon peeled and finely chopped fresh ginger
1 tablespoon finely chopped fresh coriander leaves (cilantro)
1 teaspoon lemon juice
1 teaspoon grated lemon zest
1 teaspoon pink peppercorns or green peppercorns, crushed
½ teaspoon salt or to taste

1 Lightly sprinkle the sole fillets with salt and lightly press the 2 teaspoons of pink peppercorns onto both sides of the fillets. Set aside for 10 minutes.

2 To make the butter sauce, place the butter in a small saucepan and set over medium heat. Add the chopped ginger and lightly fry. Remove from the heat and add the remaining ingredients. Mix well and place in a heatproof serving bowl or sauce boat. Set aside in very low oven or other warm spot.

3 Prepare the grill for direct grilling with medium heat. (See page 13 for charcoal and page 17 for gas.)

4 Just before you begin grilling, prepare the fish basket by placing it on the grill to preheat. Once hot, oil the fish basket. Arrange the fillets in the fish basket. Place the fillets over medium heat and grill each side for 3 to 5 minutes. As soon as the fish becomes flaky it is ready. Or, insert a needle into the fish and hold it to the back of your hand. If it feels warm the fish is done.

Grilled Fillet of Sole with Cilantro Ginger Butter

I love the subtle flavor of grilled sole, which is best when combined with other subtle and simple sides. The accompanying Cilantro Ginger Butter Sauce (right) and plain rice or boiled new potatoes are a good match for this delicate fish.

SERVES **4**
PREPARATION TIME: **20 minutes**
GRILL TIME: **7 to 9 minutes**

4 sole fillets, about 6 to 8 oz (175 to 250 g) each
Salt to season fillets
2 teaspoons crushed pink peppercorns or green peppercorns

Note Pink pepper isn't a true pepper but is a dried berry from a small tree related to the rose and found on the French island of Réunion in the Indian Ocean. The flavor is similar to that of black pepper, but fruitier. It is available freeze-dried or packed in brine or water.

Barbecued Snapper with Coconut and Green Mango

The practice of grilling fish and coconut in banana leaves is widely popular along the Malabar Coast of India. In the more southern regions of India, green mango is often added instead of kocum (a sour fruit) and curry leaves are replaced with coriander leaves, which give the fish an entirely different flavor.

SERVES **4**
PREPARATION TIME: **30 minutes**
GRILL TIME: **20 to 30 minutes**

2 large snappers, about 1 lb (500 g) each
2 teaspoons salt to season the snappers
1 green mango (not too sour variety) or under ripe regular variety, sliced
Banana leaves (or aluminum foil) to wrap the fish

SOUTH INDIAN SPICE PASTE
1 teaspoon cumin seeds, toasted
6 cloves garlic, coarsely chopped
½ teaspoon ground turmeric
8 green chilies, deseeded
1 cup (25 g) fresh coriander leaves (cilantro), coarsely chopped
½ fresh coconut grated or ½ cup (50 g) desiccated coconut soaked in warm water for 30 minutes
2 teaspoons sugar

1 Make gashes into each side of the fish and rub inside and outside with the salt. Push the salt into the gashes. Set aside for 30 minutes.

2 To make the spice paste, place the toasted cumin seeds in a mortar or food processor and grind to a powder. Add the garlic, turmeric, chili, coriander and coconut and grind to a paste. Add the sugar and stir to combine.

3 Rub the fish on the inside and outside with the spice paste, place the green mango slices on top and wrap each fish in banana leaves or aluminum foil. Let marinate in the refrigerator for about 1 hour.

4 Prepare the grill for direct grilling with two heat zones (medium and high). (See page 13 for charcoal and page 17 for gas.)

5 Just before you begin grilling, oil the hot grate. Place the wrapped fish on the grate over the high heat zone and grill for 20 to 30 minutes. If the banana leaves start to burn, move to the medium heat zone.

Chapter 4
Pork Barbecue Recipes

Pork has a long culinary history in Asia. In China, pigs began to be domesticated around 4500 B.C. By comparison, pork breeding was not introduced in Europe for another three thousand years and it did not reach America until some 600 years ago, brought by the Spanish seafarer Hernando de Soto.

Via the Chinese pork quickly spread to other parts of Asia. Many of the pork dishes in Asia are stir-fried or braised but you will find grilled pork specialties throughout Asia. Most popular cuts in these regions for grilling are pork ribs, pork neck and pork loin. The famous char siu pork, a Chinese specialty, is made with pork loin (page 113). I have included two delicious pork chop recipes that add the exciting flavors of Asia to this familiar Western cut, which has just recently become known in Asia through the influence of Western tastes.

The Thais and Vietnamese love pork and are very good at preparing barbecued pork dishes. Both the Sweet Soy Glazed Pork Kebabs (page 113) and the Thai-Style Spare Ribs with Tamarind Chili Dip (page 124) are original Thai recipes. The Caramelized Soy and Lemongrass Spareribs (page 120) are inspired by a Vietnamese recipe.

Pork has even found its way to Bali. Most of the islanders follow the Hindu religion so one would expect little pork consumption, but Bali is famous for its suckling pig, or *babi kuling*. I have included a recipe for Pork Roast with Balinese Spices (page 114) that uses pork shoulder rather than a whole pig, which is easier to prepare and serve.

The Philippines, with its strong Spanish influence, is also a large consumer of pork and one can make out the distinct Spanish influence in their recipes. In particular, the island of Cebu, like Bali, is famous for its grilled suckling pigs. I've adapted the recipe for Cebu suckling pig, which uses the unusual combination of ginger and oregano with lime, for a shoulder ham (page 122).

In India pork is only eaten in Goa, which used to be a Portuguese colony. The Portuguese influence on the local cuisine is apparent in many dishes. The most famous dish known outside India is vindaloo, a Goan specialty, and I have included Vindaloo Pork Steaks (page 116)—a spicy grilled version of this dish.

Pork Cooking Times All grill times mentioned in the table refer to direct grilling and indirect grilling at medium to high heat temperatures. For low temperature grilling the time needs to be adjusted by multiplying by 3 to 3.5, e.g. if I state in the table a grilling time of 20 to 25 minutes, then for low temperature grilling you will have to calculate 60 to 90 minutes. The cooking times in the recipe section are based on cooking to medium well.

Pork Butt Roast, Boston Butt Roast or Blade Shoulder (English Pork Shoulder) This piece, from the top of the foreleg, is very suitable for barbequing because the meat contains a lot of fat. The skin should be cut in squares, which will make it crispy.

Pork Belly or Side This is not very popular since it contains a lot of fat. But the meat is very suitable for barbecuing since the fat keeps the meat moist.

Pork Chops These are taken from the back and should have a fat layer at the outer part that prevents the meat from becoming dry during grilling. Pork chops for grilling should be about ¾ inch (2 cm) thick. If the entire back is grilled, the bones should be left in place.

Pork Steak This is a boneless pork chop.

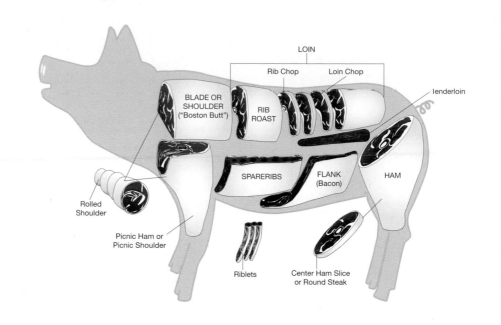

Pork Knuckle This is a German specialty. In order to successfully grill this cut you will require a rotisserie or a large closed grill.

Pork Leg or Ham This is very suitable for grilling. You can grill the entire leg or slices of it.

Pork Loin or Loin Roast or Pork Top Loin Roast is the cut of the pig between the shoulder and the leg along the top of the ribs. Pork loin is good for low temperature grilling and smoking.

Spareribs These are the ribs in the lower part of the pig and are considered a specialty cut for grilling. When you buy them make sure that there is sufficient meat on them.

Pork Tenderloin or Pork Fillet This is the piece of meat on the inner part of the back. The fillet contains less fat. It has to be treated with care because it dries out very easily. If you grill it on a rotisserie, wrap it in bacon to prevent it from drying out.

State	Internal Temperature	Pressing Test	Pricking Test	Meat Internal Color	Spareribs 2 lbs	Chops Bone-in, ½ inch thick	Shoulder	Tenderloin	Baby rack	Suckling Pig
Medium Well	150°F to 160°F 65°C to 70°C	firm	pinkish juice	white	not advisable	8 to 10 minutes	not advisable	20 to 25 minutes	20 to 30 minutes	20 to 30 minutes per lb
Well Done	160°F to 170°F 70°C to 75°C	firm	clear colorless juice	white	25 to 35 minutes	10 to 15 minutes	20 to 25 minutes per lb	20 to 25 minutes	25 to 35 minutes	35 minutes per lb

Chinese Roast Pork

This recipe is inspired by char siu—a classic Chinese specialty that has spread all over Asia, including Japan, Thailand, Vietnam and Malaysia. It is eaten as is or is used as an ingredient in other dishes such as noodle dishes, soups, salads and steamed buns. If you have leftover roast pork, it can be used the next day in noodle soup. Simply slice it thinly and spread it over the boiled noodles in chicken stock. But the best way to enjoy it is hot off the grill with crunchy Chinese Coleslaw (page 162). The marinade for this recipe uses red fermented tofu, a special ingredient that gives the marinade its red color and a distinct flavor. An all-purpose char sui marinade, which uses a little more soy and honey than this one, can be found on page 38. Both marinades can be used to make Chinese Roast Pork, each with a slightly different but equally delicous result.

SERVES **4**
PREPARATION TIME: **30 minutes**
GRILL TIME: **20 to 35 minutes for medium well**

2 lbs (1 kg) pork tenderloin
1 teaspoon salt

ROAST PORK MARINADE
1 tablespoon neutral-flavored oil
One 1-in (2.5-cm) piece fresh ginger, peeled and finely chopped
2 to 3 small green onions (scallions), finely chopped
1 tablespoon hoisin sauce
1 tablespoon Chinese dark soy sauce
1½ tablespoons honey
1 tablespoon Chinese Shaoxing wine or dry sherry
1 teaspoon red fermented tofu or dash of red food color (optional)
½ teaspoon five spice powder (page 31)

1 To make the marinade, add the oil to a skillet and place over medium heat. Add the ginger and green onion and fry slightly. Add the hoisin sauce and continue to fry. Add the soy sauce, honey, Shaoxing wine, fermented tofu, if using, five spice powder and red food color, if using. Bring to a boil and then lower the heat to let simmer for 2 to 3 minutes. Remove from the heat and let cool before using.

2 Place the tenderloin in a shallow tray and pour the marinade over. Turn to evenly coat. Let the tenderloin marinate for 3 hours in the refrigerator.

3 Remove the tenderloin from the marinade. In a small saucepan, add the leftover marinade and place over medium heat. Let simmer for a few minutes. Remove from the heat and set aside for use as a basting sauce.

4 Prepare the grill for direct grilling with two heat zones (high and medium). (See page 13 for charcoal and page 17 for gas.)

5 Just before you're ready to grill, oil the hot grate. Place the tenderloin on the grate over the high heat zone and grill each side for 2 to 3 minutes. Move the tenderloin to the medium heat zone and continue grilling for another 15 to 20 minutes, turning frequently. Baste regularly with the cooked marinade. Check for doneness by poking the meat with a finger (see page 19). If you feel that the meat is more or less ready do a pricking test. When the juices run clear the meat is done. Wrap in aluminum foil and let rest for 10 minutes in a warm place before serving.

NOTE Red fermented tofu, or *hong dou fu ru,* is a variety of tofu pickled in straw with red yeast rice added as coloring.

Sweet Soy Glazed Pork Kebabs

These delicious pork kebabs—marinated with soy sauce and sugar—are very popular as a midday snack in Thailand. One often finds office workers buying these kebabs in the early afternoon to bring them back to the office where they are shared with colleagues. They are typically dipped into a spicy dipping sauce and eaten with sticky rice. Serve with Tamarind Chili Dip (page 51) or Vietnamese Chili and Lime Dip (page 51) and jasmine rice.

SERVES **4**
PREPARATION TIME: **30 minutes**
GRILL TIME: **7 to 10 minutes for medium well**

1 lb (500 g) pork tenderloin, not too lean, cut into ¾ x 1 x ⅛-in (2 x 2.5 x 0.3-cm) pieces
12 bamboo skewers, soaked in water 30 minutes prior to grilling, or metal skewers

SWEET SOY MARINADE
1 teaspoon Thai dark soy sauce or 1 teaspoon Chinese dark soy sauce and a few drops molasses
1 tablespoon palm sugar or light brown sugar
1 tablespoon fish sauce
6 cloves garlic, finely chopped
2 green onions (scallions), finely chopped
1 tablespoon cleaned and finely chopped fresh coriander (cilantro) roots or stems
1 teaspoon black pepper
Salt to taste

1 In a small bowl, combine all of the ingredients for the marinade except for the salt. Taste to check for seasoning and add salt if needed. Combine the pork with the marinade and keep in the refrigerator for at least 1 hour.

2 Thread the pork onto bamboo skewers. Wipe off excess marinade before placing the pork skewers onto the grill.

3 Prepare the grill for direct grilling with two heat zones (high and medium). (See page 13 for charcoal and page 17 for gas.)

4 Just before you're ready to grill, oil the hot grate. Place the skewers on the grate over the high heat zone and grill each side for about 2 to 3 minutes. Move the skewers to the medium heat zone and continue to grill for another 3 to 5 minutes, turning frequently. Check doneness by poking with your finger (see page 19) or pricking the meat. The juices should run clear when done.

Pork Roast with Balinese Spices

This dish is traditionally made with a whole pig. To make it easy for a normal household, I have modified the recipe to serve six people rather than one hundred! The finely cut leeks or greens combined with the spice paste create a very smooth-textured filling. This dish can be made a day ahead and served cold the next day. Some guests claim it is even better the second day. Serve with Bean Sprout Salad (page 162) and Saffron Rice (page 167).

SERVES **6**
PREPARATION TIME: **1 hour**
GRILL TIME: **1 to 1¾ hours for medium well**

2 lbs (1 kg) pork shoulder, preferably with skin on
1½ tablespoons salt
1 tablespoon neutral-flavored oil
2 oz (50 g) leeks, or leafy green vegetable such as spinach, Swiss chard or kale cut into very fine slivers

BALINESE SPICE PASTE

½ teaspoon coriander seeds, toasted
½ teaspoon cumin seeds, toasted
½ teaspoon black peppercorns, toasted
½ teaspoon ground turmeric
Pinch of nutmeg
2 tablespoons peeled and chopped fresh ginger
5 cloves garlic, sliced
Lower two-third of 1 lemongrass stalk, outer tough leaves removed and finely chopped
4 medium shallots, sliced
1 kaffir lime leaf, finely shredded (optional)
2 finger-length chilies (preferably bird's-eye), sliced
6 candlenuts or macadamia nuts, chopped

BALINESE BASTING SAUCE

1 tablespoon reserved Balinese Spice Paste
¼ teaspoon ground turmeric
4 tablespoons water
3 tablespoons oil
Pinch of salt

1 Cut the pork shoulder into a slab following steps 1 through 4 shown on the opposite page. Or ask your butcher to cut the shoulder into a slab.

2 In a mortar add the ingredients for the spice paste one by one, crushing all ingredients to a smooth paste. If you're using a food processor, add a little water as you're crushing the ingredients to keep them from sticking to the sides. From time to time stop the motor and push the ingredients down.

3 Reserve 1 tablespoon of the spice paste for the basting sauce. Rub 2 tablespoons of the spice paste on both sides of the shoulder to thinly coat it and let marinate in the refrigerator for a few hours.

4 In a bowl, combine the leek with the rest of the spice paste. Follow steps 5 through 9 shown on the opposite page.

5 To make the basting sauce, combine the reserved 1 tablespoon of spice paste, the turmeric, water, oil and salt. Stir well and set aside for basting.

6 Skewer the pork roast onto a rotisserie skewer and make sure it is well balanced. Rub the outside of the roast with the basting sauce.

7 Prepare the grill for indirect grilling and preheat two heat zones (medium and low). (See page 14 for charcoal and page 17 for gas.) If you're using charcoal, place a drip pan in the middle and live coals around the drip pan.

8 Place the rotisserie above the drip pan in a charcoal grill or, if you're using a gas grill, over the low heat zone and grill at low temperature with the hood closed for 1 to 1½ hours. Regularly baste the meat with the basting sauce. Test for doneness by pricking. When the juices run clear the meat is done. Wrap in aluminum foil and let rest for 10 minutes in a warm place before carving.

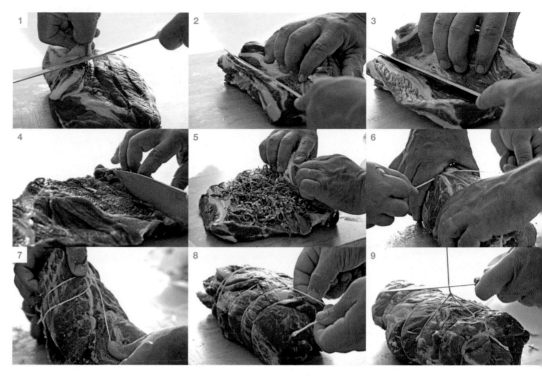

1 With a sharp knife, remove excess fat from the pork shoulder. 2 To cut the shoulder into a large slab, with a large knife, begin slicing into the shoulder (with the grain instead of against it) at a point about 1 inch (2.5 cm) up from the bottom of the shoulder. As you slice continuously unroll the top portion of the meat until you have one large slab. 3 Continue slicing and rolling back the meat in 1-inch (2.5-cm) increments. 4 The shoulder is now one large slab. 5 Distribute the vegetable and spice mixture evenly on the slab and begin to roll up the slab. 6 Tie the meat with butcher's string at one end and fix with a knot. 7 Continue to tie the meat in four to five places and make a knot at the last tie. 8 Turn the roll over and continue to make a loop around each tie working along the roll lengthwise. 9 Once you have reached the last tie make a knot and cut the ends.

Pork Roast Tip You can roast both boneless and bone-in cuts of pork. Good choices include the pork loin roast, fresh pork leg or ham and the shoulder or Boston butt, as is used here. Many barbecue enthusiasts prefer the moist, tender and flavorful pork loin roast. Tenderloin, which is a different cut from pork loin, is a favorite cut of many cooks because it is boneless and tender. However, because it is quite lean it's important to watch the grill time very carefully and not cook a minute beyond medium well doneness. The further the cuts are from the center of the pig, the less tender they will be. However, these cuts are lower priced and are very flavorful. To grill these use the low temperature grill method or smoking. This requires more time but it will render the meat tender and moist.

2 lbs (1 kg) boneless pork chops
1 tablespoon neutral-flavored oil
1 cup (250 ml) water
Salt to taste

VINDALOO MARINADE
4 cloves, toasted
One 1-inch (2.5-cm) piece cinnamon, toasted
1 teaspoon cumin seeds, toasted
1½ teaspoons chili flakes
2 teaspoons black peppercorns, crushed
1 tablespoon chopped garlic
1 tablespoon peeled and finely chopped fresh
   ginger
1 large onion, finely chopped
6 tablespoons malt vinegar

1 To make the marinade, place the toasted spices in a mortar or food processor and grind to a powder. One by one, add the chili flakes, peppercorns, garlic, ginger and onion and grind them to a fine paste. Add the vinegar and stir to combine. Rub this marinade all over the pork chops and leave in the refrigerator for 3 to 4 hours.

2 Remove the pork from the marinade and wipe off the marinade.

3 In a small saucepan, add the oil and place over medium-high heat. When hot add the leftover marinade and sauté for a few minutes. Add the water and simmer over low heat for 10 minutes. Add the salt. Set aside to be used as a basting sauce and for serving as a dipping sauce.

4 Prepare the grill for direct grilling with two heat zones (high and medium). (See page 13 for charcoal and page 17 for gas.)

5 Just before you begin grilling, oil the hot grate. Place the meat on the grate over the high heat zone and grill for about 2 to 3 minutes on each side. Move the meat to the medium heat zone and continue grilling for 5 to 7 minutes and baste regularly with the cooked marinade. Check for doneness by poking with your finger (see page 19) or pricking with a needle. If you're using the pricking test, the juice should run clear when done.

Vindaloo Pork Steaks

Vindaloo is the Indian name for the Portuguese *Vinho d'alhos* (pork with wine and garlic) and is a specialty from the Indian state of Goa, which was once colonized by the Portuguese. I used the spice combination because it works very well as a marinade but modified the cooking method to work on a grill. This gives the best of both worlds—grilled pork chops with a nice crust and a fiery vindaloo sauce. I serve this dish with a spicy vindaloo sauce made from the marinade, plain basmati rice and Yogurt Cucumber Raita (page 166) because rice and yogurt are very good for taking edge the off of spicy food.

SERVES **4**
PREPARATION TIME: **40 minutes**
GRILL TIME: **8 to 10 minutes for medium well**

Vietnamese Pork Tenderloin

Pork tenderloin is very popular in Chinese cuisine. The traditional char siu is one of the various ways to serve tenderloin (page 113). This Vietnamese version is somewhat similar but uses some more spices and shallots as well as fish sauce, which gives the dish a bit more spiciness compared to the Cantonese version. Serve with Bean Sprout Salad (page 162) or Asian Celery Salad (page 164), rice and Vietnamese Chili and Lime Dip (page 51).

SERVES **4**
PREPARATION TIME: **40 minutes**
GRILL TIME: **20 to 35 minutes for medium well**

2 lbs (1 kg) pork tenderloin
Salt
2 tablespoons neutral-flavored oil, plus extra
   for basting
Vietnamese Chili and Lime Dip (page 51)

FIVE SPICE MARINADE
4 cloves garlic, crushed to a paste
2 tablespoons finely minced shallots
½ teaspoon five spice powder (page 31)
1 tablespoon fish sauce, preferably Vietnamese
1 tablespoon sugar
¼ teaspoon black pepper

1 In a small bowl, combine the ingredients for the marinade. Stir until the sugar has dissolved. Thoroughly coat the meat with the marinade and place in the refrigerator for a few hours.
2 Remove the meat from the refrigerator ½ hour before grilling. Wipe excess marinade off the meat and rub it with salt.
3 In a small saucepan, bring the remaining marinade to a boil and add the 2 tablespoons of oil and salt to taste. Set aside for use as a basting sauce.
4 Prepare the grill for direct grilling with two heat zones (high and medium).

(See page 13 for charcoal and page 17 for gas.)
5 Just before you begin grilling, oil the hot grate. Place the tenderloin on the grate above the high heat zone and grill each side for about 2 to 3 minutes, basting with the oil from time to time. Move the tenderloin to the medium heat zone, baste with the cooked marinade and continue to grill for 15 to 20 minutes, while frequently turning, until done. Check doneness by poking with your finger (see page 19) or testing with a meat thermometer.

Honey Fruit Glazed Pork Chops

The peach tree can trace its origins to China. Not surprisingly peaches are a highly regarded fruit in China. The peach tree was later introduced into Persia and from there Alexander the Great brought it to Europe. This Chinese-inspired recipe uses peaches to marinate the pork, creating a very subtle flavor. Other fruits such as pear or pineapple can also be used. Serve these chops with Pumpkin and Potato Mash with Almonds (page 164).

SERVES **4**
PREPARATION TIME: **40 minutes**
GRILL TIME: **8 to 10 minutes for medium well**

2 lbs (1 kg) pork chops
Salt to season pork

FRUIT MARINADE AND GLAZE
2 tablespoons butter
2 lbs (1 kg) ripe peaches or other fruit peeled, deseeded and chopped
2 tablespoons peeled and finely chopped fresh ginger
6 allspice berries
One ½-in (1.25-cm) piece cinnamon
3 tablespoons Chinese light soy sauce

1 tablespoon Chinese dark soy sauce
½ cup (125 ml) red wine
2 to 3 tablespoons honey (depending on sweetness of the peaches)

1 To make the marinade and glaze, place the butter in a pot and set over medium heat. Add the peaches and, when they start to brown, add the ginger, spices, soy sauce and red wine. Continue to simmer for a few minutes. Add 2 tablespoons of the honey and stir to dissolve. Taste to check for sweetness and add another tablespoon of honey if needed. Divide into two equal portions: one portion will be used to marinate the pork and the other portion does double duty as a glaze and serving sauce. Set aside to let cool.

2 Place the pork chops and half of the cooled marinade in a shallow tray. Turn the chops to thoroughly coat with the marinade and let marinate in the refrigerator for 1 to 2 hours.

3 Prepare the grill for direct grilling with two heat zones (high and medium). (See page 13 for charcoal and page 17 for gas.)

4 Just before you're ready to grill, remove the pork from the marinade (discard this portion of the marinade), sprinkle the pork with some salt and oil the hot grate. Place the chops on the grate over the high heat zone and grill each side for about 2 to 3 minutes or until nicely browned. Move to the medium heat zone and grill each side for 2 to 3 minutes until done. Glaze regularly with the other half of the boiled peach mixture. Check doneness by pricking the meat close to the bone. If the juices run clear the meat is done. Alternatively check with a meat thermometer. Serve the leftover glaze with the pork as a sauce.

> **TIP** To quickly remove peach peels, blanch the peaches for 30 seconds in boiling water. Then drain and rinse them in cold water. The peels should slip off easily.

Juicy Sweet and Sour Baby Back Ribs

The marinade for this dish is typically used for satay, which is served on skewers. I was inspired by the flavors of this marinade but wanted to combine it with the juiciness of baby back ribs. The Chinese vinegar has a very distinctive flavor that adds a nice touch of sourness to the otherwise sweet marinade. Worcestershire sauce is an acceptable substitute.

SERVES **4**
PREPARATION TIME: **30 minutes**
GRILL TIME: **20 to 30 minutes for medium well**

3 lbs (1.5 kg) baby back ribs
1 teaspoon cornstarch mixed with ½ cup (125 ml) cold water
Neutral-flavored oil for basting

SWEET AND SOUR MARINADE
1 tablespoon neutral-flavored oil
2 green onions (scallions), finely chopped
1 tablespoon peeled and finely chopped fresh ginger
1 tablespoon finely chopped garlic
1½ tablespoons Chinese black vinegar or Worcestershire sauce
3 tablespoons Chinese light soy sauce
1 tablespoon light brown sugar
½ teaspoon five spice powder (page 31)
Pinch of salt and pepper

1 In a small bowl, combine the ingredients for the marinade. Thoroughly coat the ribs with the marinade, rubbing the ribs with the marinade, and keep in the refrigerator for a few hours or overnight.

2 One hour before grilling remove the ribs from the marinade and set aside. In a small saucepan, bring the remaining marinade to a gentle boil. Add the dissolved cornstarch and continue to boil until the marinade thickens. Remove from the heat and let cool for use as a basting sauce.

3 Prepare the grill for direct grilling with two heat zones (medium and low). (See page 13 for charcoal and page 17 for gas.)

4 Just before you're ready to grill, oil the hot grate. Place the ribs on the grate above the medium heat zone and grill about 10 to 15 minutes, turning regularly and basting regularly with the oil. When the ribs are nicely browned, move them to the low heat zone and continue to grill for another 10 to 15 minutes. About 5 to 10 minutes before the ribs are done baste a few times on each side with the cooked marinade to give a nice thick coating. Test for doneness by pricking the meat. When the juices run clear the meat is done.

Caramelized Soy and Lemongrass Spareribs

I like this Vietnamese-inspired recipe because the Caramelized Lemongrass Marinade combines sweet and salty flavors with lemongrass. The sugar is first caramelized, which gives the ribs a nice crust. This marinade is well suited to both smoking and grilling. Serve these ribs with Chinese Coleslaw (page 162) and Curried Potato Wedges (page 148) or jasmine rice.

SERVES **4**
PREPARATION TIME: **30 minutes, plus approximately 8 hours to marinate**
GRILL TIME: **20 to 30 minutes for medium well**

3 lbs (1.5 kg) pork spareribs
1 cup (250 ml) Caramelized Lemongrass
    Marinade (see page 39)
Salt for seasoning the ribs

1 Place the spareribs in a large shallow dish. Pour the Caramelized Lemongrass Marinade over, turning the ribs in the marinade to thoroughly coat them. Marinate in the refrigerator overnight.

2 Remove the ribs from the marinade and sprinkle them with salt.

3 In a small saucepan, add the leftover marinade and place over medium heat. Simmer for a few minutes and set aside for use as a basting sauce.

4 Prepare the grill for indirect grilling with low heat. (See page 14 for charcoal and page 17 for gas.) If you're using charcoal, place a drip pan in the middle and live coals around the drip pan.

5 Just before you begin grilling, oil the hot grate. Place the meat on the grate above the drip pan or, if you're using a gas grill, over the low heat zone. Grill for about 10 to 15 minutes on each side with the hood closed and baste regularly with cooked marinade.

6 Check for doneness by pricking the meat. If the juices run clear the ribs are ready.

Spicy Sweet Pork Satays with Fiery Lime Chili Dip

This recipe stems from the southern parts of Thailand bordering Malaysia, which is famous for its use of turmeric and chilies. If you prefer less spice you can replace the ground red pepper with paprika, which will give a similar flavor and color but will be much less spicy. Serve these skewers with the Fiery Lime Chili Dip (below) for dipping, jasmine rice, and Green Papaya Salad (page 165) or any kind of green salad.

SERVES **4**
PREPARATION TIME: **30 minutes**
GRILL TIME: **7 to 10 minutes for medium well**

1½ lbs (750 g) lean pork, sliced into thin
   1 x 3-in (2.5 x 7.5-cm) pieces
15 bamboo skewers, soaked in water
   30 minutes prior to grilling, or metal skewers

COCONUT SATAY MARINADE
4 garlic cloves, coarsely chopped
2 tablespoons cleaned and finely chopped
   fresh coriander (cilantro) roots or finely
   chopped fresh coriander stems
1 tablespoon light brown sugar
1 teaspoon ground red pepper (cayenne)
½ teaspoon ground turmeric
1 tablespoon neutral-flavored oil
4 tablespoons fish sauce
1 tablespoon Chinese light soy sauce
½ cup (125 ml) coconut milk

FIERY LIME CHILI DIP
1 tablespoon sugar
1 tablespoon fish sauce
2 tablespoons lime juice
1 tablespoon Chinese light soy sauce
1 teaspoon chili flakes
1 tablespoon chopped fresh coriander leaves
   (cilantro)

1 To make the marinade, grind the garlic, coriander roots and sugar to a paste in a mortar of food processor. Add the ground red pepper and turmeric and continue to grind to a paste. Add the remaining ingredients for the marinade one by one and mix well.

2 In a bowl, combine the marinade and the pork and let marinate in the refrigerator for about 1 hour. Remove the pork from the marinade. Thread the pork onto skewers.

3 In a small saucepan, add the remaining marinade and place over medium heat. Simmer for a few minutes and set aside for use as a basting sauce.

4 Prepare the grill for direct grilling with two heat zones (medium and low). (See page 13 for charcoal and page 17 for gas.)

5 In a small bowl, combine the ingredients for the dipping sauce.

6 Just before you're ready to grill, oil the hot grate. Place the meat on the grate over the medium heat zone and grill for about 7 to 10 minutes, turning frequently and basting regularly with the heated marinade. Test for doneness by poking the meat with your finger (see page 19).

Grilled Pork Shoulder with Tangy Orange Sauce

The island of Cebu in the Philippines is famous for its various preparations of suckling pig, a strong reminder of Spain's colonial influence. Among the many recipes, this one is especially interesting because it combines ginger and oregano with lime to make a zesty and very aromatic marinade. Although the original recipe was intended for an entire suckling pig, I opted to use a shoulder ham to downsize it to serve 6 people. If possible, try to find a ham shoulder with the skin left on to give you a nice crispy skin. However, even without the crispy skin, the recipe is still delicious. This recipe is very well suited for smoking since the smoke flavor combines nicely with this particular marinade. Serve with Filipino Salsa (page 54) or with the more traditional Tangy Orange Sauce (right). The orange sauce—a wonderful combination of fruit juice and spices—can also be combined with grilled pork, fish or chicken.

SERVES **6 to 8**
PREPARATION TIME: **40 minutes**
GRILL TIME: **1 to 1½ hours on low heat for medium well**

4 lbs (1.75 kg) boneless pork loin roast or pork shoulder ham, preferably with the skin on

GINGER OREGANO MARINADE
1 onion, finely chopped
8 cloves garlic, coarsely chopped
One 1-In (2.5-cm) piece fresh ginger, peeled and coarsely chopped
1½ teaspoons salt
1 teaspoon ground cumin
2 teaspoons dried oregano leaves
1 teaspoon black pepper
½ cup (125 ml) lime juice
1 teaspoon finely grated orange zest
2 tablespoons extra-virgin olive oil

TANGY ORANGE SAUCE
½ cup extra virgin-olive oil
6 cloves garlic, crushed with the side of a knife
½ cup (80 g) finely chopped red onion
One 1-in (2.5-cm) piece fresh ginger, peeled and finely chopped
1 teaspoon salt
½ teaspoon ground cumin
1 teaspoon chili flakes
½ teaspoon black pepper
1 teaspoon dried oregano
1 tablespoon sugar
½ cup (125 ml) orange juice
1 tablespoon finely grated orange zest
2 tablespoons lime juice
¼ cup (12 g) finely chopped fresh coriander leaves (cilantro)

1 In a mortar or food processor, grind the ingredients for the marinade, one by one, into a fine paste.

2 If the ham has the skin on, cut regularly spaced 2-inch (5-cm) diamond-shaped incisions about ½-inch (1-cm) deep into the skin. If you cannot find ham with the skin on there is no need to make incisions. Rub the ham with the marinade, pushing some of the marinade into the incisions with your fingers. Wrap in plastic wrap and keep in the refrigerator for at least 24 hours. Scrape excess marinade off the ham. In a small saucepan, add the leftover marinade and simmer over medium heat for a minute or so. Set aside for basting.

3 lbs (1.5 kg) pork spareribs

TANDOORI MARINADE
6 cloves garlic, coarsely chopped
6 green finger-length chilies, deseeded and
  coarsely chopped
2 tablespoons peeled and finely chopped
  fresh ginger
Juice of ½ lime
1 cup (250 ml) plain yogurt
¼ cup (125 ml) neutral-flavored oil
1 to 2 teaspoons ground red pepper (cayenne)
2 tablespoons finely chopped fresh coriander
  leaves (cilantro)
Salt and pepper to taste

1 Cut the ribs into segments with 3 to
4 ribs each.

2 To make the marinade, place the garlic,
chili, ginger and lime juice in a mortar or
food processor and grind to a fine paste.
Add the yogurt, oil, ground red pepper,
chopped coriander leaves, salt and pepper
and mix well. Divide the marinade into two
equal portions: one-half will be used as
the marinade and the other half as a
basting sauce.

3 Place the ribs in a large shallow tray and
pour half of the yogurt mixture over them.
Turn to evenly coat. Let the ribs marinate
in the refrigerator for 1½ to 2 hours. Place
the other half of the yogurt mixture in the
refrigerator.

4 Prepare the grill for direct grilling with two
heat zones (medium and low). (See page 13
for charcoal and page 17 for gas.)

5 Just before you're ready to grill, oil the
hot grate. Place the meat on the grate over
the medium zone of the grill and grill for
about 20 to 30 minutes, turning regularly.
Quickly move the ribs to the low heat zone
if the meat browns too quickly. Ten minutes
before the ribs are done baste with the
remaining yogurt mixture. Test for doneness
by pricking the meat. If the juices run clear,
the meat is done.

3 Prepare the grill for indirect grilling with
low to medium-low heat. (See page 14 for
charcoal and page 17 for gas.) If you're
using charcoal, place a drip pan in the
middle with live coals around the drip pan.

4 Just before you begin grilling, oil the hot
grate. Place the ham on the grate above
the drip pan or, if you're using a gas grill,
over the low heat zone and grill at low
temperature with the hood closed for 1 to
1½ hours. Baste regularly with the leftover
marinade. Test for doneness by using a
meat thermometer or pricking the meat with
a needle. If the juices run clear the meat
is done. When the ham is done, wrap in
aluminum foil and let rest for 10 minutes.

5 In a bowl, combine the ingredients for the
orange sauce. Keep in the refrigerator until
ready to be used.

6 Serve with the orange sauce.

Tandoori Pork Ribs

**The impact of Portuguese colonists
can be detected in various ways in
the Indian state of Goa, including its
culinary tradition of using pork, which
is rarely used outside this region. This
recipe has a touch of tandoori flavor
but, apart from ginger, garlic and red
and black pepper, is prepared with very
few spices. In other parts of India this
recipe would typically be made with
either chicken or mutton, which isn't as
juicy as when prepared with pork.**

SERVES **4**
PREPARATION TIME: **20 minutes**
GRILL TIME: **20 to 30 minutes for medium well**

Thai-Style Spareribs with Tamarind Chili Dip

These ribs are originally from the northeast of Thailand but have become very popular in central Bangkok. When you walk in the streets of Bangkok you will find this dish on the roadside. It is served with a special tamarind chili dip that in Thai is sometimes referred to as *nam jim ko moo yang*, which literally means "grilled pork neck dip." I changed the original recipe from pork neck to ribs because pork neck is too fatty for many people. These ribs go nicely with a Arugula Salad with Ginger Soy Dressing (page 162), Green Papaya Salad (page 165) Thai Glass Noodle Salad (page 165) and either sticky or jasmine rice.

SERVES **4**
PREPARATION TIME: **30 minutes**
GRILL TIME: **20 to 30 minutes for medium well**

3 lbs (1.5 kg) baby back ribs
Tamarind Chili Dip (page 51)
Fresh herbs, such as Thai basil or mint

THAI SPARERIB MARINADE
3 cloves garlic, crushed with the side of a knife
3 tablespoons fish sauce, preferably Thai
1½ tablespoons Chinese light soy sauce
1 teaspoon Thai dark soy sauce
1½ tablespoons palm sugar
1½ tablespoons sesame seeds
½ teaspoon black pepper

1 In a small bowl, combine the marinade ingredients. Stir until the sugar dissolves. Marinate the pork ribs with this mixture for about 1 hour.

2 Remove the pork from the marinade. In a small saucepan, add the leftover marinade and place over medium heat. Simmer for a few minutes and set aside to be used as a basting sauce.

3 Prepare the grill for direct grilling with two heat zones (medium and low). (See page 13 for charcoal and page 17 for gas.)

4 Just before you're ready to grill, oil the hot grate. Place the meat on the grate over the medium heat zone and grill for about 20 to 30 minutes at medium to low heat and baste regularly with the cooked marinade. If the ribs brown too quickly, move to the low heat zone. Test for doneness by pricking. When the juices run clear the meat is done.

5 When done cut the ribs into segments of 3 or 4 ribs each and serve with the Tamarind Chili Dip and the fresh herbs.

Honey Garlic Pork Chops

In this recipe I use a combination of honey, lavender and balsamic vinegar combined with zaatar—a Middle Eastern spice mixture—to give a nice very aromatic crust. This recipe works equally well with lamb chops or sirloin steaks. I like to serve these chops with Honey Ginger Vegetables (page 146) and Baked Potatoes with Chinese Chives (page 146) or Grilled Potato Salad (page 154).

SERVES **4**
PREPARATION TIME: **30 minutes**
GRILL TIME: **8 to 10 minutes for medium well**

4 bone-in pork chops, about ½ lb (250 g) each
Salt to season the chops

HONEY GARLIC MARINADE
2 tablespoons honey
2 tablespoons balsamic vinegar
6 cloves garlic, crushed to a paste
1 teaspoon dried lavender

ZAATAR SPICE MIXTURE
4 tablespoons sesame seeds, toasted
1 tablespoon dried thyme leaves
2 teaspoons dried marjoram leaves
2 teaspoons sumac

1 In a small bowl, combine the ingredients for the marinade. Combine the chops and marinade in a shallow dish and set aside to marinate for about 1 hour.

2 In a mortar or food processor, add the ingredients for the spice mixture. Crush slightly and set aside.

3 Prepare the grill for direct grilling with two heat zones (medium and low). (See page 13 for charcoal and page 17 for gas.)

4 Remove the meat from the marinade. In a small saucepan, add the leftover marinade and simmer over medium-low heat for a few minutes. Set aside to use as a basting sauce.

5 Just before you begin grilling, sprinkle some salt on the meat and oil the hot grate.

Place the meat over the medium to low heat zone and grill each side for about 2 to 3 minutes, turning regularly and basting regularly with the cooked marinade. Shortly before the meat is done baste again and turn the meat in the spice mixture until it is covered. Return to the grill and continue to cook for 2 to 3 minutes on each side or until finished. Test for doneness by pricking the meat. When the juices run clear the meat is done.

TIPS ON USING THE PRICKING TEST
When pricking pork the juices should run clear. If the juice is pink while doing the pricking test, the meat is not yet done. However, when you carve the meat after it has rested the juices will still show a slight pinkish color. So just remember: pricking—no pink!; carving—pink okay!

Chapter 5

Lamb Barbecue Recipes

Lamb, mutton, which is simply mature lamb, and more often goat are the preferred meats in northern India, Iran, central Asia, western China and the entire Middle East. Goat is hardy enough to withstand the arid climate of these regions and people have chosen these animals as their primary meat source. To accommodate Western tastes, this chapter offers lamb recipes, though some of them are adapted from traditional recipes for goat or mutton.

The Rack of Lamb with Olive Oil and Fresh Herbs (page 138) can be combined with the Tomato Pomegranate Dip (page 50), which is a typical Middle Eastern combination. I have featured some of my absolute favorites of Indian cuisine, which I often prepare on my charcoal grill. Indian Frontier Lamb Chops (page 132) and a stuffed boneless lamb recipe—Stuffed Lamb Roast (page 135)—have proven to be dinner highlights. I have served these dishes on several occasions because of my friends' repeated requests for them.

The Fragrant Pomegranate Scented Lamb Burgers (page 138) are based on a traditional kebab version and are served like their original counterpart on crispy grilled pita bread.

Three very different recipes for easy-to-work-with lamb chops and cutlets are includedand—one from Persia using a saffron marinade (page 131), and two Indian recipes based on a fragrant yogurt marinade (page 129) and one with a nut crust (page 132).

The Thai, Japanese and most Chinese, except for the western and northern Muslim minorities in China, are not particular fans of lamb hence it is rarely served in mainstream Chinese cuisine. However, in the northeast of China, which was formerly Manchuria and Mongolia, as well as in Xinjiang Province to the west, lamb is commonly available and the Lamb Shish Kebabs (page 136) in this chapter pays tribute to this fact. The lamb steak with a selection of three Asian sauces (page 130) is also based on these local cuisines.

Lamb Cooking Times All grill times mentioned in the following table refer to direct grilling and indirect grilling at medium to high heat temperatures. For low temperature grilling the time needs to be adjusted by multiplying by 3 to 3.5, e.g. if I state in the table a grilling time of 20 to 25 minutes, then for low temperature grilling you will have to calculate 60 to 90 minutes. The cooking times in the recipe section are based on cooking to medium rare to medium.

Lamb Chops These are from the rack of lamb. When you grill them be careful not to overdo it. They can become dry very quickly.

Lamb Shoulder This is usually rolled and grilled as a whole or cut into cubes and grilled on skewers. It is best to use a rotisserie when grilling it whole.

Lamb Steak is sliced leg of lamb and has the same qualities as leg of lamb. When grilling make incisions into the outer fat layer to keep the steak from curling when placed onto the grill. If you have a small group to serve, this piece is as good as leg of lamb and much easier to handle.

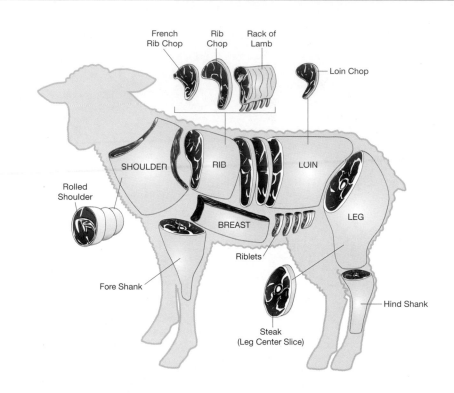

Leg of Lamb (Gigot) This is an excellent piece of meat for grilling, and it is my personal favorite. It can be grilled whole. You can remove the bone and grill it butterflied or roll it with a stuffing. If you have only a few people to serve, it is best to buy slices.

Rack of Lamb This is taken from the rib section of the lamb. It can be grilled as a whole or cut into lamb chops. I personally prefer to grill it whole and cut it prior to serving. This leaves it much more juicy.

State	Internal Temperature	Pressing Test	Pricking Test	Meat Internal Color	Skewers 1 inch cubes	Chops with bones	Leg sliced 3/4 inch thick	Rack 2/3 to 1 lb	Leg with bone	Leg without bone
Rare (Bleu)	125°F to 130°F 45°C to 55°C	soft touch	red juice	red	5 to 7 minutes	5 to 8 minutes	6 to 10 minutes	15 to 20 minutes		
Medium Rare	130°F to 135°F 55°C to 60°C	soft to firm	dark pink juice	pinkish red	6 to 8 minutes	6 to 10 minutes	8 to 12 minutes	18 to 25 minutes	18 to 25 minutes per lb	20 to 25 minutes per lb
Medium	140°F to 150°F 60°C to 65°C	slighty yielding	pink juice	traces of pink	7 to 10 minutes	8 to 12 minutes	10 to 16 minutes	25 to 30 minutes		
Medium Well	150°F to 160°F 65°C to 70°C	firm	pinkish juice	no traces of pink	8 to 12 minutes	10 to 16 minutes	14 to 18 minutes	30 to 35 minutes		
Well Done	160°F to 170°F 70°C to 75°C	firm and hard	clear colorless juice	greyish brown	6 to 8	7 to 9	7 to 9	15 to 24	24 to 26 minutes per lb	20 to 25

Tandoori Lamb Chops

Tandoori is a classic north Indian or Punjabi dish that is served in almost every Indian restaurant around the world. There are many variations on how to prepare the marinade. This recipe uses a combination of cardamom, cinnamon and nutmeg, which makes it especially fragrant. The yogurt not only gives a creamy coating but also tenderizes the meat.

SERVES **4**
PREPARATION TIME: **1 hour**
GRILL TIME: **6 to 10 minutes for medium rare**

One 1-in (2.5-cm) piece fresh ginger, peeled and chopped
6 cloves garlic, chopped 2 lbs (1kg) lamb chops
5 green cardamom pods, toasted
2 pieces mace, toasted
One ½-in (1-cm) piece cinnamon, toasted
½ teaspoon cumin seeds, toasted
½ teaspoon coriander seeds, toasted
¼ teaspoon ground nutmeg
1 tablespoon black pepper
2 teaspoons chili flakes
½ cup (125 ml) plain yogurt

1 In a mortar or food processor, crush the ginger and garlic to paste. Rub the lamb chops with this paste. Set aside for 30 minutes.

2 In a mortar or food processor, add the toasted spices and grind to a powder. Pass through a fine sieve and regrind the larger parts. Remove any remaining unground pieces of cardamom pod. Add the nutmeg, black pepper, chili flakes and yogurt and mix well.

3 Apply half of the yogurt-spice mixture to the lamb chops and let marinate in the refrigerator for a few hours or preferably overnight. Reserve the remaining half of the yogurt mixture for basting.

4 Prepare the grill for direct grilling with two heat zones (medium and high). (See page 13 for charcoal and page 17 for gas.)

5 Remove the meat from the marinade and wipe excess marinade off the chops. Use the other half of the marinade for use as a basting sauce.

6 Just before you begin grilling, oil the hot grate. Place the meat on the grate over the high heat zone and grill each side for about 2 to 3 minutes until nicely browned. Move the meat to the medium heat zone and continue grilling each side for 2 to 4 minutes, turning regularly and basting with the yogurt-spice mixture. Test for doneness by poking the meat with your finger (see page 19).

4 lamb steaks, approximately 6 to 7 oz (175 to 200 g) each
Neutral-flavored oil for basting
⅓ cup (80 ml) Soy Garlic Sauce (page 46) for dipping
⅓ cup (80 ml) Mongolian Sesame Soy Dip (page 52) for dipping
⅓ cup (80 ml) Green Onion Sesame Sauce (page 48) for dipping

SOY MARINADE
1 tablespoon Chinese light soy sauce
1 tablespoon Chinese Shaoxing wine or dry sherry
2 tablespoons neutral-flavored oil

1 In a small bowl, combine the ingredients for the marinade. Set the lamb steaks in a shallow tray and pour the marinade over, turning to evenly coat. Set the steaks aside to marinate for 30 minutes.

2 Prepare the grill for direct grilling with two heat zones (medium and high). (See page 13 for charcoal and page 17 for gas.)

3 Just before you begin grilling oil the hot grate. Place the meat on the grate over the high heat zone and grill each side for about 2 to 3 minutes. If the meat becomes too browned, move the meat to the medium heat zone and continue to grill for 5 to 6 minutes, turning regularly and basting once in a while with oil. Test for doneness by poking with your finger (see page 19).

Lamb Steaks with Three Asian Sauces

The marinade used in this Chinese-inspired recipe uses very little flavoring—thus the three dipping sauces are the key flavor accents. Soy Garlic Sauce is a mild aromatic sauce that greatly enhances the flavor of the grilled lamb. Mongolian Sesame Soy Dip is normally served with boiled lamb in Beijing and is the accompaniment for the famous Mongolian hot pot, which features slices of lamb simmered in a broth. The Green Onion Sesame Sauce is of Korean origin and often served with boiled or grilled lamb. Serve these steaks with one or more of the dipping sauces and Potato Cucumber Salad with Fresh Herbs (page 166) or Japanese Grilled Eggplant (page 151).

SERVES **4**
PREPARATION TIME: **1 hour**
GRILL TIME: **8 to 12 minutes for medium rare**

Saffron Lamb Loin Chops

A traditional Persian recipe for kebabs was the inspiration for this elegant dish. I changed the meat to lamb chops but stayed true to the original spice and herb combination, which gives saffron a starring role. Sumac gives an additional astringent and perfumed note, but the dish is still delicious without it. Serve with long grain rice and The Famous Mango Chutney (page 53) or Sweet and Sour Tomato Chutney (page 54) and Pistachio Rice Salad (page 166).

SERVES **4**
PREPARATION TIME: **30 minutes**
GRILL TIME: **6 to 10 minutes for medium rare**

2 lbs (1 kg) lamb loin chops

SAFFRON MARINADE
2 tablespoons extra-virgin olive oil
3 onions, finely chopped
2 cloves garlic, crushed
½ teaspoon saffron
½ teaspoon black pepper
½ teaspoon sumac (optional)
Pinch of salt

1 In a bowl, combine the ingredients for the marinade. Set the lamb chops in a shallow tray and pour the marinade over, turning to evenly coat. Let the chops marinate for 3 hours in the refrigerator.

2 Remove the meat from the marinade. In a saucepan, bring the leftover marinade to a simmer for a few minutes and set aside for basting.   Prepare the grill for direct grilling with two heat zones (medium and high). (See page 13 for charcoal and page 17 for gas.)

3 Just before you begin grilling oil the hot grate. Place the meat on the grate over the high heat zone and grill each side for about 2 to 3 minutes. If the meat becomes too browned, move the meat to the medium heat zone and continue grilling for 2 to 4 minutes, turning regularly and basting regularly with the cooked marinade.

4 Test for doneness by poking the meat with your finger (see page 19) or inserting a meat thermometer.

Indian Frontier Lamb Chops

This recipe was inspired by a classic Indian recipe. My version uses a simplified spice combination, which makes it relatively easy to prepare, and adds a delicious nut crust made of pistachios, hazelnuts and sesame seeds and flavored with spices and fresh herbs. Ideal sides for this dish are Yogurt Cucumber Sauce (page 166) and Grilled Potato Salad (page 154) or plain or Saffron Rice (page 167).

SERVES **4**
PREPARATION TIME: **30 minutes**
GRILL TIME: **6 to 10 minutes for medium rare**

12 lamb chops

FRONTIER SPICE RUB
1½ teaspoons coriander seeds, toasted
½ teaspoon black peppercorns, toasted
1 teaspoon cumin seeds, toasted
6 cloves garlic, chopped
1 teaspoon chili flakes (optional)
1 teaspoon lime zest
2 tablespoons chopped fresh mint leaves
1 tablespoon chopped fresh coriander leaves (cilantro)

FRONTIER NUT CRUST
2 tablespoons extra-virgin olive oil
2 tablespoons unsalted pistachios, shelled and lightly crushed
2 tablespoons hazelnuts, lightly crushed
2 tablespoons sesame seeds

1 To make the spice rub, place the toasted spices in a mortar or food processor and grind to a powder. Add the garlic, chili flakes, if using, lime zest, mint and coriander leaves and grind to a paste.

2 Rub the paste on all sides of the chops and let marinate in the refrigerator for 3 hours.

3 In a small bowl, combine the ingredients for the nut crust.

4 Prepare the grill for direct grilling with two heat zones (medium and high). (See page 13 for charcoal and page 17 for gas.)

5 Just before you begin grilling oil the hot grate. Place the chops on the grate over the high heat zone and grill each side for about 2 to 3 minutes. Baste again with spice paste and apply the nut mixture onto the moist meat. Continue to grill for 2 to 4 minutes, turning frequently until a nice crust has formed. Poke with your finger to test for doneness (see page 19).

3 lbs (1.5 kg) lamb chops
Salt to season lamb
¼ cup (65 ml) pomegranate concentrate for glazing

POMEGRANATE MARINADE
3 tomatoes, peeled, deseeded and chopped
2 tablespoons neutral-flavored oil
Juice of 1 lime
Zest of 1 lemon
2 tablespoons pomegranate concentrate
1 large onion, finely chopped
¼ cup (12 g) chopped fresh coriander leaves (cilantro)
¼ cup (6 g) chopped fresh mint leaves
½ teaspoon ground cinnamon
¼ teaspoon ground cloves
3 green cardamom pods, crushed to a powder with larger pieces of unground shell removed
Heaping ¼ teaspoon grains of paradise seeds, crushed to a powder
Pinch of ground nutmeg

1 In a food processor or blender, add the ingredients for the marinade and grind until smooth.

2 Rub the lamb chops with the spice paste and let them marinate in the refrigerator for a few hours or preferably overnight.

3 Scrape excess marinade off the meat and sprinkle the meat with some salt. In a saucepan, bring the leftover marinade to a simmer for a few minutes. Remove from the heat and set aside as a dipping sauce.

4 Prepare the grill for direct grilling with two heat zones (medium and high). (See page 13 for charcoal and page 17 for gas.)

5 Just before you begin grilling the meat, oil the hot grate. Place the meat on the grate over the high heat zone and grill each side for about 2 to 3 minutes. Move the meat to the medium heat zone and continue grilling for 2 to 4 minutes, turning regularly and glaze regularly with the pomegranate concentrate.

6 Test for doneness by poking the meat with your finger (page 19) or pricking the meat.

Lamb Chops with Sweet Pomegranate Glaze

My sister-in-law Mouna is an excellent cook. She introduced me to pomegranate concentrate years ago and I've been a big fan of it ever since. I'm always on the lookout for new ways to use it and this fragrant north Indian recipe is the perfect showcase for this delicious ingredient. This dish is best served with an Indian-style eggplant purée called Baingan Bhurta (page 144), which can be served hot or cold, and Quick Pita Bread (page 160), Tandoori Naan (page 160) or rice.

SERVES **4**
PREPARATION TIME: **30 minutes**
GRILL TIME: **6 to 10 minutes for medium rare**

Roast Leg of Lamb with Moghul Spices

This dish was served at the table of maharajahs and is truly fit for kings. The lamb is covered in a paste of various nuts, yogurt and spices. The crushed nuts turn crispy on the outside and leave the meat very moist inside. This delicacy takes a bit of time to prepare but the result is worth the extra effort. I usually serve this lamb with a simple sauce made from the drippings, Tandoori Naan (page 160) and a salad.

SERVES **6 to 8**
PREPARATION TIME: **45 minutes**
GRILL TIME: **1⅓ to 2 hours for medium rare**

One 4-lb (2-kg) leg of lamb, bone-in
Salt
3 tablespoons melted butter for basting
⅓ cup (80 ml) red wine
½ cup (125 ml) beef stock

MOGHUL SPICE PASTE

One 1-in (2.5-cm) stick cinnamon, toasted
5 green cardamom pods, toasted
Heaping ½ teaspoon grains of paradise seeds, toasted
5 cloves, toasted
1 piece mace, toasted
1 teaspoon aniseeed, toasted
½ teaspoon ground nutmeg
Pinch of asafetida (optional)
1½ teaspoons chili flakes
2 medium onions, chopped

1 tablespoon peeled and chopped fresh ginger
1 tablespoon poppy seeds soaked in ¼ cup (65 ml) milk
2 tablespoons grated coconut (if you use desiccated coconut, soaked for 30 minutes in ½ cup/125 ml warm water and drained)
2 tablespoons almond slivers
2 Indian bay leaves or regular bay leaves
Pinch of salt
1 cup (250 ml) plain yogurt

1 To make the spice paste, place the toasted spices in a food processor or mortar and grind to a powder. Pass through a fine sieve and regrind the larger parts. Remove any remaining unground pieces of cardamom pod. One by one, add the nutmeg, asafaetida, if using, chili flakes, onions, ginger, soaked poppy seeds, grated coconut, almond slivers, bay leaves and salt to the mortar or food processor and grind to a coarse paste. Add the yogurt and stir to combine.

2 Remove all the fat from the leg of lamb and prick the meat with a fork down to the bone. The deep pricks will allow the yogurt, which is a natural tenderizer, to fully penetrate the meat and render it very soft and juicy. Rub the meat with the spice paste, wrap tightly with plastic wrap and let marinate overnight in the refrigerator.

3 Remove the lamb from the spice paste and wipe off excess paste. In a saucepan, bring the leftover paste to a simmer for a few minutes and set aside. Generously rub the lamb with salt.

4 Prepare the charcoal grill for indirect grilling (see page 14). Place a drip pan in the middle and live coals around the drip pan.

5 If you're using a gas grill, prepare the grill for two zones (high and low). (See page 17.)

6 Just before you begin grilling, oil the hot grate. Place the meat on the grate above the drip pan or, if you're using a gas grill, over the low heat zone and grill initially at high temperature for about 10 minutes while turning often. When all the sides are browned, move to the medium heat zone and continue to grill with the hood closed for 80 minutes to 2 hours. Regularly baste the meat with butter and apply a layer of the heated spice paste during the last 10 minutes of the grilling.

7 Test for doneness by pricking or inserting a meat thermometer. The juices should run clear when pricking.

8 In a saucepan, add the remaining yogurt spice paste, the drippings with fat removed, the wine and beef stock. Bring to a boil and add salt if needed. Serve this sauce as a side dish with the lamb.

Stuffed Lamb Roast

Cooked over low heat, this dish combines crusty grilled lamb with a delicious stuffing of moist plumped fruits. The stuffing is inspired by the famous north Indian dish called "korma." This dish is best served with Pistachio Rice Salad (page 166) and Lemon Chutney (page 54) or Sweet and Sour Tomato Chutney (page 54). Or, you can serve it with plain long-grain rice or couscous.

SERVES **6 to 8**
PREPARATION TIME: **1 hour**
GRILL TIME: **1⅓ to 1¾ hours for medium rare**

One 4-lb (2-kg) leg of lamb, de-boned and butterflied
3 tablespoons melted butter for basting

KORMA SPICE PASTE
1 teaspoon coriander seeds, toasted
1 teaspoon cumin seeds, toasted
3 pods cardamom, toasted
Heaping ¼ teaspoon grain of paradise seeds, toasted
1 piece mace, toasted
Pinch of nutmeg
1 bay leaf
1 tablespoon peeled and finely chopped fresh ginger
1 tablespoon finely chopped garlic

KORMA STUFFING
One 1-in (2.5-cm) piece cinnamon, toasted
3 cloves, toasted
1 teaspoon coriander seeds, toasted

3 tablespoons oil
1 large onion, finely chopped
6 prunes, pitted and coarsely chopped
6 dried apricots, coarsely chopped
½ cup (30 g) almond slices, lightly toasted
¼ cup (30 g) cashew nuts, lightly toasted
3 tablespoons chopped fresh coriander leaves (cilantro)
Salt to taste

1 To make the spice paste, grind the toasted spices to a powder in a mortar or food processor. Add the nutmeg, bay leaf, chopped ginger and garlic and grind to a paste.

2 Rub the spice paste onto the lamb and let marinate in the refrigerator for 2 to 4 hours.

3 To make the stuffing, grind the toasted spices to a powder in a mortar or food processor. In a large skillet, add the oil and place over medium heat. Add the onion and fry until softened. Add the ground spices and continue to sauté for a few minutes. Remove from the heat and transfer to a large bowl. Add the chopped dried fruits, toasted almond and cashew nuts, fresh

coriander and salt. Stir to combine.

4 Lay the butterflied lamb open and place the stuffing in the center. Roll up and close and secure with toothpicks and butcher's string.

5 Prepare the charcoal grill for indirect grilling with low heat (see page 14). Place a drip pan in the middle and live coals around the drip pan.

6 If you're using a gas grill, prepare the grill for indirect grilling with low heat (See page 17.)

7 Place the meat above the drip pan or, if you're using a gas grill, over the low heat zone and grill initially at high temperature over direct heat for about 10 minutes while turning often to brown all sides and continue at medium to low temperature with indirect heat with the hood closed for 80 minutes to 1¾ hours.

8 Regularly baste the meat with the butter during the later stage of grilling. Test for doneness by pricking or inserting a meat thermometer.

Lamb Shish Kebabs

These ground lamb kebabs are based on the Indian shish kebab. These kebabs are traditionally cooked in the tandoor on long flat steel skewers. I grill them on a conventional grill using square steel skewers. These kebabs are usually served with Tandoori Naan (page 160) and Mint and Coriander Chutney (page 53).

SERVES **4**
PREPARATION TIME: **1 hour**
GRILL TIME: **6 to 10 minutes for medium**

1½ teaspoons coriander seeds, toasted
4 pods green cardamom, toasted
Heaping ¼ teaspoon grains of paradise seeds, toasted
½ teaspoon aniseed, toasted
½ piece mace, toasted
3 cloves, toasted
½ teaspoon cumin seeds, toasted
½ teaspoon black peppercorns, toasted
2 eggs
2 lbs (1 kg) ground lamb or ground beef, not too lean
½ cup (80 g) cashew nuts, chopped and ground to a paste
2 tablespoons melted butter for basting
½ cup (85 g) finely chopped onion
1 tablespoon peeled and finely chopped fresh ginger
8 finger-length green chilies, deseeded and finely chopped
½ cup (25 g) finely chopped fresh coriander leaves (cilantro)
20 bamboo skewers, soaked in water for 30 minutes prior to grilling, or metal skewers

1 In a mortar or food processor, grind the toasted spices to a powder. Set aside 1 teaspoon of the ground spices for the basting butter.

2 In a large bowl, whisk the eggs. Add the ground meat and mix to combine. Add the cashew nut paste and all but the reserved teaspoon of the ground spices. Knead the mixture until all of the ingredients are completely combined. Let rest in the refrigerator for 1 hour.

3 In a small bowl, mix the melted butter with the remaining teaspoon of ground spices and set aside for use as a basting sauce.

4 Wet your hands and spread the ground meat onto the skewers. Leave enough room on one end of the skewer to easily handle it. If you're using bamboo skewers, the kebab should be not more than ½ inch (1.25 cm) in diameter; for larger metal skewers, the kebabs can be up to ¾ inch (2 cm) in diameter.

5 Prepare the grill for direct grilling with one heat zone (high). (See page 13 for charcoal and page 17 for gas.)

6 Just before you begin grilling oil the hot grate. Place the skewers on the grate over the high heat zone and grill each side for about 2 to 3 minutes while basting regularly with the spiced butter. Remove from the grill and set the kebabs on top of a wire rack to cool slightly (this will allow you to give the kebabs a nice crust without overcooking them). After a few minutes place the skewers on the grill over the high heat zone and baste with the spiced butter. Grill for an additional 2 to 3 minutes or until a nice crust has formed. Serve hot.

Mongolian Lamb Kebabs

Xinjiang is the most western province of China and its food is similar to central Asian food. This dish is sold on the streets of Beijing and one can smell the grilled meat when you walk along the markets. The skewers are large compared to the typically smaller skewers served in East Asian countries and one portion is quite a big helping. Serve these skewers with Grilled Stuffed Eggplants (page 143) or Grilled Bell Peppers (page 142) and Quick Pita Bread (page 160) or plain rice.

SERVES **4**
PREPARATION TIME: **30 minutes**
GRILL TIME: **6 to 10 minutes for medium rare**

2 lbs (1 kg) lean boneless lamb, cut into 1-in (2.5-cm) cubes
2 large onions, quartered
2 large green bell peppers, deseeded and cut into squares
12 bamboo skewers, soaked in water for 30 minutes prior to grilling, or metal skewers
Salt for seasoning the skewers

SOY SCALLION MARINADE
½ teaspoon black pepper
1 tablespoon Chinese light soy sauce
1 teaspoon cumin seeds, toasted and crushed
1 to 2 teaspoons chili flakes
1 tablespoon finely chopped green onion (scallion)
1½ teaspoons peeled and chopped fresh ginger

1 In a large bowl, combine the ingredients for the marinade. Add the lamb cubes, toss to coat, cover and let marinate in the refrigerator for 2 hours.

2 Remove the meat from the marinade. In a saucepan, bring the leftover marinade to a simmer for a few minutes. Remove from the heat and set aside for basting.

3 Thread the meat cubes, onion quarters and green pepper squares onto the skewers, alternating them as you go. Sprinkle with some salt.

4 Prepare the grill for direct grilling with two heat zones (medium and high). (See page 13 for charcoal and page 17 for gas.)

5 Just before you begin grilling oil the hot grate. Place the skewers on the grate over the high heat zone and grill each side for 2 to 3 minutes. Move the skewers to the medium heat zone and continue grilling for about 3 to 5 minutes, turning regularly and basting regularly with the cooked marinade.

6 Test for doneness by poking the meat with your finger (see page 19).

Fragrant Pomegranate Scented Lamb Burgers

Pomegranate is a popular ingredient in north Indian cuisine, which still shows the strong influence of the Moghul emperors. This delicious recipe combines heady pomegranate concentrate with an underlying scent of cardamom and cloves and the fresh aroma of coriander (cilantro). Serve these burgers on Quick Pita Bread (page 160) with a few sprigs of fresh coriander and either with Yogurt Cucumber Raita (page 166), Sweet and Sour Tomato Chutney (page 54) or Tomato Pomegranate Dip (page 50). If you wish to serve a salad alongside, Farmer's Salad (page 163) is a good choice.

MAKES **6 burgers, about ⅓ lb (150 g) each**
PREPARATION TIME: **45 minutes**
GRILL TIME: **6 to 12 minutes for medium**

2 slices white bread
1 teaspoon cumin seeds, toasted
4 green cardamom pods, toasted
4 cloves, toasted
1 teaspoon coriander seeds, toasted
2 lbs (1 kg) ground lamb
3 tablespoons extra-virgin olive oil
5 cloves garlic, finely chopped
½ cup (30 g) finely chopped fresh flat-leaf parsley
1 egg
½ cup (85 g) finely chopped onion
3 tablespoons pomegranate concentrate
3 teaspoons sumac
Salt to taste
2 tablespoons melted butter for basting

1 Remove the crusts from the bread, cut into small cubes and soak in warm water until soft.

2 In a mortar or food processor, add the toasted spices and grind to a powder.

3 In a large bowl, add the ground lamb, bread, ground toasted spices, olive oil, garlic, parsley, egg, onion, 1 tablespoon of the pomegranate concentrate, sumac and salt and knead well. Let rest for 30 minutes in the refrigerator. Moisten hands and make patties.

4 Prepare the grill for direct grilling with two heat zones (medium and high). (See page 13 for charcoal and page 17 for gas.)

5 Just before you begin grilling, oil the hot grate. Place the burgers on the grate over the medium heat zone and grill for about 6 to 12 minutes while basting regularly with the butter. Towards the end of the grilling time baste with the remaining 2 tablespoons of pomegranate concentrate to give the burgers a nice flavored glazing.

Rack of Lamb with Olive Oil and Fresh Herbs

Rack of lamb is one of my favorite cuts to prepare. I prefer lamb racks because they tend to be juicier than lamb chops. This recipe works also with leg of lamb. This dish is best served with either Tomato Pomegranate Dip (page 50) or Garlic Sauce (page 47) and Rosemary Roast Potatoes (page 148) or Potato Cucumber Salad with Fresh Herbs (page 166).

SERVES **4**
PREPARATION TIME: **1 hour**
GRILL TIME: **18 to 25 minutes for medium rare**

2 lbs (1 kg) rack of lamb
Salt to season the lamb

OLIVE OIL HERB MARINADE
6 cloves garlic, chopped
1 teaspoon black pepper
3 tablespoons extra-virgin olive oil
2 teaspoons dried rosemary leaves
2 teaspoons dried oregano leaves
½ teaspoon Garam Masala (page 31)
Zest of ½ lemon
2 tablespoons lemon juice

1 In a mortar or food processor, crush the garlic to a paste. Add the black pepper, olive oil, rosemary, oregano, and lemon zest and continue to crush lightly. Add the lemon juice and mix well.

2 Place the lamb rack in a shallow tray. Sprinkle some salt over both sides of the lamb and pour the marinade mixture on top. Rub the marinade on all sides of the rack.

Set aside to marinate for about ½ hour.

3 Remove the lamb from the marinade. In a saucepan, bring the leftover marinade to a simmer for a few minutes. Remove from the heat and set aside for use as a basting sauce.

4 Prepare the grill for direct grilling with two heat zones (medium and high). (See page 13 for charcoal and page 17 for gas.)

5 Just before you begin grilling oil the hot grate. Place the meat on the grate over the high heat zone and grill each side for about 2 to 3 minutes until it is nicely browned. Move the meat to the medium heat zone and continue grilling for 15 to 20 minutes, turning regularly and basting often with the cooked marinade. Test for doneness by poking the meat with your finger (see page 19). Wrap the rack in aluminum foil and let rest for about 5 to 10 minutes. Cut the rack into chops and serve.

Lamb Steaks with Cherry Sauce

Cherries originated in central Asia and were brought during the Greek and Roman era to Europe. Persian and north Indian cooks often use fruits such as apricots, prunes and pomegranates and combine them with cashew nuts, almonds or other nuts. This practice was introduced by the Moghul emperors coming from central Asia. I use cherries instead but combine them with mild Indian spices. Serve with the slightly perfumed Saffron Rice (page 167), which complements the cherry sauce in flavor and in color.

SERVES **4**
PREPARATION TIME: **1 hour**
GRILL TIME: **8 to 12 minutes for medium rare**

2 lbs (1 kg) lamb steaks

CHERRY MARINADE
One ½-in (1.25-cm) piece cinnamon, toasted
½ teaspoon black peppercorns, toasted
3 green cardamom pods, toasted
½ piece mace, toasted
1 tablespoon vegetable oil
1 tablespoon peeled and finely chopped fresh ginger
1½ cups (200g) fresh pitted sweet black cherries or sour cherries (see note)
½ cup (125 ml) water
2 tablespoons lime juice
Zest of ½ lime

1 To make the marinade, grind the toasted spices to a powder in a mortar or small food processor.

2 In a small saucepan, add the oil and place over medium heat. Add the ginger and sauté until soft. Add the cherries, ground spices, water, lime juice and lime zest. Stir to combine.

3 Simmer for a few minutes then remove from the heat to let cool.

4 Set the lamb steaks in a shallow tray and pour the cooled marinade over, turning to evenly coat. Let the steaks marinate for 3 hours in the refrigerator. One hour before grilling remove the meat from the marinade. In a saucepan bring the leftover marinade to a simmer for a few minutes. Remove from the heat and set aside for use as a basting and serving sauce.

5 Prepare the grill for direct grilling with two heat zones (medium and high). (See page 13 for charcoal and page 17 for gas.)

6 Just before you begin grilling, oil the hot grate. Place the meat on the grate over the high heat zone and grill each side for about 2 to 3 minutes. If the meat becomes too browned, move the meat to the medium heat zone and continue grilling for 2 to 4 minutes, turning regularly and basting regularly with the marinade.

7 Test for doneness by poking the meat with your finger (see page 19) or inserting a meat thermometer.

> **Note** Though harder to find than sweet black cherries, sour cherries, such as Griotte cherries, are a more authentic choice for this dish. If you can find sour cherries, do use them. If using sour cherries, add 1 tablespoon of sugar and omit the lime juice.

Chapter 6

Vegetable Barbecue Recipes

With the exception of Japan, China and India, which have their own traditions of grilled vegetables, most Asian cuisines feature vegetables either in stir-fries or curries. There are a few exceptions here and there—such as the grilled banana chili pepper or eggplant one can find along the roadsides in Thailand. The recipe for Grilled Stuffed Chiles (page 144) is inspired by this roadside fare.

The vegetarian heritage in India goes back millennia, making it the foundation of one of the most diverse vegetarian cuisines in the world. Many entirely vegetarian and vegan dishes have been created which imitate meat. Marinating and grilling vegetables is widely applied and I have added a few recipes based on this method. Making shish kebabs with vegetables, potatoes and legumes is a truly unique Indian specialty and is the inspiration for Vegetarian Shish Kebabs (page 147). Another famous dish and one of my favorites in Bombay is the vegetable cutlet. It is usually deep-fried but I have adapted the recipe for my grilled Spicy Vegetable Burgers (page 150).

In Japan, the style of grilling vegetables is stripped down to the essentials. Typically vegetables are simply rubbed with salt, with no marinade used at all. They are then threaded on fine metal skewers and broiled until just done. Grilled vegetables are served with a soy- or vinegar-based sauce or dip. This method ensures that the pure taste of the vegetable is maintained. Therefore only the freshest, most crunchy vegetables should be used.

In China, vegetables are typically stir-fried. The Grilled Vegetable Pack (page 152) is inspried by Chinese vegetables dishes, but adapted for the grill.

In the Middle East region from Iran to Turkey it is very common to stuff vegetables with rice, minced meat, and nuts and cook them in a clay oven. Interestingly the name for these stuffed dishes—*dolme-e* in Persian and *dolmades* in Turkish and Greek—is from the same root word and originated most likely in Persia. I love these stuffed vegetables and have included a few recipes for them in this chapter. Along with the recipe for Honey Ginger Vegetables (page 146), these stuffed vegetables can be combined with any dish with Middle Eastern flavors, or any Western dish for that matter.

Grilled Stuffed Chilies

Grilled chilies are very popular. They are either skewered like a satay and placed on the grill or they are stuffed, normally with a minced meat filling. I modified the stuffing for our vegetarian friends and found that this dish is a hit among vegetarians and non-vegetarians alike.

SERVES **6 to 8**
PREPARATION TIME: **20 minutes**
GRILL TIME: **2 to 4 minutes**

12 medium-size banana chilies, about 3 in/ 7.5 cm long
1 tablespoon extra-virgin olive oil plus extra for basting and drizzling
½ cup (80 g) coarsely chopped white button mushrooms
1 clove garlic, finely chopped
Salt for rubbing chilies and seasoning stuffing
½ cup (80 g) crumbled feta cheese
1 tablespoon chopped fresh mint leaves
1 tablespoon chopped fresh coriander leaves (cilantro)
Pinch of pepper

1 Slice off the top (stalk end) of the chilies. Remove the inner membrane and seeds. Sprinkle some salt on the inside and outside of the chilies.

2 In a small skillet, add 1 tablespoon of olive oil and place over medium heat. When hot add the mushrooms and garlic. Sauté for a few minutes or until the mushrooms just begin to soften. Season with a pinch of salt. Remove from the heat and let cool.

3 While the mixture is cooling, prepare the grill for direct grilling and preheat to high heat. (See page 13 for charcoal and page 17 for gas.)

4 In a bowl, add the cooled mushrooms and garlic, the feta cheese, herbs and pepper. Stir to combine. Taste for seasoning and, if needed, add a little more salt. Stuff this mixture into the banana chilies. Baste the chilies with some olive oil.

5 Place the stuffed chilies on the hot grate and grill over high heat for 2 to 4 minutes. Remove from the fire and drizzle on some olive oil before serving.

Baingan Bhurta

Baingan Bhurta is a typical north Indian dish and is often served as part of the main course together with other vegetarian dishes or with meat dishes. Like Grilled Eggplant Purée (page 153) it has a creamy texture and balances well with grilled food. It can be combined with any kind of Indian- or Middle Eastern-inspired recipes in this book.

SERVES **4**
PREPARATION TIME: **30 minutes**
GRILL TIME: **15 to 20 minutes**

4 eggplants, about ⅓ lb (150 g) each
1 teaspoon cumin seeds, toasted
2 tablespoons extra-virgin olive oil
1 medium onion, finely chopped
2 finger-length green chilies, deseeded and chopped
1 tablespoon peeled and finely chopped fresh ginger
1 teaspoon sugar
Salt
Fresh coriander leaves (cilantro) for garnish

Zucchini with Pesto

This dish is very easy to prepare and is suitable as a side dish for almost every recipe in this book. Try to find small zucchini since they are more tender than large ones.

SERVES **2**
PREPARATION TIME: **30 minutes**
GRILL TIME: **3 to 5 minutes**

1 lb (500 g) zucchini

PESTO
3 cloves garlic, crushed to a paste
1 tablespoon finely chopped fresh mint leaves
1 teaspoon dried oregano leaves
5 tablespoons shelled pistachio nuts
¼ cup (60 ml) extra-virgin olive oil
Salt to taste

1 To make the pesto, place the garlic, mint, oregano and pistachios in a mortar or food processor and grind to a coarse paste. Add the olive oil and salt and stir.

2 Cut the zucchini in half lengthwise. If the zucchini are larger than 1 inch (2.5 cm) in diameter, cut them lengthwise into ½-inch (1.25-cm)-thick slices.

3 Place the zucchini in a large shallow dish and pour half of the pesto marinade over the zucchini. Set aside for 30 minutes.

4 Prepare the grill for direct grilling with two heat zones (medium and high). (See page 13 for charcoal and page 17 for gas.)

5 Just before you begin grilling, oil the hot grate. Place the zucchini on the grate over the high heat zone and grill for 3 to 5 minutes. Turn once and add the remaining pesto on top of the grilled side of the zucchini. Continue to grill with the hood closed for another 3 minutes or until done.

1 Prepare the grill for direct grilling with one heat zone (medium). (See page 13 for charcoal and page 17 for gas.)

2 Make four lengthwise incisions into each eggplant. As soon as the grill is hot, place the eggplants on the grate over medium heat and grill with the hood closed. When the skin starts to burn and blister remove from the fire and let cool.

3 When the eggplants are cool enough to handle, remove the burnt skin and discard. Mash the flesh in a food processor until it becomes a coarse purée.

4 In a small mortar or food processor, grind the toasted cumin seeds to a powder.

5 In a large skillet, add the oil and place over medium heat. Add the onion and sauté until soft. Add the green chilies and ginger and cook until soft. Add the ground cumin and fry briefly. Don't let the cumin burn. Add the eggplant purée and stir-fry for a few minutes. Add the sugar and salt to taste and remove from the heat. Place in a serving bowl and set aside at room temperature or place in the refrigerator to chill. Just before serving, sprinkle with coriander leaves.

Honey Ginger Vegetables

These aromatic vegetables are a wonderful side dish for any of the recipes given in this book.

SERVES **6**
PREPARATION TIME: **30 minutes**
GRILL TIME: **10 to 15 minutes**

½ lb (250 g) carrots, cut into matchsticks about 2 in (5 cm) long and ¼ in (6 mm) thick
½ lb (250 g) celery, cut into 1-in (2.5-cm)-thick slices
½ lb (250 g) zucchini, cut into 1-in (2.5-cm)-thick cubes
½ lb (250 g) onions, cut into 1-in (2.5-cm)-thick slices
2 tablespoons extra-virgin olive oil
Generous pinch of salt

HONEY GINGER GLAZE
2 tablespoons honey

One ½-in (1.25-cm)-piece fresh ginger, peeled, chopped and crushed to a paste
½ teaspoon ground cinnamon
1 teaspoon dried lavender flowers
1 tablespoon lime juice

1 In a small saucepan, add the ingredients for the glaze. Place over medium heat and stir occasionally. When the honey is dissolved remove from the heat and set aside to let cool.

2 In a large bowl, add the vegetables, olive oil and salt. Toss the vegetables to evenly distribute the oil and salt. Set aside for 20 minutes.

3 Prepare the grill for direct grilling with two heat zones (medium and high). (See page 13 for charcoal and page 17 for gas.)

4 When the grill is hot, place the vegetables in a grill tray and place on the grate over the high heat zone. Grill for 3 to 5 minutes. If the vegetables begin to cook too quickly, move them to the medium heat zone and continue to grill for another 5 to 12 minutes until they have just begun to soften. When the vegetables are almost done, glaze with the honey ginger mixture and continue to grill for a few minutes until a nice glaze has formed.

Baked Potatoes with Chinese Chives

Everybody knows that baked potatoes are not originally Asian. However, they have found their way to almost every barbecue party in Asia. The difference is the sour cream, which is often given a local touch by adding spices and herbs. Here I've used a nice paprika and Chinese chive sour cream filling, but any favorite combination of Asian herbs and spices will be delicous.

SERVES **4**
PREPARATION TIME: **20 minutes**
GRILL TIME: **40 to 50 minutes**

4 large baking potatoes
2 cloves garlic, coarsely chopped
½ teaspoon salt
¾ cup (180 g) sour cream
1 teaspoon ground paprika
4 tablespoons finely chopped Chinese chives or regular chives

1 Prepare the grill for direct grilling with medium-high heat. (See page 13 for charcoal and page 17 for gas.)

2 Wrap the potatoes in aluminum foil and bury them in the hot embers and let cook for about 40 to 50 minutes or until done. If you're using a gas grill, place the wrapped potatoes onto the hot grill grate and close the hood.

3 In a mortar, crush the garlic with the salt to a paste.

4 In a bowl, combine the sour cream, paprika, crushed garlic and salt and chives. Set the sour cream mixture in the refrigerator until ready to use.

5 Test the potatoes for doneness by inserting a small knife. If the knife goes in quite easily, they are done.

6 Remove the potatoes from the fire, slice open and fill with the sour cream sauce.

Vegetarian Shish Kebabs

This shish kebab recipe hails from India, a country with a major vegetarian population. The trick to success is to make the kebab mixture smooth yet not so soft that it cannot be molded over the skewers. Also, square skewers, rather than rounded ones, will hold the kebab mixture more easily. This dish is best served with Sweet and Sour Tomato Chutney (page 54), or another chutney of your choice, or Spicy Tomato Sauce (page 50).

SERVES **4**
PREPARATION TIME: **50 minutes**
GRILL TIME: **6 to 8 minutes**

1 cup (150 g) dried chickpeas, soaked overnight in water, or 2 cups (400 g) drained canned chickpeas
2 large potatoes
3 tablespoons neutral-flavored oil
2 cups (350 g) fresh or frozen green peas
1 large onion, finely chopped
1 tablespoon finely chopped garlic
4 finger-length green chilies, deseeded and finely chopped
1 tablespoon peeled and finely chopped fresh ginger
½ lb (250 g) fresh spinach
1 egg, beaten
2 teaspoons ground cumin, toasted
2 teaspoons ground coriander, toasted
3 green cardamom pods, toasted
1 teaspoon black peppercorns, toasted
1 piece mace, toasted
½ teaspoon ground nutmeg
2 tablespoons coarsely chopped fresh coriander leaves (cilantro)
1 tablespoon coarsely chopped fresh mint leaves
1 teaspoon lemon juice
1 tablespoon tomato paste
Pinch of salt

Twenty-five 8¼-in (20 cm)-long bamboo skewers, soaked in water for 30 minutes, or flat metal skewers

1 If you're using dried chickpeas, bring water to a boil in a large saucepan and cook the soaked chickpeas until tender, then drain. In a large bowl, add the drained chickpeas and mash.

2 In the same saucepan, bring salted water to a boil, add the potatoes and cook until soft. Remove from the heat, drain, let cool just enough to handle and peel. Mash the potatoes and add to the mashed chickpeas.

3 In the same saucepan, add 1 tablespoon of the oil and place over medium heat. Sauté the green peas and mash coarsely before combining with the mashed chickpeas and potatoes.

4 In a large skillet, heat the remaining 2 tablespoons of oil and slightly fry the onion. Add the garlic, green chilies and ginger and continue to fry. Add the spinach and sauté until all liquid has evaporated. Remove from the heat and let cool. Finely chop the cooked spinach, onion and garlic and add to the chickpea mixture.

5 Fold the egg into the vegetable chickpea mixture. In a mortar or small food processor, add the toasted spices and grind to a powder. Pass through a fine sieve and regrind the larger parts. Remove any remaining unground pieces of cardamom pod. Add the ground toasted spices and the rest of the ingredients to the chickpea mixture. Stir until completely combined.

6 Wet your hands and place the chickpea mixture on the skewers. Leave enough room on one end of the skewer to easily handle it. The kebab should be not more than ½ inch (1.25 cm) in diameter. Prepare the grill for direct grilling with two heat zones (medium and high). (See page 13 for charcoal and page 17 for gas.)

7 Just before you begin grilling, oil the hot grate. Place the skewers on the grate over the high heat zone and grill each side for 3 to 4 minutes. If the skewers begin to cook too quickly, move them to the medium heat zone.

Curried Potato Wedges

These versatile potato wedges can be served with almost any dish in this book. A mild curry blend is rubbed onto the potatoes before being grilled.

SERVES **4**
PREPARATION TIME: **5 minutes**
GRILL TIME: **35 to 40 minutes**

4 large potatoes, each cut into 6 wedges

CURRY RUB
2 cloves garlic, crushed to a paste
½ teaspoon black pepper
½ to 1 teaspoon ground red pepper (cayenne)
½ teaspoon ground cumin
½ teaspoon curry powder
2 teaspoons salt

1 In a large bowl, combine the ingredients for the Curry Rub. Add the potato wedges and rub the spice mixture onto the wedges with your hands. Let the potatoes marinate for 30 minutes.

2 Prepare the grill for direct grilling with two heat zones (medium and low). (See page 13 for charcoal and page 17 for gas.)

3 Just before you begin grilling, oil the hot grate. Place the potato wedges on the grate over the medium hot zone and grill for about 35 to 40 minutes. Move the wedges to the lower heat zone if they begin to cook too quickly. It's important to not let the wedges become too browned as the curry rub will taste bitter.

Rosemary Roast Potatoes

Grilled potatoes are nowadays used in most international cuisines and have found their way into Asia as well. Many restaurants in Asia, even those that are strictly Asian, serve all kinds of grilled potatoes. This version is of Western origin but is often served in Asia combined with Asian grilled foods.

SERVES **4**
PREPARATION TIME: **20 minutes**
GRILL TIME: **20 minutes**

1 lb (500 g) small new potatoes
3 tablespoons extra-virgin olive oil
1 sprig fresh rosemary or 2 teaspoons dried rosemary leaves
Generous pinch of salt and pepper

1 In a large saucepan, bring salted water to a boil, add the potatoes and cook for 10 minutes until almost cooked (they should still be firm). Remove from the heat, drain, let cool just enough to handle and peel.

2 In a large bowl, add the peeled potatoes, olive oil, rosemary, salt and pepper and toss to evenly coat the potatoes with the oil and spices. Set aside for 30 minutes.

3 Prepare the grill for direct grilling with medium heat. (See page 13 for charcoal and page 17 for gas.)

4 Just before you begin grilling, oil the hot grate. Place the potatoes on the grate and grill for 20 minutes with the hood closed. Baste a few times with the leftover olive oil mixture until the potatoes become browned and crispy.

Teriyaki Tofu Skewers

For these simple yet delicious skewers, the tofu is marinated in a teriyaki sauce, grilled and garnished with a drizzle of dark sesame oil and a sprinkling of green onion. This recipe uses firm tofu. I prefer tofu which is not too hard with a firm and smooth texture.

SERVES **3**
PREPARATION TIME: **15 minutes**
GRILL TIME: **4 to 6 minutes**

½ lb (250 g) firm tofu, cut into rectangular
   pieces (about 1½ in/3.75 cm long, 1 in/2.5
   cm wide and ½ in/1.25 cm thick)
6 bamboo skewers, soaked in water for
   30 minutes, or metal skewers
Dark sesame oil
1 green onion (scallion), finely chopped

TERIYAKI SAUCE
2 tablespoons soy sauce
2 tablespoons mirin
1 tablespoon sugar, preferably superfine

1 In a large bowl, combine the ingredients for the teriyaki sauce. Stir until the sugar has dissolved.

2 Add the tofu pieces and toss to evenly coat in the marinade. Let the tofu marinate for 30 minutes.

3 Thread the tofu onto skewers. To secure the tofu use double metal skewers or two bamboo skewers for each kebab.

4 Prepare the grill for direct grilling with two heat zones (medium and high). (See page 13 for charcoal and page 17 for gas.)

5 Just before you begin grilling, oil the hot grate. Place the tofu on the grate over the high heat zone and grill for 4 to 6 minutes, turning once or twice by carefully holding the two skewers. Baste a few times with the teriyaki sauce to form a nice crust. If the tofu becomes browned too quickly, move the skewers to the medium heat zone and continue to grill till a nice crust has formed.

6 When done place the skewers on a serving platter. Drizzle on some sesame oil and sprinkle on the chopped green onion.

Tandoori Vegetables

These grilled broccoli and cauliflower pieces are marinated in a yogurt spice combination inspired by south Indian cuisine. If you don't care for a spicy vegetable dish, replace the ground red pepper with paprika.

SERVES **4**
PREPARATION TIME: **15 minutes**
GRILLING TIME: **10 to 12 minutes**

1 lb (500 g) broccoli, cut into bite-size pieces
1 lb (500 g) cauliflower, cut into bite-size pieces
12 bamboo skewers soaked 30 minutes in water

YOGURT MARINADE
1 teaspoon cumin seeds, toasted
1 teaspoon coriander seeds, toasted
½ teaspoon peeled and coarsely chopped fresh ginger
1 tablespoon coarsely chopped garlic
½ teaspoon ground turmeric
½ teaspoon ground red pepper (cayenne) or paprika
½ teaspoon black pepper
¼ cup plus 2 tablespoons (100 ml) plain yogurt
Salt to taste

SPICY BASTING SAUCE
½ teaspoon ground red pepper (cayenne) or 1 teaspoon paprika
3 tablespoons neutral-flavored vegetable oil

1 To make the marinade, place the toasted spices in a mortar or food processor and grind to a powder. Add the ginger and garlic and crush to a paste.

2 In a large bowl, add the garlic-spice paste and the rest of the marinade ingredients. Whisk the yogurt mixture until smooth.

3 Add the broccoli and cauliflower to the bowl with marinade and toss to evenly coat. Let marinate for 30 minutes. Remove from the marinade and thread alternating one broccoli and one cauliflower onto the bamboo skewers.

4 In a small bowl, add the ingredients for the basting sauce. Stir until combined.

5 Prepare the grill for direct grilling with medium heat. (See page 13 for charcoal and page 17 for gas.)

6 Just before you begin grilling, oil the hot grate. Place the skewers on the grate over the medium heat zone and grill for about 10 to 12 minutes or until done. Baste regularly with the spiced oil.

Spicy Vegetable Burgers

Vegetable burgers, or vegetable cutlet as they are called in India, are usually deep-fried and are a very popular snack. This dish is quite spicy and is usually served with Spicy Tomato Sauce (page 50) and french fries or salads. If you want to counter the spiciness serve with Mint and Coriander Yogurt Sauce (page 48).

SERVES **4**
PREPARATION TIME: **40 minutes**
GRILL TIME: **4 to 6 minutes**
MAKES **about 12 patties**

2 large potatoes
1 cup (150 g) dried red kidney beans, soaked overnight and boiled until soft, or 2 cups (300 g) drained canned red kidney beans
1 carrot, peeled and boiled until soft and coarsely mashed
2 tablespoons neutral-flavored oil
2 cups (100 g) finely chopped red cabbage
½ cup (80 g) finely chopped green beans
1 egg
½ cup (80 g) finely ground nuts, such as hazelnuts or cashew nuts
½ cup (25 g) finely chopped fresh coriander leaves (cilantro)
1 onion, finely chopped
3 cloves garlic, finely chopped
1 tablespoon peeled and minced fresh ginger
1 teaspoon cumin seeds, toasted and ground

Japanese Grilled Eggplant

Eggplant is one vegetable that I almost always have on hand. It's easy to grill and is a good match for almost any marinade. In this recipe the eggplant is marinated with soy sauce and garlic and then sprinkled with crunchy sesame seeds just before serving.

SERVES **2**
PREPARATION TIME: **15 minutes**
GRILL TIME: **10 to 15 minutes**

1 large eggplant (about 6 to 7 oz /175 to 200 g), cut into ½-in (1.25 cm)-thick slices
Salt
2 tablespoons sesame seeds, toasted

SWEET SOY MARINADE
4 green onions (scallions), finely chopped
1 tablespoon Japanese soy sauce
1 tablespoon sugar
1 tablespoon neutral-flavored vegetable oil
2 cloves garlic, finely chopped

1 Sprinkle the eggplant slices with some salt and set aside for 30 minutes. Rinse and pat dry.
2 In a small bowl combine the ingredients for the marinade.
3 Prepare the grill for direct grilling with two heat zones (medium and high). (See page 13 for charcoal and page 17 for gas.)
4 Just before you begin grilling, oil the hot grate. Place the eggplant on the grate over the high heat zone and grill each side for 3 to 4 minutes. Move to the medium heat and continue to grill for another 4 to 5 minutes or until the eggplant becomes very soft. Baste from time to time with the marinade.
5 When done place the grilled eggplant slices on a serving platter and drizzle the remaining marinade over top. Sprinkle on the sesame seeds and serve immediately.

½ teaspoon ground turmeric
1 teaspoon chili flakes
Generous pinch of salt and pepper
1 to 2 tablespoons bread crumbs (for binding) plus 1 cup (180 g) bread crumbs (for panade) in a plate for turning the patties

1 In a large saucepan, bring salted water to a boil, add the potatoes and cook until soft. Remove from the heat, drain, let cool just enough to handle and peel.
2 In a large bowl, combine the cooked potatoes, kidney beans and carrot and coarsely mash.
3 In a wok or skillet, add the oil and place over medium-high heat. Add the cabbage and green beans with a little salt and water and stir-fry until the water has evaporated. Set aside and let cool. Add the cabbage and

green beans to the mashed kidney beans and potatoes and stir to combine. Add the rest of the ingredients, except for the bread crumbs. If the mixture is too wet add 1 to 2 tablespoons of bread crumbs. Form patties that are about 3 to 4 inches (7.5 to 10 cm) in diameter and 1 inch (2.5 cm) thick. Turn the patties in the bread crumbs.
4 Prepare the grill for direct grilling with two heat zones (medium and high). (See page 13 for charcoal and page 17 for gas.)
5 Place a grill plate or grill tray on the grill grate over high heat to preheat it. When hot oil the plate and add the burgers. Grill about 4 to 6 minutes or until browned, turning once. Move the grill plate to the medium heat zone if the burgers begin to cook too quickly. Handle carefully because they fall apart easily.

Vegetable Barbecue Recipes   151

Grilled Vegetable Pack

This is an easy way to prepare vegetables on the grill or open fire. It may even bring back memories of your campfire days. These vegetables can be served with grilled fish, meat or chicken.

SERVES **4**
PREPARATION TIME: **10 minutes**
GRILL TIME: **10 to 15 minutes**

½ cup (40 g) dried black Chinese fungus (wood ear mushroom) or dried shiitake
½ lb (250 g) snow peas
½ lb (250 g) carrots, cut into thin slices
½ cup (50 g) bean sprouts
½ lb (250 g) zucchini, cut into thin slices
1 tablespoon Chinese light soy sauce
1 tablespoon peeled and finely chopped fresh ginger
2 cloves garlic, finely chopped
3 tablespoons white wine
Generous pinch of salt
Large sheet of aluminum foil to form the pouch

1 Soak the Chinese fungus in 1 cup (250 ml) hot water for about 1 hour. Drain and rinse several times to remove sand.

2 In a large bowl, combine all of the ingredients and toss to mix. Place in an aluminum pouch and tightly seal.

3 Prepare the grill for direct grilling with medium heat. (See page 13 for charcoal and page 17 for gas.)

4 When the grill is hot, place the pouch directly over the heat and grill for about 15 minutes.

Soy Sesame Vegetables

This dish is equivalent to a grilled vegetable salad. The veggies are first grilled and then a vinaigrette is added. Any kind of vegetable can be used for this dish.

SERVES **4**
PREPARATION TIME: **40 minutes**
GRILL TIME: **6 to 10 minutes**

¼ lb (100 g) green beans, preferably small and slender ones
¼ lb (100 g) asparagus, preferably slender
2 red bell peppers, cut into long slices
Kosher salt or sea salt
¼ cup (65 ml) Sesame Soy Vinaigrette (page 53)

1 If the green beans and asparagus aren't slender, cut in half lengthwise.

2 Prepare the grill for direct grilling with two heat zones (medium and high). (See page 13 for charcoal and page 17 for gas.)

3 Just before you begin grilling, oil the hot grate. Place the vegetables on the grate over the high heat zone and grill for 2 to 3 minutes, then move to the medium heat zone and continue to grill for another 4 to 8 minutes. Just before the vegetables are finished grilling, sprinkle them with some coarse salt.

4 Arrange the grilled vegetables on a serving platter and drizzle on the Soy Sesame Vinaigrette.

Grilled Eggplant Purée

Eggplant purée is often served with grilled meats or as a dip with pita bread or vegetable crudité. If you prefer a less creamy purée, as I do, use 1 tablespoon of tahini; if you like it creamier, use 2 tablespoons. I don't like to use a food processor when making eggplant purée as it makes it too smooth.

SERVES **4**
PREPARATION TIME: **20 minutes**
GRILL TIME: **15 to 20 minutes**

4 eggplants, about ⅓ lb (150 g) each
1 to 2 tablespoons tahini
Juice of 1 lemon
2 cloves garlic, crushed to a paste
Salt to taste
2 tablespoons extra-virgin olive oil
Fresh mint leaves for garnish

1 Prepare the grill for direct grilling with medium heat. (See page 13 for charcoal and page 17 for gas.)
2 Just before you begin grilling, oil the hot grate. Make four shallow lengthwise incisions into each eggplant. Place the eggplants on the grate and grill with the hood closed until the skin starts burning and blistering. Remove from the fire and let cool.
3 Remove the burnt skin from the eggplants. Coarsely chop the flesh and add it to a large bowl. Mash the flesh with a fork to a coarse paste. Add the tahini, lemon juice, garlic paste and a little salt. Continue to mash to a coarse purée. Place the purée in a serving bowl. Place a few mint leaves in the center of the bowl and drizzle on the olive oil.

Grilled Stuffed Mushrooms

Portobello mushrooms are great to grill because they maintain a firm toothsome texture and they absorb marinades very nicely. This simple dish goes great with many of the recipes in this book.

SERVES **2 as a main dish/4 as a side dish**
PREPARATION TIME: **15 minutes**
GRILL TIME: **6 to 10 minutes**

3 cloves garlic, crushed to a paste
2 tablespoons extra-virgin olive oil
4 large portobello mushrooms, stems removed
6 tablespoons pine nuts, lightly toasted and cooled
⅓ lb (150 g) feta cheese
3 tablespoons chopped fresh flat-leaf parsley
3 tablespoons chopped fresh mint leaves
Salt to taste

1 In a small bowl, combine the garlic paste and olive oil. Rub this mixture all over the mushroom caps and let them marinate for about 30 minutes.
2 In a bowl, combine the cooled toasted pine nuts, feta cheese, herbs and salt. Stuff the mushroom caps with this mixture.
3 If you're using a charcoal grill, prepare it for indirect grilling (see page 14). Place a drip pan in the middle and live coals around the pan. If you're using a gas grill, prepare it for direct grilling with two heat zones (medium and high). (See page 17.)
4 Just before you begin grilling, oil the hot grate. Grill for 6 to 10 minutes and move to medium heat if too hot.

Grilled Potato Salad

This refreshing salad is packed with lots of fresh herbs. It goes well with most dishes in the book.

SERVES **4**
PREPARATION TIME: **40 minutes**
GRILL TIME: **7 to 10 minutes**

2 lbs (1 kg) potatoes
2 tablespoons extra-virgin olive oil for basting

HERB SALAD DRESSING
2 cloves garlic, finely chopped
2 tablespoons finely chopped fresh flat-leaf parsley
1 tablespoon finely chopped fresh mint leaves
1 tablespoon finely chopped fresh coriander leaves (cilantro)
2 tablespoons chopped green onion (scallion)
1 teaspoon ground paprika
1 teaspoon cumin seeds, toasted and crushed to a powder
3 tablespoons extra-virgin olive oil
Juice of 1 lemon

1 To make the salad dressing, combine the garlic, parsley, mint, coriander, green onion, paprika, crushed cumin seeds and olive oil in a large serving bowl. Add the lemon juice and stir to combine.

2 Bring a large pot of salted water to a boil. Add the potatoes and cook until almost done. Drain, peel and quarter the potatoes.

3 Prepare the grill for direct grilling with medium heat. (See page 13 for charcoal and page 17 for gas.)

4 Just before you begin grilling, oil the hot grate. Place the potato wedges on the grate and grill until each side has formed a nice brown crust. Regularly baste with the olive oil.

5 Remove from the grill and add to the bowl with the salad dressing. Toss and serve warm.

Grilled Goat Cheese

Hot molten cheese is always a crowd-pleaser at BBQ parties. Serve with crackers or some thin slices of black bread. Do not use fresh goat cheese (chèvre) for this recipe. You need a moderately aged goat cheese to hold up to the heat of the grill.

SERVES **2 as a side dish/4 as a starter**
PREPARATION TIME: **20 minutes**
GRILL TIME: **4 to 6 minutes**

One ½-lb (250-g) piece aged goat cheese or a Brie or tomme-style cheese made with goat's milk

CASHEW PANADE
2 tablespoons extra-virgin olive oil
2 to 3 tablespoons roasted and coarsely chopped cashew nuts
2 dried apricots, finely chopped
1 tablespoon bread crumbs
1 tablespoon finely chopped fresh mint leaves
1 tablespoon finely chopped celery leaves or fresh flat-leaf parsley
Pinch of salt and black pepper

1 Prepare the grill for indirect grilling and preheat two heat zones (medium and high). (See page 14 for charcoal and page 17 for gas.) If you're using charcoal, place a drip pan in the middle and live coals around the drip pan.
2 In a small bowl, mix together the ingredients for the panade.
3 Pat the panade over the entire surface of the cheese, firmly pressing it so that it sticks to the cheese. Place the panade-covered cheese on a sheet of aluminum foil that has been wiped with a little neutral-flavored oil. Lay another sheet of foil over the top. Don't wrap the aluminum foil around the cheese since you want the two sheets to come off very easily.
4 When the grill is hot place the cheese in the aluminum foil directly above the drip pan or,

if you're using a gas grill, over the low heat zone. Grill with the hood closed at high temperature until the cheese starts to melt. After a few minutes, carefully turn the cheese and remove the top piece of foil. Scrape any panade that has stuck to the foil and place it back on the cheese. Continue to grill with the hood closed for a few minutes until the cheese has become molten and the panade turns slightly crisp. The cheese should just start oozing out of the crust. Discard the remaining piece of foil before serving.

Asparagus, Snow Peas and Mushrooms Pouch

I learned how to make these vegetable pouches from my Aussie sailing friend Gary, who can often be spotted cheerfully folding foil pouches at our parties.

SERVES **4**
PREPARATION TIME: **15 minutes**
GRILL TIME: **10 minutes**

One 12 x 20-in (30 x 50-cm) sheet aluminum foil, folded into a pouch
¼ lb (100 g) asparagus, cut into 1½-in (3.75-cm) pieces
¼ lb (100 g) snow peas
¼ lb (100 g) Chinese wood ear mushrooms or shiitake mushrooms
2 cloves garlic, crushed with the side of a knife
1 tablespoon soy sauce
2 tablespoons white wine
1 tablespoon dark sesame oil

1 Prepare the grill for direct grilling with medium heat. (See page 13 for charcoal and page 17 for gas.)
2 Fill the foil pouch with the vegetables. In a small bowl, combine the rest of the ingredients and pour over the vegetables. Loosely close the pouch, leaving room for the expanding steam.
3 Place the vegetable parcel on the hot grate over the high heat zone and grill for about 10 minutes.

Chapter 7

Side Dishes and Desserts

From hot and cold sides to tempting starters and sweets, this chapter is filled with recipes that will bring a contrast of color, texture and flavors to a delicious array of barbecued foods.

Satisfying flat breads, such as Tandoori Naan (page 160) and Quick Pita Bread (page 160), and rice dishes, such as the subtle Saffron Rice (page 167) and Grilled Rice Cakes (page 167) provide the perfect neutral base to accompany flavorful barbecued meats.

A refreshing salad is the perfect side dish for a barbecue. Here you will find a variety of salads that reflect renditions available throughout Asia. Chinese Coleslaw (page 162), originally a Chinese recipe, was slightly adapted to Western cuisine and can easily be combined with Chinese, Japanese or Western dishes.

In Thailand unripe fruit like green papaya and green mango are often made into salads and are served with grilled or deep-fried food. I have included recipes for both Green Papaya Salad (page 165) and Green Mango Salad (page 161) as their refreshing sourness offers a welcome contrast to the richness of grilled food. Usually Green Papaya Salad is served with meat dishes and Green Mango Salad with fish or seafood, however, feel free to mix things up. Even in Asia this rule is not adhered to very strictly.

In India salads have only recently become popular. I have included both the traditional Yogurt Cucumber Raita (page 166) and a recipe for Tomato and Pepper Salad (page 163), which reflects the new style of salad that's becoming popular there. These salads can be combined with any Indian recipe in this book.

The Middle East, in particular Lebanon and Turkey, is famous for its very aromatic and herby salads like the Tabbouleh Salad (page 161), the Pistachio Rice Salad (page 166) and the Farmer's Salad (page 163). These salads, along with Potato and Cucumber Salad (page 166), can be combined easily with any food originating from the Middle East to northern India.

Rounding out the chapter are some tempting grilled fruits served with or without ice cream or sorbet such as Caramelized Mangoes (page 168) or Fresh Grilled Pineapple with Pineapple Sorbet (page 168). Asians usually serve fruit after a meal and it's this tradition that inspired the fruit-based desserts here.

Asian Crostini Platter

Crostinis, which means "little toasts" in Italian, are easy to make and make great starters at a party. To create the base for the crostini, simply grill ½-inch (1.25-cm)-thick slices of French bread over a hot grill until they turn very crisp. Then set them aside to be topped with a delicious spread, such as hummus, or grilled meats, seafood or vegetables. To make a crostini platter for a party, make one, or preferably two or more of the crostinis that follow. When making crostinis for four people I generally grill a 12-inch (30-cm) loaf of French bread, which gives about twenty slices between ½ and ¾ inch (1.5 cm) thick, or five slices per person.

Grilled Chicken Crostini

This crostini is inspired by the banh mi thit—a Vietnamese sandwich that combines marinated and grilled meat, radish pickles, fresh cucumber, herbs and lettuce over which a delicious Soy Sesame Sauce is drizzled. The variety of tastes and textures makes this crostini a real treat.

SERVES **4**
PREPARATION TIME: **30 minutes**
GRILL TIME: **7 to 9 minutes**

2 chicken breasts, skinned
20 grilled crostini slices
2 tablespoons Sri Racha Chili Sauce Mayonnaise (page 57)
A few lettuce leaves washed and torn into bite-size pieces
½ cucumber, peeled, deseeded and cut into thin 1-inch (2.5-cm)-long matchsticks
½ cup (100 g) Carrot and Radish Pickle (page 57)
Leaves from 8 to 10 sprigs fresh coriander (cilantro)

BANH MI SPICE PASTE
3 black peppercorns
2 cloves garlic
Lower half of 1 lemongrass stalk, outer tough leaves removed and finely chopped
1 tablespoon fish sauce, preferably Vietnamese
1 teaspoon Chinese light soy sauce
1½ teaspoons palm sugar or light brown sugar
Salt to taste

SOY SESAME SAUCE
1 tablespoon light soy sauce
1 tablespoon dark sesame oil
1 teaspoon lime juice

1 To make the spice paste, crush the peppercorns and garlic in a mortar. Add the lemongrass and crush together with the peppercorns and garlic. Add the remaining ingredients except the salt. Taste for seasoning and add salt if needed.

2 Rub the chicken with the spice paste. Place in the refrigerator to marinate for 1 hour.

3 In a small bowl, combine the ingredients for the soy sesame sauce.

4 Prepare the grill for direct grilling and preheat two heat zones (medium and high). (See page 13 for charcoal and page 17 for gas.)

5 Just before you begin grilling, oil the hot grate. Place the chicken breasts over the high heat zone and just before done move to the medium heat zone of the grill and grill each side for about 3 to 5 minutes, turning regularly and basting regularly with the spice paste. If the chicken becomes browned too quickly move to lower zone.

6 When done remove from the fire and let the chicken rest for about 5 minutes. Cut diagonally into ¼-inch (6-mm)-thick slices.

7 On a crostini slice, spread about ½ teaspoon of the Sri Racha Chili Sauce Mayonnaise. Then follow with a couple of the bite-size lettuce pieces, a few cucumber strips, some chicken slices and then about ½ teaspoon of the Carrot and Radish Pickle. Garnish with a few fresh coriander leaves and drizzle on about ¼ teaspoon of the Soy Sesame Sauce. Repeat with the remaining crostini slices.

Fish Tataki Crostini

This spicy crostini is drizzled with a delicious balsamic dressing.

SERVES **4**
PREPARATION TIME: **10 to 15 minutes**
GRILLING TIME: **3 to 5 minutes**

¼ lb (100 g) cod or snapper fillets
12 fresh shiso leaves (or use a fresh mint and a fresh coriander leaf for each shiso leaf)
20 grilled crostini slices
1 tablespoon wasabi paste

BALSAMIC DRESSING
2 tablespoons extra-virgin olive oil
1 tablespoon balsamic vinegar

1 In a small bowl, whisk together the ingredients for the dressing.

2 Prepare the grill for direct grilling with high heat. (See page 13 for charcoal and page 17 for gas.)

3 Just before you begin grilling, oil the hot grate. Place the fish fillets on the grate over high heat and grill to your preferred doneness. (Asians will grill them just to give them some crust while the inside remains raw.) Remove the fish from the grill and cut into thin slices. Place 2 shiso leaves on a crostini. Arrange the grilled fish on top and add a pinch or two of the wasabi paste. Drizzle with the dressing.

Feta and Eggplant Crostini

This crostini is made of a mixture of strips of grilled eggplants and crumbled feta cheese.

SERVES **4**
PREPARATION TIME: **15 minutes**
GRILL TIME: **4 to 6 minutes**

1 eggplant, about ⅓ to ½ lb (150 to 250 g), cut into ½-in (1.25)-thick slices
¼ lb (100 g) feta cheese, crumbled
20 grilled crostini slices
Extra-virgin olive oil for drizzling
Fresh flat-leaf parsley for garnish

1 Prepare the grill for direct grilling and preheat to high heat. (See page 13 for charcoal and page 17 for gas.)
2 Just before you begin grilling, oil the hot grate. Place the eggplant slices over high heat and grill until they become soft. Cut the grilled slices into thin slivers. In a bowl, add the warm eggplant slivers and feta cheese. Use a fork to work the two into a coarse mixture. Drizzle the bread with olive oil and arrange this mixture on top. Garnish with some parsley.

Grilled Curry Shrimp Crostini

This crostini features shrimp marinated in Thai red curry paste.

SERVES **4**
PREPARATION TIME: **20 minutes**
GRILL TIME: **3 to 5 minutes**

¼ lb (100 g) medium shrimp
3 tablespoons coconut milk
20 grilled crostini slices
Fresh coriander leaves (cilantro) for garnish

RED CURRY PASTE
1 shallot
2 red chilies, deseeded and chopped
2 cloves garlic, coarsely chopped
½ teaspoon lime zest
Pinch of ground coriander
Pinch of ground cumin
1 teaspoon lime juice
1 teaspoon neutral-flavored oil
Pinch of salt

1 In a food processor or mortar, crush the ingredients for the curry paste. In a bowl, add the shrimp and half of the curry paste. Toss to coat the shrimp with the paste. Marinate in the refrigerator for 20 minutes.
2 In a small saucepan, add the coconut milk and remaining half of the curry paste. Gently simmer for a few minutes. Remove from the heat and keep ready for basting.
3 Prepare the grill for direct grilling with high heat. (See page 13 for charcoal and page 17 for gas.)
4 Just before you begin grilling, oil the hot grate. Place the shrimp over high heat. Baste the shrimp with the coconut milk curry sauce. When done place the shrimp onto the crostini and drizzle with some additional red curry sauce or plain coconut milk. Garnish with some fresh coriander leaves.

Hummus Crostini

This vegetarian crostini consists of a few sticks of just-tender grilled vegetables topped with some creamy hummus.

SERVES **4**
PREPARATION TIME: **30 minutes**
GRILLING TIME: **3 to 5 minutes**

½ cup (100 g) dried chickpeas, soaked overnight, or 1 cup (200 g) drained canned chickpeas
2 tablespoons extra-virgin olive oil
1½ tablespoons lemon juice
1½ teaspoons tahini
Pinch of toasted and ground coriander seeds
Pinch of salt and pepper
1 carrot, cut into 2-in (5-cm)-long matchsticks
1 stalk celery, cut into 2-in (5-cm)-long matchsticks
1 radish, cut into 2-in (5-cm)-long matchsticks
20 grilled crostini slices
Paprika for garnish
Fresh flat-leaf parsley for garnish
Extra-virgin olive oil for drizzling

1 In a large saucepan, bring water to a boil and add the soaked chickpeas. (*Note:* Do not add salt when cooking dried beans or peas as they will not become soft.) Boil the chickpeas until soft. Drain the chickpeas. If you're using canned chickpeas, boil for about 3 minutes and then drain.
2 To make the hummus, place the chickpeas in a bowl and mash them to a fine paste. Add the olive oil, lemon juice, tahini, toasted and ground coriander seeds, salt and pepper.
3 Prepare the grill for direct grilling with high heat. (See page 13 for charcoal and page 17 for gas.)
4 Place the vegetable sticks in a grilling tray and place on the hot grate for a few minutes. Arrange the grilled vegetable sticks on top of the toasted crostini and top each with 1 tablespoon of hummus. To garnish, lightly sprinkle on the paprika, top with some parsley leaves and drizzle on the olive oil.

Quick Pita Bread

This traditional flat bread has become a favorite in most Western and Asian cities as a wrap for endless fillings, including kebabs. My sister-in-law bought me a special device from Egypt to make these flat breads. It is a copper bowl that is inverted on top of a charcoal fire. The bread is spread on top of this copper shell and it is nicely baked from underneath. The result is a very thin and crisp bread. I've adapted the traditional pita bread recipe to work on a standard grill. The resulting pita is great for making pouches and wraps or as a side dish for grilled foods.

SERVES **6**
PREPARATION TIME: **30 minutes**
GRILL TIME: **3 to 6 minutes**

3 tablespoons fresh yeast or 1 tablespoon
   active dry yeast
4 tablespoons plus 2 cups (500 ml) lukewarm
   water
2 lbs (1 kg) whole-wheat flour plus extra for
   working the dough
1½ teaspoons salt
¼ cup (65 ml) olive oil

1 In a small bowl, add the yeast and the 4 tablespoons of lukewarm water. Set aside for a few minutes or until the yeast has begun to foam.

2 In a large bowl, sift in the flour and add the salt and yeast mixture. Add the olive oil and, while stirring, slowly add the 2 cups (500 ml) of lukewarm water until you get a firm dough. Knead well until the dough becomes soft and smooth. Cover with a damp towel and let rest in a warm place for 2 hours or until it has doubled in size.

3 After it has doubled in size, knead once more and divide into eight equal-size pieces. Form the pieces into small balls. Roll each ball into a disk about 8 inches (20 cm) in diameter. Set aside for 20 minutes.

4 Prepare the grill for direct grilling with medium heat. (See page 13 for charcoal and page 17 for gas.)

5 Just before you begin grilling, oil the hot grate. Place the disks on the grate and let cook for about 3 to 5 minutes. When the bottom starts to blister and become browned, turn once and continue to grill until the bottom starts blistering.

Vietnamese Garlic Bread

Garlic bread is French in origin but it has become so popular in Asia—from India to Thailand and Vietnam—that an Asian version has evolved. The special Asian touch is the addition of fresh mint and coriander.

SERVES **4**
PREPARATION: **10 minutes**
GRILL TIME: **3 to 5 minutes**

1 tablespoon softened butter
2 cloves garlic, finely chopped
1 tablespoon finely chopped fresh coriander
   leaves (cilantro)
1 teaspoon finely chopped fresh mint leaves
Pinch of taste (if using unsalted butter)
1 baguette

1 In a small bowl, mix the softened butter with the garlic, coriander and mint leaves, and salt, if using.

2 Make slices into the baguette every ½ inch (2 cm)—do not slice through the bottom of the baguette. Spread the garlic herb butter between the slices.

3 Prepare the grill for direct grilling with medium heat. (See page 13 for charcoal and page 17 for gas.)

4 When the grill is hot, place the baguette on the grate and grill with the hood closed for 3 to 5 minutes. Turn once to evenly grill the loaf.

Tandoori Naan

Traditionally this bread, which is eaten in most parts of central Asia from Turkey to India, is baked on the inside wall of a clay oven. I adapted the recipe for baking it on a conventional grill.

SERVES **6**
PREPARATION TIME: **30 minutes**
GRILL TIME: **3 to 5 minutes**

1½ lbs (750 g) flour
½ teaspoon salt
½ oz (10 g) active dry yeast
2 teaspoons sugar
1 egg
5 tablespoons plain yogurt
3 tablespoons milk
Cold water to mix and knead

1 In a large bowl, sift the flower and add the salt, yeast, sugar, egg, yogurt and milk. Mix with your hands and knead, adding some cold water little by little until you get a soft and smooth dough. Cover with a damp towel and let rest in a warm place and for about 2 hours or until the dough has risen to double its size.

2 Divide into 8 equal-size balls. Flatten each ball into an oval shape about 10 inches (25 cm) long and 4 inches (10 cm) wide.

3 Prepare the grill for direct grilling with medium heat. (See page 13 for charcoal and page 17 for gas.)

4 Just before you begin grilling, oil the hot grate. Place the ovals on the grate and grill for about 2 to 3 minutes. As soon as the bottom starts to get blackened and blisters, turn and continue to grill for another 1 to 2 minutes. Naan should remain soft and should not become crisp.

Chinese Vegetable Salad

This vegetable salad is preferably prepared one hour before you fire up the grill. The sauce is added to the blanched vegetables and left in the fridge until ready to be served.

SERVES 4
PREPARATION TIME: **20 minutes**

½ lb (250 g) bean sprouts
½ lb (250 g) celery, cut into ¼-in (6-mm) slices
1 large carrot, cut into fine slivers
1 tablespoon Chinese light soy sauce
1 tablespoon white vinegar
1 tablespoon sugar
2 tablespoons dark sesame oil
1 teaspoon Szechuan peppercorns
1 teaspoon ground red pepper (cayenne)

1 Blanch the bean sprouts, celery and carrot in boiling water for 30 seconds and toss into ice water. Drain the blanched vegetables and place in a large serving bowl.
2 Add the soy sauce and vinegar and stir to evenly coat the vegetables. Sprinkle the sugar over top.

3 In a small skillet, add the sesame oil and place over medium heat. When the oil is hot add the Szechuan peppercorns and ground red pepper. Quickly remove from the heat and stir for a few minutes. When the oil has absorbed the color of the ground red pepper pour the hot oil over the vegetables and stir well. Place in the refrigerator to completely cool before serving.

Tabbouleh Salad

A refreshing salad comprised mostly of cracked wheat (bulgur) with a generous amount of fresh parsley. It is a very versatile side dish and can be served with several of the recipes in this book.

SERVES 4
PREPARATION TIME: **30 minutes**

½ cup (80 g) bulgur
4 bunches fresh flat-leaf parsley (about ¾ lb/350 g total)
1 bunch fresh mint (about ¼ lb/100g)
2 shallots, finely chopped

2 green onions (scallions), finely chopped
3 firm tomatoes, diced
½ cucumber, diced
Juice of 3 lemons
4 tablespoons extra-virgin olive oil
Salt and pepper to taste

1 Soften the bulgur in cold water for about 30 minutes. Rinse and thoroughly dry the parsley and mint. Coarsely chop the parsley and mint leaves.
2 In a large bowl, add the shallots, green onion, tomatoes, cucumber and chopped parsley and mint leaves. Drain the bulgur and add to the bowl. Toss to combine.
3 Add the lemon juice, olive oil, salt and pepper. Toss to combine and taste for seasoning, adding more salt if needed.

Green Mango Salad

This delicious salad is often served in Thailand with grilled or fried seafood. The mangoes should be slightly sour and firm.

SERVES 2
PREPARATION TIME: **15 minutes**

1 tablespoon fish sauce, preferably Thai
1 tablespoon lime juice
2 teaspoons sugar
2 finger-length green chilies, cut diagonally into three pieces
1 shallot, halved and sliced into thin half-moons
2 cloves garlic, finely chopped
2 tablespoons finely chopped fresh coriander leaves (cilantro)
Salt to taste
1 green mango, peeled, pitted and cut into thin slivers

In a bowl, combine the fish sauce, lime juice and sugar. Stir until the sugar has dissolved. Add the rest of the ingredients, except the mango, and stir to combine. Add the mango, toss and serve immediately.

Chinese Cole Slaw

For good reason, this fresh and crunchy cole slaw with festive color is a universally popular BBQ side dish.

SERVES **4**
PREPARATION TIME: **20 minutes**

½ head Chinese (napa) cabbage
½ head red cabbage
2 carrots, peeled and cut into thin slivers
1 yellow bell pepper, deseeded and cut into thin slices
4 green onions, cut into thin slivers about 2 in (5 cm) long
2 tablespoons coarsely chopped fresh coriander leaves (cilantro)
2 teaspoons salt
1 teaspoon black pepper
1 tablespoon sesame seeds, toasted

RICE VINEGAR DRESSING
2 tablespoons lime juice
1 tablespoon Chinese light soy sauce
1 tablespoon rice vinegar or apple cider vinegar
1 tablespoon honey
2 teaspoons peeled and finely grated fresh ginger
2 cloves garlic, finely chopped
1 tablespoon dark sesame oil
¼ cup plus 2 tablespoons (100 ml) neutral-flavored oil

1 Remove the tough outer leaves from the Chinese cabbage and red cabbage, core the cabbages and slice them into very thin shreds.

2 In a large serving bowl, add the cabbage shreds, carrots, bell pepper, green onions, coriander leaves, salt and pepper.

3 Combine the ingredients for the dressing in a small bowl. Stir until the honey dissolves. Just before serving pour the dressing over the vegetables and toss to combine. Sprinkle on the toasted sesame seeds.

Bean Sprout Salad

This easy-to-prepare salad—which is essentially a pickled side dish—is served on the roadside in Vietnam with grilled foods. It goes great with any of the grilled recipes in this book. The sprouts used in this salad are the ubiquitous mung bean sprout—the most popular bean sprout in Asia and widely available in the West.

SERVES **4**
PREPARATION TIME: **25 minutes plus 2 hours to pickle**

½ cup (80 g) sugar
1 teaspoon salt
1 cup (250 ml) boiling water
1 cup (250 ml) white vinegar
1 lb (500 g) fresh bean sprouts
5 small green onions (scallions), cut to about the same length as the bean sprouts
1 small bunch fresh coriander (cilantro), coarsely chopped

1 In a large bowl, add the sugar, salt and boiling water. Stir until the sugar and salt

are dissolved. Immediately add the vinegar, bean sprouts, green onions and coriander. Toss to combine and evenly coat the vegetables with the brine.

2 Keep in the refrigerator for two hours, turning the vegetables once in a while. Shortly before serving drain the liquid and serve on a plate.

Arugula Salad with Ginger Soy Dressing

Balsamic vinegar is nowadays often used in Asian cuisines as well and it goes very well in combination with soy sauce and sesame oil.

SERVES **4**
PREPARATION TIME: **20 minutes**

½ lb (250 g) arugula or any other kind of firm green lettuce like oak leaf
12 cherry tomatoes, halved
1 teaspoon sesame seeds, lightly toasted, for garnish

GINGER SOY DRESSING

3 tablespoons light Chinese soy sauce or Japanese soy sauce
2 tablespoons balsamic vinegar
1 teaspoon sugar
1 teaspoon peeled and finely chopped fresh ginger
2 tablespoons neutral-flavored oil
1 tablespoon dark sesame oil
Pinch of salt and pepper

1 In a large bowl, combine the ingredients for the dressing.
2 Add the arugula or other lettuce and cherry tomatoes. Toss to evenly coat the vegetables in the dressing and arrange on 4 salad plates. Sprinkle some of the sesame seeds over each salad.

Tomato and Pepper Salad

This refreshingly sour and spicy salad can be combined with most of the Indian and central Asian–based recipes in this book. Variations on this salad are served all over the region. In Burma peanuts are added to give it extra crunch. If you don't have tomatoes or bell pepper on hand, this flexible salad can be made with almost any salad vegetable you have on hand—including cucumber, carrots or radish.

SERVES **4**
PREPARATION TIME: **20 minutes**

½ lb (250 g) tomatoes, deseeded and diced
½ lb (250 g) bell peppers, diced
2 red onions, finely sliced
2 tablespoons coarsely chopped fresh coriander leaves (cilantro)
2 finger-length green chilies, deseeded and sliced
Salt to taste
3 to 5 tablespoons lime juice

In a large serving bowl, combine the tomatoes, bell pepper, onions, coriander leaves, chilies and salt. Add 3 tablespoons

of the lime juice and taste. If you prefer it more sour, add up to 2 more tablespoons of lime juice and add more salt if needed. Set aside for 20 minutes in the refrigerator before serving.

Farmer's Salad

This hearty farmer's salad or "fatoush," is typically tossed with freshly grilled pita bread, which gives a nice crunch to the salad. Alternatively, you can leave out the pita bread and use it to wrap the salad together with hamburgers or other grilled meats.

SERVES **4**
PREPARATION TIME: **30 minutes**

5 tablespoons extra-virgin olive oil
3 tablespoons lemon juice
1 tablespoon pomegranate concentrate

Pinch of salt and pepper
2 teaspoons sumac
2 tablespoons pine nuts, toasted
2 pita bread, grilled until crisp and torn into small pieces (optional)
1 large cucumber, cut into bite-size pieces
6 green onions (scallions), sliced
1 green bell pepper, cut into bite-size pieces
4 medium tomatoes, cut into bite-size pieces
1 bunch fresh flat-leaf parsley, coarsely chopped
1 small bunch fresh coriander (cilantro), coarsely chopped
1 small bunch fresh mint, coarsely chopped

1 In a small bowl, combine the olive oil, lemon juice, pomegranate concentrate, salt, pepper, sumac and toasted pine nuts (let the pine nuts cool before adding them).
2 In a large serving bowl, add the vegetables and herbs. Just before serving add the grilled pita bread pieces, if using, and the olive oil mixture and toss to combine.

Asian Celery Salad

The Chinese enjoy cold vegetables that are usually served with white vinegar, a little sugar, salt and sesame oil or sesame seeds. In particular around Shanghai, where my wife comes from the art of making small cold dishes (*leng pan*) is extremely well developed. One of my favorite Chinese vegetables used for a cold salad is *wo sun*, which resembles a large broccoli stalk but the inside is very soft and tender, close to cucumber. It is very difficult to come by in other countries and I've substituted it with celery. If you don't have celery on hand, you can use cucumber, which is another good substitute for wo sun.

SERVES **4**
PREPARATION TIME: **20 minutes plus 30 minutes to soak dried mushrooms**

½ cup (40 g) dried black Chinese fungus (wood ear mushroom) or dried shiitake
1 lb (500 g) celery stalks, thinly sliced

SWEET SESAME DRESSING
3 tablespoons white vinegar
1½ teaspoons sugar
Pinch of salt
1 tablespoon dark sesame oil
1 teaspoon chili oil

1 Soak the Chinese fungus in warm water for about 30 minutes. When soft drain the mushrooms.

2 To make the dressing, in a large bowl, add the vinegar, sugar and salt. Stir until the sugar is dissolved. Add the oils and stir to combine.

3 Add the celery and drained mushrooms to the bowl and toss to combine. Taste for seasoning and add more salt if needed. Arrange on a serving plate and serve.

Pumpkin and Potato Mash with Almonds

This satisfying side dish is a good match for many different kinds of grilled meats. The fresh coriander provides a bright flavor and unique Asian touch. If you'd like to serve this dish with a Western-style meal—Thanksgiving comes to mind!—simply omit the coriander.

SERVES **4**
PREPARATION TIME: **45 minutes**

½ lb (250 g) potatoes
1 lb (500 g) fresh pumpkin
1 tablespoon butter
Small pinch of ground nutmeg
½ cup (125 ml) warm milk
Salt to taste
½ cup (80 g) almond slivers, lightly roasted
1 tablespoon chopped fresh coriander leaves (cilantro) (optional)

1 In a large saucepan, bring salted water to a boil, add the potatoes and cook until soft. Remove from the heat, drain, let cool just enough to handle and peel.

2 Peel the pumpkin, remove the seeds and cut the flesh into slices.

3 In a skillet, add the butter and place over medium heat. Add the pumpkin slices and cook until they become very soft and can be mashed with a fork. If necessary, add a little water to keep the pumpkin from sticking to the pan. Mash to a coarse purée.

4 In a large saucepan or bowl, mash the potatoes. Add the pumpkin purée and mix to combine. Add the nutmeg and the warmed milk, little by little, until you achieve the consistency of a smooth purée. Add salt as needed and place in a serving bowl. Sprinkle on the toasted almonds sprinkle and chopped coriander leaves, if using.

Thai Glass Noodle Salad

To make a good glass noodle salad it is important that the glass noodles are freshly soaked and are not too soft. They should have a little bite to them. Glass noodles absorb the flavors of the sauce and thus give a full aroma to the salad.

SERVES **4**
PREPARATION TIME: **30 minutes**

⅓ lb (150 g) dried glass noodles
2 cups (500 ml) boiling water
1 carrot, cut into thin matchsticks
4 small green onions (scallions), cut into thin strips about 1½ in (3.75 cm) long
1 small celery stalk, cut into thin strips about 1½ in (3.75 cm) long
1 tomato, cut into eight wedges
One 1-in (2.5-cm)-piece fresh ginger, peeled and cut into thin slivers
½ cup (60 g) fresh coriander leaves (cilantro)
2 tablespoons fresh mint leaves
3 tablespoons lightly crushed roasted peanuts

THAI SALAD DRESSING
2 cloves garlic, finely chopped
2 jalapeno peppers, preferably red, deseeded and crushed with the side of a knife
1 tablespoon sugar
3 tablespoons lime juice
2 tablespoons fish sauce

1 In a heatproof bowl, combine the glass noodles and water. Soak the noodles for 5 minutes. Drain the noodles and rinse with cold water. Cut the soaked glass noodles into 2-inch (5-cm)-long strands.
2 In a serving bowl, combine the noodles, vegetables, ginger, herbs and peanuts.
3 In a small bowl, combine the ingredients for the dressing. Just before serving, pour the dressing over the glass noodles and vegetables and toss.

Green Papaya Salad

Thai papaya salad, or *som tam*, as it is called in Thai, is an absolute must for any kind of grilled Thai dish. It is typically made with raw papaya but any other kind of sour-tasting raw fruit, such as green mango or Indian goose-berry, will work. You can even use lettuce, carrots or celery—which have recently been introduced into the Thai kitchen—or any other crisp vegetable that has a neutral flavor.

SERVES **4**
PREPARATION TIME: **20 minutes**

4 cloves garlic
3 to 5 red bird's-eye chilies or serrano chilies, slit open lengthwise
2 tablespoons fish sauce, preferably Thai
2 tablespoons palm sugar or light brown sugar
2 tablespoons lime juice
2 tablespoons dried shrimp
6 green beans, coarsely chopped
4 tablespoons roasted peanuts
2 small firm tomatoes, quartered
1 lb (500 g) green papaya, peeled, deseeded and cut into thin slivers

In a large mortar, add the garlic and crush slightly. Add one by one the chilies, fish sauce, palm sugar, lime juice and mix well in the mortar with a spoon. Then continue to pound and add one by one the dried shrimp, green beans, roasted peanuts, tomato wedges and finally the green papaya. Slightly pound the mixture in the mortar until the papaya has absorbed some of the juices. Serve immediately.

Yogurt Cucumber Raita

The combination of yogurt and cucumbers or other fresh vegetables is popular from India to Greece. It is a very refreshing dish and goes well with virtually any Indian or Middle Eastern recipe. This raita is served often with grilled lamb and vegetables.

SERVES **4**
PREPARATION TIME: **30 minutes**

1 clove garlic, crushed to a paste
1 large cucumber, cut in half, deseeded and grated
1 tablespoon finely chopped fresh mint leaves
1 tablespoon finely chopped fresh coriander leaves (cilantro)
2 finger-length green chilies, finely chopped (optional)
1 cup (250 ml) plain yogurt
Salt and pepper to taste

In a bowl, combine the garlic, cucumber, herbs and chilies, if using. Whisk the yogurt and combine with the cucumber. Add the salt and pepper. Mix well.

Potato Cucumber Salad with Fresh Herbs

The combination of potato and cucumber with a touch of savory makes this potato salad very refreshing and well suited for a warm summer afternoon BBQ. If you cannot find savory, replace it with ¹/₂ teaspoon ground thyme. The addition of mineral water and beef stock in potato salad is a traditional German practice that I learned from my mother.

SERVES **4**
PREPARATION TIME: **30 minutes**

4 medium potatoes
1 cucumber, peeled, cut in half lengthwise and deseeded
2 tablespoons coarsely chopped fresh flat-leaf parsley
1 tablespoon finely chopped fresh rosemary leaves
1 teaspoon ground savory or ½ teaspoon ground thyme
2 medium shallots, finely sliced
3 tablespoons extra-virgin olive oil

3 tablespoons white wine vinegar
1 tablespoon Dijon mustard
Salt and pepper to taste
1 cup (65 ml) sparkling mineral water
½ cup (125 ml) beef stock

1 Bring a pot of salted water to a boil. Add the potatoes and cook until just soft. Drain, let cool and peel. Thinly slice the potatoes and add to a large serving bowl.
2 Thinly slice the cucumber halves and add to the sliced potatoes.
3 In a small bowl, combine the herbs, shallots, olive oil, vinegar, mustard, salt and pepper. Add the potato and cucumber slices. Toss to combine.
4 In a large measuring cup, combine the mineral water and beef stock. Add the mineral water mixture to the salad little by little until the potatoes have a glassy and smooth appearance.

Pistachio Rice Salad

This rice salad is inspired by flavors and ingredient pairings typically used in Middle Eastern cuisine. It is simple and combines the flavors of parsley, mint and pistachios. Its light and subtle flavor makes it a good side dish for almost any of the recipes in this book.

SERVES **4**
PREPARATION TIME: **30 minutes**
COOKING TIME: **20 minutes**

1 tablespoon neutral-flavored oil
1 cup (180 g) uncooked basmati rice
1½ cups (375 ml) water
½ cup (80 g) shelled pistachios

LEMON HERB DRESSING
5 tablespoons extra virgin olive oil
3 tablespoons lemon juice
Zest of 1 lemon, finely chopped
2 tablespoons fresh flat-leaf parsley, chopped
2 tablespoons fresh mint leaves, chopped
4 green onions (scallions), finely chopped

1 In a saucepan with a tight-fitting lid, add the oil and place over medium heat. Add the rice and sauté for a few minutes or until the rice becomes glassy. Add the water, lower the heat and simmer half covered until done. Remove from the heat and let cool.

2 In a small bowl, combine the dressing ingredients.

3 In a large serving bowl, add the cooled rice and pistachios. Pour the dressing over and mix together. Let chill in the refrigerator for about 1 hour before serving.

Grilled Rice Cakes

Grilled rice cakes are often served in Japan with grilled food. I tasted these grilled rice cakes in Japan where they were basted with butter and salt, dark miso, soy sauce and light miso sauce. If you find making Onigiri rice cakes from scratch too labor-intensive, ready-made cakes are available in Japanese markets.

MAKES **12 rice cakes**
PREPARATION TIME: **50 minutes**
GRILL TIME: **5 to 8 minutes**

2 cups (400 g) short-grain "sushi" rice
2⅓ cups (550 ml) water
6 thin bamboo skewers, soaked in water for 30 minutes, or metal skewers

SUSHI DRESSING
¼ cup plus 2 tablespoons (100 ml) rice vinegar
1 tablespoon sugar
1 teaspoon salt

MISO BASTING SAUCE
2 tablespoon Japanese soy sauce
1 tablespoon mirin
1 teaspoon sugar
2 teaspoons miso, preferably red

SALTED BUTTER BASTING SAUCE
2 tablespoons melted butter
Salt to taste

TERIYAKI BASTING SAUCE
2 tablespoons Japanese soy sauce
1 teaspoon sake
1 tablespoon mirin

1 Rinse the rice with fresh water and drain. Do this 3 to 5 times, or until the water runs clear. Drain the rice. In a medium saucepan (with a lid), combine the rinsed and drained rice with thewater. Bring to a boil over high heat. Once the water is boiling, place the lid on the pan slightly askew (or else it will boil over) and cook the rice for a full 10 minutes at a boil. Reduce the heat to low, cover, and simmer for 10 to 15 minutes. When the rice is soft and fluffy it is ready. Let cool completely before using to make the Grilled Rice Cakes.

2 In a small saucepan, add the ingredients for the sushi dressing and place over low heat. As soon as the sugar and salt are dissolved remove from the heat. Let cool before mixing with the rice.

3 While the sushi dressing is cooling, make one of the three basting sauces that you'd like to use by combining the ingredients in a small bowl. If you're making the Miso Basting Sauce, combine the first 3 ingredients and stir until the sugar dissolves. Then add the miso and stir to combine.

4 Wet your hands and prepare round or triangular rice patties about ¾ inch (2 cm) thick and 2 inches (5 cm) in diameter or side length respectively. Press tightly and keep the patties in the refrigerator until used.

5 Prepare the grill for direct grilling with one heat zone (medium to low). (See page 13 for charcoal and page 17 for gas.)

6 Skewer the patties. Just before you begin grilling, oil the hot grate. Place the rice cakes on the grate and grill until each side has developed a nice crust, about 1 to 2 per side, while basting regularly with either the Miso Basting Sauce, Salted Butter or Teriyaki Basting Sauce.

Saffron Rice

This biryani-style rice is slightly perfumed with saffron, cardamom and rose petals. This recipe is also delicious when stripped down to just saffron, a little salt and stock.

SERVES **4**
PREPARATION TIME: **30 minutes**
COOKING TIME: **20 minutes**

1 tablespoon neutral-flavored oil
2 cups (360 g) uncooked basmati rice
3 cups (750 ml) chicken or beef stock or water
Pinch of salt
4 green cardamom pods (optional)
½ teaspoon saffron dissolved in 3 tablespoons milk
2 tablespoons almond slivers
2 teaspoons dried rose petals (optional)

In a large saucepan with a tight-fitting lid, add the oil and place over medium heat. Add the rice and fry until it just starts to become golden brown. Add the stock or water, salt and cardamom pods, if using, and cover. Cook for 10 minutes and then add the saffron milk and the rose petals, if using. Reduce the heat to low and let steam for another 5 to 10 minutes. Serve warm.

> **Note** Rose petals are sold as dried whole buds or petals. It is said that the best rose flavor is made from damask roses. If you cannot find rosebuds, replace with rose water, which is the liquid extract from rose petals.

Caramelized Mangoes

This quick-to-make dessert is always a popular ending to barbecue meals.

SERVES **4**
PREPARATION TIME: **15 minutes**
GRILL TIME. **3 to 5 minutes**

¾ cup (120 g) sugar
Juice of 3 limes
1 tablespoon peeled and finely chopped
   fresh ginger
3 medium mangoes, peeled, halved and stones
   removed

1 In a saucepan, add the sugar and lime juice and place over medium heat. When the sugar is dissolved add the ginger. Cook for about 6 minutes or until the sauce begins to thicken.

2 Prepare the grill for direct grilling with medium heat. (See page 13 for charcoal and page 17 for gas.)

3 Just before you begin grilling, oil the hot grate. Place the mango halves on the grate and grill for a few minutes, turning once.

4 Place on a serving plate and drizzle with the ginger lime sauce. Serve hot.

Fresh Grilled Pineapple with Pineapple Sorbet

Sweet grilled pineapple served with cooling pineapple sorbet is a just-right combo after a hot and spicy meal.

SERVES **4**
PREPARATION TIME: **15 minutes plus 1½ to 2 hours for
   sorbet to set up**
GRILL TIME: **4 to 6 minutes**

1 medium pineapple, peeled, cored and cut
   into quarters
A few fresh mint leaves for garnish

PINEAPPLE SORBET
1 medium pineapple, peeled, cored and cut
   into large chunks

1 tablespoon sugar
1 tablespoon lime juice

1 To make the sorbet, place the pineapple chunks in a food processor or blender and process until you have a fine purée.

2 In a bowl, combine 2 cups (500 ml) of the pineapple purée with the sugar and lime juice. Place in the freezer. Stir thoroughly after 30 minutes to avoid large ice crystals. Put the sorbet back into the freezer and repeat the process twice more after 30-minute intervals. The sorbet should be frozen after about 1½ to 2 hours.

3 Prepare the grill for direct grilling with medium heat. (See page 13 for charcoal and page 17 for gas.)

4 Just before you begin grilling, oil the hot grate. Place the pineapple quarters on the grate and grill for 5 to 6 minutes. Serve hot with the Pineapple Sorbet and garnish with some mint leaves.

Grilled Honeydew Melon with Honey and Almonds

In Asia melons are a highly regarded fruit. In central Asia fruits are often perfumed with rose petals but lavender equally is delicious and exotic. Lavender goes nicely with melons or any other very sweet fruit such as apricots and prunes.

SERVES **4**
PREPARATION TIME: **30 minutes**
GRILL TIME: **3 to 5 minutes**

2 tablespoons butter
4 tablespoons sugar
4 tablespoons almond slivers
½ cup (125 ml) honey
3 tablespoons water
1 tablespoon dried lavender flowers
1 large honeydew melon, cut into eight slices

1 In a small skillet, add the butter and place over medium-low heat. When the butter has melted, add the sugar. When the sugar has dissolved, add the almond slivers and heat until the slivers are covered with a caramel crust. Set aside on a plate and let cool.

2 In a small saucepan, add the honey, water and dried lavender flowers and place over low heat. When the lavender is softened set aside for 30 minutes to cool and allow the lavender to infuse its flavor and aroma. Strain the lavender and retain the liquid.

3 Prepare the grill for direct grilling with medium heat. (See page 13 for charcoal and page 17 for gas.)

4 Just before you begin grilling, oil the hot grate. Place the melon slices on the grate and grill each side for a few minutes. When the melon begins to brown, remove from the heat and place 2 slices on each plate. Sprinkle with the caramelized almonds and drizzle on the lavender-infused honey.

Sweet Ginger and Mint Fruit Skewers

In Asia it is very common to serve a mixed fruit platter after a spicy meal and in Thailand fruit is usually served with salt or sugar mixed with a little ground red pepper (cayenne). To appeal to the our Western friends I created this recipe of mixed grilled fruit skewers with a refreshing ginger and mint basting sauce.

SERVES **4**
PREPARATION TIME: **30 minutes**
GRILL TIME: **2 to 4 minutes**

3 tablespoons sugar
2 tablespoons lemon juice
1 tablespoon peeled and finely chopped
   fresh ginger
1 tablespoon finely chopped fresh mint leaves
1 cup (180 g) pineapple cubes
1 orange, cut into 8 wedges
1 cup (180 g) mango cubes
12 bamboo skewers, soaked in water for
   30 minutes, or metal skewers

1 In a saucepan, add the sugar and lemon juice and place over medium-low heat. When the sugar has dissolved, add the ginger and simmer for a few minutes. Add the mint leaves and set aside to cool.

2 Prepare the grill for direct grilling with medium heat. (See page 13 for charcoal and page 17 for gas.)

3 Just before you begin grilling, thread the fruit cubes and orange wedges onto skewers and oil the hot grate.

4 Place the skewers on the grate and grill for 1 to 2 minutes on each side, basting with the ginger and mint mixture. Remove from the grill and pour the remaining mint mixture over the grilled fruit skewers and serve hot.

Grilled Bananas with Chocolate and Coconut

Chocolate and grated coconut go well together. This recipe combines the two with bananas and a lovely orange aroma.

SERVES **4**
TIME TO PREPARE: **10 minutes**
GRILL TIME: **5 to 7 minutes**

4 firm bananas (not too ripe)
2 oz (50 g) bittersweet chocolate, cut into slivers and divided into 4 portions
2 tablespoons grated coconut or desiccated coconut, soaked in water for 30 minutes
2 teaspoons Grand Marnier or other orange liqueur
Aluminum foil to wrap the bananas

1 With their peels on, make a lengthwise slit in each banana. Be careful not to cut the banana in half. Place one portion of the chocolate slivers into the split in each banana. Follow with a sprinkling of the grated coconut and a drizzle of the Grand Marnier.

2 Prepare the grill for direct grilling with medium heat. (See page 13 for charcoal and page 17 for gas.)

3 When the grill is hot, wrap the bananas in aluminum foil and place them on the grate and grill for 5 to 7 minutes. Serve hot.

Honey Prunes with Cinnamon Ice Cream

A very simple dessert but nonetheless very good. I personally like the blend of prunes with cinnamon ice cream.

SERVES **4**
PREPARATION TIME: **10 minutes plus 30 minutes to macerate the dried prunes**
GRILL TIME: **2 to 4 minutes**

12 prunes
⅓ cup (80 ml) port wine
⅓ cup (80 ml) cognac
2 tablespoons honey
One 1-in (2.5-cm) piece cinnamon

2 cloves
4 bamboo skewers, soaked in water for 30 minutes, or metal skewers
4 scoops cinnamon or vanilla ice cream

1 In a bowl, combine the prunes, port and cognac. Let soak for 30 minutes. Remove the prunes and set aside. Reserve the soaking liquid.

2 In a saucepan, add the port and cognac mixture and the honey and place over medium-low heat. When the honey has dissolved remove from the heat. Add the cinnamon and cloves and let rest to allow the spices to infuse the port and cognac.

3 Prepare the grill for direct grilling with medium heat. (See page 13 for charcoal and page 17 for gas.)

4 Just before you begin grilling, thread three prunes on a skewer and oil the hot grate.

5 Place the skewers on the grate and grill for 1 to 2 minutes on each side.

6 Place the hot prunes on a plate, drizzle with the honey-port mixture and serve with one scoop of cinnamon or vanilla ice cream.

Index

The Tuttle Story: "Books to Span the East and West"

Most people are surprised when they learn that the world's largest publisher of books on Asia had its beginnings in the tiny American state of Vermont. The company's founder, Charles Tuttle, came from a New England family steeped in publishing, and his first love was books—especially old and rare editions.

Tuttle's father was a noted antiquarian dealer in Rutland, Vermont. Young Charles honed his knowledge of the trade working in the family bookstore, and later in the rare books section of Columbia University Library. His passion for beautiful books—old and new—never wavered through his long career as a bookseller and publisher.

After graduating from Harvard, Tuttle enlisted in the military and in 1945 was sent to Tokyo to work on General Douglas MacArthur's staff. He was tasked with helping to revive the Japanese publishing industry, which had been utterly devastated by the war. After his tour of duty was completed, he left the military, married a talented and beautiful singer, Reiko Chiba, and in 1948 began several successful business ventures.

To his astonishment, Tuttle discovered that postwar Tokyo was actually a book-lover's paradise. He befriended dealers in the Kanda district and began supplying rare Japanese editions to American libraries. He also imported American books to sell to the thousands of GIs stationed in Japan. By 1949, Tuttle's business was thriving, and he opened Tokyo's very first English-language bookstore in the Takashimaya Department Store in Ginza, to great success. Two years later, he began publishing books to fulfill the growing interest of foreigners in all things Asian.

Though a westerner, Charles Tuttle was hugely instrumental in bringing knowledge of Japan and Asia to a world hungry for information about the East. By the time of his death in 1993, he had published over 6,000 books on Asian culture, history and art—a legacy honored by Emperor Hirohito in 1983 with the "Order of the Sacred Treasure," the highest honor Japan bestows upon non-Japanese.

The Tuttle company today maintains an active backlist of some 1,500 titles, many of which have been continuously in print since the 1950s and 1960s—a great testament to Charles Tuttle's skill as a publisher. More than 60 years after its founding, Tuttle Publishing is more active today than at any time in its history, still inspired by Charles' core mission—to publish fine books to span the East and West and provide a greater understanding of each.